. . . And the Sun Will Rise from the West

. . . And the Sun Will Rise from the West

The Predicament of "Islamic Terrorism" and the Way Out

Rafaat Ludin and Windham Loopesko

Copyedited by Chris Anthony Ferrer

Library of Congress Control Number:		2016907017
ISBN:	Hardcover	978-1-5144-8890-4
	Softcover	978-1-5144-8889-8
	eBook	978-1-5144-8888-1

Print information available on the last page.

Rev. date: 02/23/2018

To order additional copies of this book, contact:
Xlibris
1-888-795-4274
www.Xlibris.com
Orders@Xlibris.com
734841

CONTENTS

Preface

How This Book Came to Be

Rafaat

I woke up on a Tuesday morning in September 2001 and helped to prepare our three children—Nurin, Modather, and Mozamel—to go to their new school, the New Horizon Elementary School in Irvine, California, a private elementary school that complemented the regular public school curriculum with Islamic religious education. The school's focus was to bring up American Muslims to be successful in America while enshrining a strong religious belief and love of God and His prophet. I had helped in realizing this project over the past twelve months and had volunteered to raise institutional funds for the school. Monday, September 10, 2001, had been the first day of school, and our children were very excited about being part of this new experiment in their lives.

On Monday morning, upon arriving at the school, I met an Afghan American friend who asked me in an excited tone of voice if I had heard the news. I inquired what news, and he told me of the assassination of Ahmad Shah Masood, the legendary mujahideen commander known as the Lion of Panjshir (a district about sixty kilometers [thirty-five miles] north of Kabul along the Kabul-Mazar highway). He had fought with bravery and skills against the Soviets during the 1980s and gained the reputation as one of the best mujahideen, not only within Afghanistan but throughout the world. My friend informed me that on September 8, a team posing as an Arab television cameraman and a journalist visited him in his Takhar Province base to interview him. They had apparently hidden explosives in their camera, resulting in their own death and Ahmad Shah Masood's fatal injury. This attack was probably the first suicide bombing carried out on Afghan soil, notwithstanding its twenty-three years of war and civil strife. It was only later that I realized the importance of this news in the context of Islamic terrorism and Afghanistan's involvement in terrorism.

On Tuesday, September 11, 2001, I had not yet finished preparing the kids to go to school when I received a call from my brother-in-law, Hares, who, in an excited and dramatic voice, told my wife about some airplane attacks in New York. We had chosen not to own a TV set; leaving our children at home with my mother, we immediately drove to his apartment to see what was happening. When we arrived, I saw footage of the second plane hitting the Twin Towers and the buildings' collapse. My jaw fell, my heart pounded, and my brain filled with shock at the images of all that would happen as a result of this incident. The captions read "War on America," "America Under Attack," etc. One of the first sentences I uttered was "Now they will bomb Afghanistan and kill thousands of innocents!" And so it happened, starting a few months later but still going on some fourteen years later.

This day forever changed not only my life but those of more than 1.6 billion Muslims throughout the world. The repercussions of this incident woke all American and European Muslims from a deep slumber, opening their eyes to a new reality—a war against Islam and Muslims, waged by hatemongers on both sides from within and outside the United States, non-Muslims as well as Muslims. Ignorance, hate, prejudice, and racism came to play an increasing role in our world for a long time after that defining moment.

September 11, 2001, was my first day of a one-week orientation at University of California in Irvine's (UCI) Paul Mirage School of Business. I was entering a two-year executive MBA program to jump-start my management and executive career in my new home, the United States of America. At around 9:00 a.m., I received a call from UCI informing me that the program was still on and that I should be there at 10:00 a.m. as scheduled.

Clearly we did not take our children to their new school. My wife, Farah, and I had an intense discussion on how to deal with this situation, especially since I would be gone for a week, staying day and night at the Hyatt Regency in Irvine. She would be on her own, albeit with the support of my mother and her family, who lived nearby.

I arrived at the Hyatt stunned, not knowing how to deal with this situation. I looked around and found that others were no different from me. Everyone was in shock—heads shaking, tears rolling down cheeks, and sad faces everywhere. My heart continued to pound, albeit somewhat slower, overwhelmed not just by the sheer cruelty of the action against my new homeland, but also by its possible consequences for Afghanistan—my place of birth, my source of pride, my emotional homeland—and for all Muslims. After all, I had just moved to the United States a year earlier, after having spent, with interruptions, about twenty-three years in Germany and the previous six years (1993–1999) in Peshawar, Pakistan.

It was during this week with my new classmates that I had my first conversations on Islam in the United States. I was forced to explain that what those criminals did had nothing to do with Islam and that theirs were the acts of individuals or groups that did not represent the community of Islam and Muslims.

On September 12, I received a call from an *Orange County Register* journalist who wanted to have a reaction from an Afghan Muslim on the terrorist attacks. I received him at the hotel and tried to explain that these tragic events had nothing to do with Islam as we understand and live it and that al-Qaida, which by then had been stamped as the culprit behind it, had nothing to do with Afghanistan. Afghanistan was merely a place of residence for Osama bin Laden and his henchmen after others had denied them a place to live. I tried to explain that the Taliban would likely not turn bin Laden over to the United States and that the attacks might lead to war in Afghanistan, causing further pain and destruction in this already war-torn and grieving country.

Our days started at 7:00 a.m. and ended after midnight. There was a lot to be learned and read, numerous group works and projects to be completed. It was a great blessing that we were all locked up in a hotel for a week and did not have the time or the mind-set to deal with all that was going on outside of the hotel. We were not immediate witnesses to the hate and anger that exploded in the media and engulfed the whole country. By the time we came out, things had calmed down a bit and people were strategizing rather than reacting.

Let me here relate an anecdote that demonstrates the level of sensitivity in the post–9/11 environment. At the time I was accepted at UCI's executive MBA program, I was working with an engineering and product-certification firm called Intertek Testing Services, testing products for compliance with OSHA,[1] NFPA,[2] ANSI,[3] UL,[4] IEC,[5] and other standards. My MBA classes were scheduled for every other Friday and Saturday. Thus I had to skip work on alternate Fridays to attend classes, and my boss was not willing to give me the time off to go to class, even though I offered to work afterhours, work on Saturdays, or have the time deducted from my paid leave days. I felt that the cause of this unreasonable denial was the cost of the MBA (around $60,000) and ITS's policy to pay 100 percent of the tuition fees for continuing education. He suggested that I should go to a less-favorably-rated school and thus avoid UCI's high cost. I chose to resign, believing that that my boss was not committed to my career advancement. My last day of work was Friday, September 7, 2001.

During my last days, I was given the task to start testing for a device that required laboratory experiments using a large propane gas cylinder. Finding such a gas cylinder was not easy; I had to inquire at many companies. Finally, the Thursday before my resignation, I was able to order a gas cylinder to be delivered to the office. The following Tuesday was 9/11; the media started to portray every Muslim as a potential enemy of America. A number of the companies that I had called to inquire about the gas cylinder contacted the FBI to give them tips about this foreign-sounding person with a likely Muslim name who was inquiring about a large gas cylinder. The company that delivered the gas cylinder called the FBI.

One day I received a call from my colleagues at ITS informing me that the office had been visited by multiple FBI agents inquiring about

---

1 Occupational Safety and Health Administration.

2 National Fire Protection Agency.

3 American National Standards Institute.

4 Underwriters' Laboratories.

5 International Electrical Commission.

me. They had the full details of the gas cylinder and knew quite a lot about me as well. My colleagues had calmed them down and shown them the gas cylinder and the project assignment that required testing with propane gas, as a result of which they left, satisfied. I had no further encounters with the FBI until 2015, when I rear-ended an FBI agent's car when my Volvo slipped on ice near my office in Denver, Colorado.

My family's history with the United States goes back to 1934, when my late uncle, Mohammad Kabir Ludin, came to the United States on a US government scholarship to study civil engineering at Cornell University. He returned to Afghanistan and eventually became minister of public works, followed by diplomatic assignments as ambassador in Washington, DC, New York (United Nations), London, and India. He passed away in India while serving as Afghanistan's ambassador.

My late father, Mohammad Bashir Ludin, was also able to win a scholarship to study civil engineering at Princeton University, followed by a master's degree specializing in dam construction from George Washington University. He also returned to Afghanistan to move up the ladder and eventually become the youngest minister in the cabinet of Nur Mohammad Etemadi in 1968. Later, in 1977, he was appointed ambassador to the then West Germany. I remember leaving Afghanistan on a first-class seat onboard Ariana Afghan Airlines. As my wife, Farah, never fails to remind me, while I sat on a first class seat and flew out of the country with dignity and pride (as a thirteen-year-old boy), she had to ride for fourteen days and nights on backs of donkeys and travel by foot to avoid Soviet helicopters and find refuge in Pakistan.

Soon after we arrived in Germany, my father gave us all a lecture about how we should behave. He said that he was not the only ambassador of Afghanistan and Islam in this country, but that each one of us was an ambassador of our country and our religion. How we behaved and acted showed the type of culture and mind-set we represented. He told us that we were no longer children with free spirits and the license to make mistakes without significant consequences. We had become adults at a young age and had a responsibility toward our people, our country, our society, and most of all, our religion. This conversation was a continuous feature of our family time, when we were able to report what we did to differentiate us from others in a positive manner. It was in this matter that we encountered the Islamic concept of *ihsan*, or consistent striving for excellence in intentions and in actions—our first conscious lesson in learning Islam in a majority non-Islamic society. The lessons of those years still define and guide us in our daily lives. My father was a great man with great ideas—a true Muslim in heart and soul. He was an example of excellence in intentions and actions and enjoyed the same reputation in Afghanistan and with everyone he came in contact.

In April of 1978, about a year after we had arrived in Germany, the Afghan Communists with Soviet support staged a coup d'etat in Afghanistan, killing President Daud and overthrowing his government. My father knew most of the Communists who had killed their way into power and refused to work with them. He resigned his post and sought to return to Afghanistan. My mother, Maria Shamim Ludin, a highly educated and accomplished teacher in her own right, managed to convince him that returning to Afghanistan would be fatal and that he should stay in the West until the situation in Afghanistan stabilized. My father conceded and approached a friend in San Francisco, who in return offered him a job at the International Engineering Company (IEC).

My father requested a work visa from the US consulate in Munich. The consular officer refused to issue him a visa and suggested that he should request an immigration visa for the United States, which would take about six months to approve. After significant hesitation my father agreed, and we were forced to stay in Germany, awaiting the visa.

During those six to eight months, we children received some of the most critical and valuable education of our lives. For the first time, we had continuous daily contact with our father, who no longer had work. We spent the days camping in the forests, picnicking in autobahn rest areas, or just hanging out in our pension,[6] where we would talk about religion, politics, education, science, and social matters. It was the most valuable educational experience of my life. I had full access to possibly one of the smartest persons in Afghanistan and a great wise man of the world. It was during these interactions that we learned what it meant to develop an in-depth understanding of concepts, to be able to analyze situations and themes and understand the underlying causes of issues, and to develop effective solutions that do not betray the essence of the value system upon which life is based. It was during these intense conversations that we learned to dive deeper into situations and ideas

6 A German bed-and-breakfast.

to seek what others may not immediately find. Wisdom's seed was planted in us during those six to eight months, on which all of us built our future—my two brothers, two sisters, and I. Islam was no longer an abstract practice; it had value and philosophies enshrined. The prophet Muhammad was no longer the subject of stories but rather a model for excellence in behavior and action. The Quran was no longer just a book to read, but rather a world to explore.

Our visas for the United States came, but the consular officer refused to issue them to us because we were not permanent residents of Germany. He knew this fact from the beginning and could have told us, but for some reason, he chose not to do so. Now we believe that it was God's will to enable us to get that important foundational basis for our lives during those months of waiting for the immigration visa. There were many other occasions in our lives before and after that that helped us to better understand the Quranic verse

> It is quite possible be that something which you do not like is good for you and something which you love is bad for you. Allah knows, and you do not know.[7]

After this major visa setback, my parents decided to drive to Saudi Arabia and perform the hajj (pilgrimage) while adhering to the recommendation of IEC lawyers to go to a third country, so that they would send the visa to us there. We started a twenty-day road trip via Austria, Yugoslavia, Bulgaria, Turkey, Syria, and Jordan to arrive in Jeddah, Saudi Arabia. I was tasked with navigation and sat next to my father to guide him through the long but beautiful route. Every mile was an education in God's creations and His will to create the diversity of people, nations, and tribes, so that we could get to know them.[8] Every country generated in us respect and appreciation for their hospitality, kindness of the heart, and achievement of peace and stability. Every religion that we were exposed to made it clearer to us that the best

7 Surah Al Baqarah (2), verse 216. In citing the Quran, we are using the *English Translation of the Meaning of AL-QUR'AN*, Muhammad Farooq-i-Azam Malik, The Institute of Islamic Knowledge, Houston, Texas (1997). All quotes will be from this version. Phrases in *italics* appear as in the text.

8 Reference is made to Quran Sura Al Hujarat (49), verse 13.

among us are those who are the most God-conscious,[9] whatever their religion or orientation may be.

For reasons not relevant here, our parents chose to remain in Saudi Arabia, and my father, through yet another miracle of fate, was hired by Saudi Arabian Airlines as a master engineer. Unfortunately, only about five months after arriving in Jeddah, my father passed away from a heart attack. We were left stranded in this new country where we did not know the language, the culture, or anyone who would care for us. I was fifteen years old and was supposed to be in the midst of my wild teenage years, but I was left with the burden of caring for myself and contributing to our family's fight for survival. My oldest brother, Monir, was called to abandon his premed school at the University of Maryland in Munich, Germany, and come to Jeddah. At only eighteen years of age, Monir immediately switched to the role of the eldest son and offered to stay, work, and take care of the whole family. Overnight, Monir became our father figure and fairly soon became a wise, honorable, compassionate, and hardworking father to all of us.

During the next six years of our life in Saudi Arabia, we learned that faith could create compassion, love, and mercy in the hearts of people. We met many people who, from pure compassion and love of their neighbor, were willing to go to great lengths and personal hardships to help us and others. Their only motivation was to please God and do good deeds. On the other hand, we learned that oppressive governments could denigrate people, abuse the religion, and create an atmosphere of hate, cruelty, injustice, and mischief on earth. We met people with soft and merciful hearts and a government with a hard, merciless attitude toward its people. For the first time, we were confronted head-on with cruelty difficult to find anywhere on earth, when a person is without any rights, any hope, or any say in anything that involves him and others. These defining years in our lives taught us that there can be a great divide between words and actions, between individuals and governments, and between free-minded religious scholars and "bonded by the government" religious scholars. We learned to differentiate, to be careful not to reach fast and thoughtless conclusions, and not to judge people because of what others of their culture and faith or their governments do.

---

9 Ibid.

In 1985 I returned to Germany to pursue my education in electrical engineering at the University of Applied Sciences in Darmstadt. I went back to Germany equipped with my foundational knowledge that

- we must not be judgmental,
- there is no such thing as pure black-and-white,
- there is a difference between people and governments,
- the Quran is not just a book of words but rather a style of life,
- the prophet Muhammad is not just a guide but a role model for us to emulate, and
- God-consciousness is not reserved by Muslims alone but can be anyone's from any religion or denomination.

I became involved with Muslim organizations such as the House of Islam in Luetzelbach am Odenwald and the Muslimische Gemeinschaft. I started to focus my reading more on Islamic books, primarily by European and US scholars such as Ahmad von Denffer, Murad Hofmann, Jamal Badawi, and others. When I engaged with people, it was based on mutual respect and understanding for other people's faiths, even if their views ran completely contrary to mine. As a twenty-one-year-old, I started to learn my religion and the value systems it incorporated from a different perspective, one influenced by wisdom and knowledge.

A Quranic verse became a foundation for me:

> Call *people* to the Way of your Rabb [Lord] with wisdom and best advice, and reason with them, *if you have to*, in the most courteous manner: for your Rabb knows best who strays from His Way and He knows best who is rightly guided.[10]

Through this verse I found a different meaning in my life—one filled with a desire to please God by spreading positivity and kindness rather than intolerance and hate.

Over the next years, I met and married my wife, Farah, who showed me the incredible blessing from God that had always been bestowed

10 Quran, Surah Al Nahl (16), verse 125.

upon me. She lost her brother to the Communist atrocities in early 1980. Her father and younger brother had to escape the country soon thereafter and migrate to India via incredibly difficult routes. Her youngest sister, still a preteen, had to leave the country for India with a family friend. Farah and her sister (with her husband) left Afghanistan in 1984 by foot and donkey to Pakistan. She was later joined in Pakistan by her mother. A few months later, she and her mother left for India with the help of human smugglers. After over ten days of riding a camel through India's Rajastan deserts they arrived in New Delhi and were reunited with their father, brother and sister. Only one sister was left in Pakistan. Farah's hardships and her resilience showed me that a strong faith and complete reliance on God could help one overcome seemingly impossible situations. Her strength has accompanied me from 1990 until today and has enabled me to get up and walk straight every time I fell from challenges.

In 1993 I accepted an offer by the German Agency for International Cooperation (GIZ) to head one of their projects in Pakistan and Afghanistan named the Domestic Energy Saving Project (DESP). As managing director of GIZ-DESP, I helped restructure the organization into a nongovernmental organization named the Agency for Rehabilitation and Energy Conservation in Afghanistan (AREA). I participated in growing AREA into one of the largest organizations in Afghanistan during 1994–2000 and beyond. The AREA experience took me to various parts of Pakistan and Afghanistan as well as to many other countries of the world. I saw people who suffered from hunger, lack of health care, lack of basic safety, lack of clean water, land mines spread throughout the country, lack of basic infrastructure, inadequate education, and corrupt leadership. In spite of all of these challenges, these poor and disadvantaged people could laugh and were genuinely happy. They appreciated the smallest things in their lives and the least that anyone did for them. They were generous with all the little they had and were ready to lose their life to protect their guests. I learned that they were neither radical nor terrorists. They did not hate; their hearts were filled with love and appreciation. They were people just like you and me, wanting to live a peaceful and happy life. The categorization of such people into terrorists—uneducated, ignorantly radical people in Muslim countries—by some Western media and Western politicians is far from reality. Those who have met them develop a deep respect for these people.

By 1999 our children had reached school age, and my wife and I agreed that they needed to be in a stable environment. So we returned to Germany, and to please my wife, I agreed to move to California to be close to her family. As a result, my career was reset to zero, leading me to seek the MBA from UCI.

In the post–9/11 world, I learned that in everything that I did with every person I met, under every circumstance, I had to justify myself and my religion. People were asking me questions like "Why don't Muslims distance themselves from or raise their voices against the terrorists?" "Why do Muslims hate us?" "Why is the Quran calling for violence against non-Muslims?" "Who is ISIS?" "Why are there wars in all Muslim countries?" and others.

Over the years, I have been consistently studying the situation and looking for the root causes of Islam's present situation. I have slowly and carefully sought answers to these questions and have dug deeper to understand the situation of Muslims. I have also spent a lot of time thinking about the way out for Muslims. What will the future be like for young Muslims? Will we be able to come out of this quagmire? If yes, then how, and with whose help?

And then on a fateful December 2014 day, I met Professor Windham Loopesko. It was during a wonderful dinner at Windham's home that the idea of a book to address this situation took an initial shape. You have before you the result.

Windham

My story is briefer and, thankfully, less eventful than Rafaat's. I had almost no contact with Islam throughout my young and early adult life, growing up in a Los Angeles suburb and studying at Dartmouth, the University of Chicago, and Harvard. A year working in France and studying in Belgium, in graduate school (1973–74), gave me a lifelong passion for studying cultures, and cultural adaptation became a (very agreeable) necessity when I met my future wife in Paris on a business trip in 1984. Part of that adaptation was exposure to a different religious tradition, as my wife comes from a family with a strong Catholic tradition,[11] and we raised our three children ecumenically—"Dad is Protestant; Mom's Catholic. When you grow up, you'll figure it out." I joined Montview Boulevard Presbyterian Church in 1991 and have had the privilege of serving as an elder, a member of the church's governing body.

While I started my career as a lawyer, I migrated to business in 1981, working as the only American in a Swiss company in Bern, Switzerland. I returned to the United States in 1983 to start an international consulting practice that I pursued full-time until 2011, when I became an adjunct professor at University of Colorado Denver (UCD), teaching globalization and international business. Since January 2011, I have taught a course entitled Global Perspectives every term. I have enjoyed wide latitude in developing the course materials; in this course, I seek to present my students with the pressing international issues of the day, as well as the more transnational issues that I believe will influence them throughout their careers.

UCD is fortunate in having a large number of foreign students and students whose families have recently immigrated to the United States. I thus have had the privilege of having a number of Muslim students in my classes and quickly came to regard them as an extraordinarily valuable asset in teaching my Global Perspectives course. In my course, I teach my students that one of the two great issues of the twenty-first century is the relationship between Islam and the West;[12] having Muslim students who can present their perspective on the issues that we discuss is a priceless advantage.

In my summer 2014 semester, I had an Afghan student, Modather Ludin. He was the outstanding student of that semester, and after the semester ended, I asked him to be my teaching assistant for the coming academic year. Modather was equally extraordinary as my teaching assistant, and to thank him, I invited him and his parents over for dinner. I found the conversation that evening spellbinding; never have I had such a far-ranging and thoughtful conversation with Muslims, and the stories that Rafaat and Farah related were humbling for my

---

11 As we like to say in our family, "Dad belongs to the Presbyterian Church. Mom belongs to the Church."

12 The other is the relationship between the United States and China.

wife, my son, and me. A lunch soon followed that dinner, and the idea for this book was born.

The authors believe that the conjunction of these two very different paths gives this book a unique point of view. We try to show the perspective of a thoughtful Muslim seeking to make sense of the state of Islam today and the terrible challenges that Islam faces. We examine Islam's sources—the Quran and the sayings and stories of the prophet Muhammad (*ahadith*), the history (both ancient and modern), and the current context (both political and social). Many of the subjects we treat deserve much greater depth, but providing this depth would make the book much longer and, we fear, too easy to put down.

We don't seek to convince, but rather to challenge and to stimulate discussion—particularly between Muslims and non-Muslims. Recent exchanges between Western and Muslim communities have too often been a dialogue of the deaf, where the two sides talk past one another with little real communication occurring.

Our intended audience is both non-Muslim Westerners who seek to understand the different currents within Islam and Muslims concerned about the state of the *ummah* (the community of believers). Again, we hope to encourage a conversation between them. May the dialogue begin.

We dedicate this book to our wives, Farah and Anne, for the insights and wisdom they have shown us (and for the jobs they have done raising our children), to our children, who may (we hope) live in a world of greatly improved understanding among the Abrahamic religions, and to our parents. Where will we be without our parents? We owe our lives, our upbringing, and our value systems to our parents. May God bless the souls of the deceased parents, bless the living parents, and grant them all eternal peace in this world and the hereafter.

Chapter 1

Islam's Place in a Twenty-First-Century Context

The mission of religion in the 21st century must be to contribute concretely to the peaceful coexistence of humankind.

—*Daisaku Ikeda*[13]

To understand Islam and its future, we propose to start with the context of the twenty-first century and the challenges it poses not only for religions but for all persons living in it.

For the authors, the defining characteristic of the twenty-first century is the accelerating rate of change—in every corner of the world, at every level of society, for virtually every person in the world (except, perhaps, that vanishingly small number of indigenous peoples in places like the Amazon or New Guinea who are not yet in contact with civilization). Three simple facts demonstrate the overwhelming scope of this change:

- The quantity of information available in the world increases by a factor of ten every five years.[14]

---

13 http://www.brainyquote.com/quotes/quotes/d/daisakuike469584.html.

14 *The Economist*, "Data, Data Everywhere," February 25, 2010, http://www.economist.com/node/15557443.

- If we place the beginning of the human species at 250,000 years ago,[15] it took approximately 99.8% of human history for the world's population to reach one billion (which it hit in 1804[16])—in the life of one of the authors' fathers, born in 1919 and still with us (as of April 2016), that population has increased from under two billion to over seven billion today.
- Some 6.5% of the people who have ever lived are alive today.[17]

For almost everyone in the world today, simply coping with the staggeringly complex world of today is a full-time task; adding the dizzyingly rapid (and again, accelerating) changes can be and often is overwhelming—which, for the authors, explains in large part the disturbing rise of populism in many areas (Muslim and non-Muslim) of the world today.

Throughout human history religion has been a source of wisdom, comfort, solace, and understanding to men and women in their day-to-day lives and particularly during times of change. It seems (at least to the authors) to be part and parcel of the human experience, a presence—more or less strong, and felt differently by different individuals—in every civilization and at every time and place.

Religions too must confront and deal with the complex world of today and the accelerating rate of change. But all of the world's great religions began and spent most of their time developing in worlds almost impossibly remote from that of our time. If they are to be able to continue to perform the functions mentioned above, they must address and offer assistance in meeting the everyday concerns of today's adherents, far different from and unimaginable for those involved in the creation and initial elaboration of these religions, and change as rapidly as their lives change, in order to adapt to the daily changes that we experience in our lives.

Although the youngest of what are generally considered the world's great religions, due to its theology and history, Islam faces some unique

---

15 Whether you choose 150,000 or 400,000 years—or any other figure—for such beginning, it makes no substantial difference to the argument.

16 http://www.learner.org/courses/envsci/unit/text.php?unit = 5&secNum = 4.

17 http://www.prb.org/Publications/Articles/2002/HowManyPeopleHaveEverLivedonEarth.aspx .

issues in meeting these challenges, which we will discuss throughout this book. No other major religion is growing as fast or inspires both the level of fervor among its practitioners and fear among many of its nonadherents. Seeking an understanding and a modus vivendi between the Western and Islamic worlds is, we believe, one of the world's two great challenges of the first half of the twenty-first century (the other being finding a similar arrangement between the United States and China).

We will argue that one of the approaches that many people claiming the banner of Islam have taken—namely radical Islamism and the intolerance, terrorism, and barbarism it employs—is not consistent with the teachings and history of Islam and is a recent aberration. We will argue further that this brand of Islam has its root causes in a combination of hundreds of years of mismanagement of the religion by leaders of various countries both inside and outside the Muslim world. Exacerbating the development of radical Islamism as well are the more recent actions of the Western world, including and especially the United States of America, in the global arena, such as

- aid to questionable fringe armed groups,
- unequivocal support for the State of Israel, and
- active support for corrupt governments in Muslim-majority countries.

All of these policies have caused significant pain and distress to Muslims throughout the world. We also argue that terrorist organizations associated with radical Muslims can and must be opposed and that they will, inshallah,[18] be defeated—but only if both the Islamic world more generally and the Western world take the steps to combat the cancer that radical people, including radical Muslims, represent. These steps are quite different for the two camps, and must be done consistently, with determination, and over the long term. We will also argue that if left to its natural dynamic, Islam will evolve in a significant way by virtue of the effects of Western Muslims on Muslim-majority countries through the use of modern technologies such as the Internet, YouTube, Facebook, and other social media.

---

18 "If God wills it."

Religious and Spiritual Belief and Practice in the Twenty-First Century

By at least some measures, the twenty-first-century Western world is becoming increasingly secular. In the United States, the fastest growing religious preference is "none," increasing from 2% in the 1950s to 7% in the 1970s and nearly 20% today.[19] A Eurobarometer poll in 2010 showed that 20% of EU inhabitants believed that there was "no sort of spirit, God or life force" (with higher figures in a number of larger, richer European countries—e.g., France, 40%; Germany, 27%; United Kingdom, 25%; Netherlands, 30%; and Sweden, 34%).[20] Research across 65 countries showed that in 16 of 20 developed countries, church attendance has been declining.[21]

Numerous factors explain this decline in religious belief and observance:

- Reactions against a pervasive fundamentalist or conservative religious upbringing.
- Events such as 9/11, which are difficult to understand how a just and merciful God could allow to happen[22]—also, the behavior of the committed religionists on both sides making many consider how religious belief could allow such behavior.[23]

---

19 Information from the Pew Research Center, cited in http://graceuniversity.edu/iip/2013/04/13-04-20-1/.

20 http://ec.europa.eu/public_opinion/archives/ebs/ebs_341_en.pdf, p. 381, cited in http://en.wikipedia.org/wiki/Religion_in_Europe.

21 http://my.fit.edu/~gabrenya/cultural/readings/Inglehart-Baker-2000.pdf, cited in http://en.wikipedia.org/wiki/Church_attendance.

22 We note that this phenomenon is not strictly a twenty-first century occurrence. The Lisbon earthquake and tidal wave, occurring on November 1, 1755 (All Saints' Day), during the time when Mass was being celebrated, caused similar reflections during the Enlightenment.

23 http://thehumanist.com/magazine/july-august-2012/features/nonbeliever-nation-the-rise-of-secular-americans.

- Children's sports (in the United States, at least).[24]
- Choice in types of upbringing and multiculturalism.
- Education, particularly the exposure to teaching about different religions.
- Bad press, particularly that concerning the misdeeds of religious figures (e.g., stories of abuses of power and money by certain evangelical Christian pastors or of pedophilia in the Catholic Church).
- The increasing spread of scientific knowledge, much of which is considered contrary to religious observance.[25]

In developing countries the tendencies seem to be more toward support for religions and religiosity and less toward secularism. According to a 2009 survey by Gallup,[26] in 40 out of the total 114 surveyed countries (35%) more than 90% of the population categorized religion as an important part of their daily life; this number increases to 64 countries (or 56%) when the threshold is lowered to 80%. The greater the per capita income of the country, the smaller is the proportion of the population considering religion as an important part of daily life, with more than 77% of all countries showing greater than 50% of their population as inclined to religion in their daily life. Among Muslim-majority countries, only Kazakhstan fell below 50%, primarily because of the high share of the non-Muslim population of the country and the religious suppression during the nearly seventy-year Soviet rule. Only five Muslim-majority countries (all from the ex-Soviet bloc) showed less than 80% of their population considering religion as an important part of daily life. These figures indicate clearly that there is a significant gap between the developed and developing world in terms of their populations' religiosity and yet an even greater gap between Muslim-majority and non-Muslim countries of the world, with Muslim-majority countries being significantly more religious than others.

---

24 http://www.christianitytoday.com/gleanings/2013/april/main-reason-for-declining-church-attendance-childrens.html?paging = off.

25 http://philanthropy2012.hubpages.com/hub/God-Is-A-Sadist.

26 http://www.gallup.com/poll/142727/religiosity-highest-world-poorest-nations.aspx.

Is religion an important part of your daily life?
Median responses among countries at each per-capita income level

Per-capita income	Yes	No
$0-$2,000	95%	5%
$2,001-$5,000	92%	7%
$5,001-$12,500	82%	17%
$12,501-$25,000	70%	28%
$25,001+	47%	52%

GALLUP

In analyzing these figures, Gallup notes that

> social scientists have put forth numerous possible explanations for the relationship between the religiosity of a population and its average income level. One theory is that religion plays a more functional role in the world's poorest countries, helping many residents cope with a daily struggle to provide for themselves and their families. A previous Gallup analysis supports this idea, revealing that the relationship between religiosity and emotional wellbeing is stronger among poor countries than among those in the developed world.[27]

Some observers, however, sense that, across the board, including in developed countries, there is a return to spiritual concerns or religious observance.[28] This return to religious observance—and, particularly, fundamentalism—may be a reaction to the increasing pace of change in the twenty-first century world and globalization, as some people seek a mooring to help them in dealing with the increasing changes and insecurities in their lives.[29] A 2013 study suggests that a number of religions are growing faster than the world rate of population increase

---

27 Ibid.

28 See, e.g., http://www.christianpost.com/news/study-world-is-turning-more-religious-atheism-declining-100518/.

29 http://www.gmu.edu/programs/icar/ijps/vol1_1/smoker.html.

(1.1% annually)—Baha'i at 1.7%, Islam at 1.6%, and Christianity at 1.2%.[30]

What seems incontestable is that religious or spiritual belief and observance is not spared from the accelerating rates of changes experienced by all areas of human activity as the twenty-first century advances.

The Abrahamic Religions

In Islam, Christians and Jews are considered intimately close to Muslims, as their belief system stems from the same source, namely a monotheistic god. All the Jewish prophets, including Jesus as well as the prophet of Islam, Muhammad,[31] take their inspiration from the same ancestor, namely the prophet Abraham (Ibrahim in Arabic). These religions are often referred to as the Abrahamic religions, referring to Abraham, whose story is told in chapters 11–25 of the Book of Genesis[32]

---

30 "Christianity In Its Global Context, 1970–2010" (conducted by the Center for the Study of Global Christianity at Gordon Conwell Theological Seminary in Massachusetts), cited in "Study: World Is Turning More Religious; Atheism Declining," http://www.christianpost.com/news/study-world-is-turning-more-religious-atheism-declining-100518/.

31 It is customary in the Muslim community to add the phrase "peace be upon him" (sometimes abbreviated "pbuh" or "saw"—the abbreviation in Arabic) after each mention of the Prophet. In this book, we have chosen to omit such usage, but our Muslim readers should assume that this phrase is included in each such reference. We certainly intend no disrespect.

32 Mercer Dictionary of the Bible, p. 5, http://books.google.com/books?id = goq0VWw9rGIC&pg = PA5#v = onepage&q = Abraham%20 %22founding%20father%22&f = false, cited in the Wikipedia article "Abraham," http://en.wikipedia.org/wiki/Abraham#CITEREFAndrews1990. The article further states that "by the beginning of the 21st century, archaeologists had 'given up hope of recovering any context that would make Abraham, Isaac or Jacob credible 'historical figures.'" Given the importance of the Abraham figure in the three religions, whether or not he existed historically ultimately makes little difference.

and who is venerated as a founding patriarch of all three religions. The Quran calls upon Christians and Jews as believers of the same God:

> Say: O People of the Book! Let us get together on what is common between us and you: that we shall worship none but Allah, that we shall not associate any partners with Him; that we shall not take from among ourselves any lords beside Allah. And if they reject your invitation then tell them: Bear witness that we are Muslims (*who have surrendered to Allah*).[33]

While the world probably has thousands of different religions, the majority of people in the world—some 54%, or approximately 3.9 billion persons as of early 2015—belong to one of these three related religions. An early twenty-first-century source[34] provided the following breakdown:

- Christianity—2.04 billion (32.9%, based upon a then world population of 6.2 billion).
- Islam—1.625 billion (22.5%).
- Judaism—14 million (0.2%).

Muslims see Islam as a continuation (and indeed the culmination) of Judaism and Christianity; they believe that the revelations (themselves divine) given first to the Jews and then to the Christians come from the same God, in Arabic called Allah.[35] Muslims believe that these revelations were given through Adam, Noah, Abraham, Moses, and Jesus, whom they consider prophets, and perfected through the revelation given to Muhammad; the earlier revelations to these prophets

33 Sura A'l-e-'Imran (3), verse 64.

34 Encyclopedia Britannica Online, 2002: http://web.archive.org/web/20070312004028/http://www.britannica.com/eb/table?tocId = 9394911.

35 The word *Allah* is a contraction of the Arabic definite article *al* and the word for god, *ilah*; it is thus not the name of God. Arabic-speaking Christians speaking of their God use the word *Allah* as well. We refer to Allah when speaking about the Muslim God, and God when talking about a notion of God outside a specifically Muslim context.

have been misinterpreted and altered over time. Jesus is thus the second-holiest person in Islam; his message was divinely inspired, but (unlike the Christians) Muslims believe that Jesus (and Muhammad, for that matter) was entirely human and did not have a divine nature.

As an Abrahamic religion, Islam shares with Judaism and Christianity the following beliefs:[36]

- *Monotheism.* Islam holds that Allah is one and incomparable. Like Judaism and Christianity, it believes that God creates, rules, reveals, loves, judges, and forgives. The Muslim conception of God is similar to Judaism's; Muslims reject the notion of a god in three persons (the Christian notion of the Trinity), which they consider to be polytheistic and idolatrous (*shirk*).
- *Theological continuity.* All the Abrahamic religions believe in an eternal God ruling the universe and history. God reveals his message through prophets and angels. All believers owe obedience to this God, who will one day intervene unilaterally in history to judge the then living and the dead.
- *Scripture.* All three religions believe that God guides humanity with revelations through angels and prophets, resulting in scripture, which has a divine character.
- *An ethical orientation.* The three religions share the belief that a choice exists between good and evil, which is related to obedience and disobedience to God's law as revealed in the scriptures.
- *An eschatological worldview.* Each religion views the world eschatologically, meaning that history has an end, which will come with the resurrection of the dead and final judgment.
- *The importance of Jerusalem.* All three religions accord enormous importance to the city of Jerusalem, albeit for different reasons:

    - For Jews, Jerusalem was established by David as the capital of the United Kingdom of Israel; his son Solomon built the First Temple on Mount Moriah, where Abraham's sacrifice of Isaac took place.

---

36 http://en.wikipedia.org/wiki/Abrahamic_religions.

- o For Christians, Jesus preached and healed in Jerusalem, drove the money changers from the temple, held the Last Supper, and was crucified there.
- o For Muslims, Jerusalem was the first *qibla,* toward which Muslims turned in prayer. Also, Muhammad traveled to the al-Aqsa mosque in Jerusalem and from there to heaven in the Night Journey, where he communicated with Allah and the other prophets, receiving instructions to take back to the faithful concerning prayer.

The Islamic World Today

The Muslim population as of 2010 (an estimated 1.625 billion persons of a then total world population of 7.21 billion, or 22.5%)[37] represents an increase from 361 million Muslims in 1950 (of a then total world population of 2.52 billion—14.3%). The number of Muslims in the world is estimated to increase to 1.92 billion in 2025 (of a then world estimated population of 7.93 billion—24.2%) and to 2.58 billion in 2050 (of a then world estimated population of 9.32 billion—27.7%).[38]

This projected increase is due less to conversions than to the high total fertility rates[39] in large Muslim countries[40] (e.g., Pakistan, 2.86; Bangladesh, 2.45; India, 2.51; Egypt, 2.87; Yemen, 4.09; Algeria, 2.78[41]); in comparison, in the four largest Christian countries,[42] the rates are United States, 2.01; Brazil, 1.79; Mexico, 2.29; and Russia,

---

37 http://www.photius.com/rankings/muslim_population_projections.html.

38 Ibid.

39 *The World Factbook*, Central Intelligence Agency, https://www.cia.gov/library/publications/the-world-factbook/docs/notesanddefs.html?countryName = France&countryCode = fr®ionCode = eu#2127, cited in Wikipedia, "Total Fertility Rate," http://en.wikipedia.org/wiki/Total_fertility_rate.

40 http://www.prb.org/Publications/Articles/2009/karimpolicyseminar.aspx.

41 https://www.cia.gov/library/publications/the-world-factbook/rankorder/2127rank.html.

42 http://www.pewforum.org/2011/12/19/global-christianity-exec/.

1.61. In Europe, for example, the total fertility rate for the period 2005–2010 for Muslims is estimated at 2.2, while the rate for non-Muslim populations is 1.5.[43]

As of 2010, there were forty-nine countries in the world with a Muslim-majority population (Nigeria, with a total fertility rate of 5.25, is expected to become the fiftieth such country by 2030).[44] All Muslim-majority countries are in the Global South, or less-developed regions of the world, with the exception of Bosnia-Herzegovina, Albania, and Kosovo in Europe. Some 1.2 billion Muslims live in Muslim-majority countries (74% of the world Muslim population); 376 million (23%) live in non Muslim-majority Global South countries, and 42 million Muslims (3%) live in the Global North (more developed countries).

43 http://www.pewforum.org/2011/01/27/future-of-the-global-muslim-population-regional-europe/. It is worth noting that this study projects for the period 2025-2030 rates of 2.0 for Muslims and 1.6 for non-Muslims.

44 http://www.pewforum.org/2011/01/27/future-of-the-global-muslim-population-muslim-majority/.

Chapter 2

Islam and Muslims

An Overview of the Religion and the People

O reassured soul, Return to your Lord, well-pleased and pleasing [to Him], And enter among My [righteous] servants, And enter My Paradise.[45]

What Is Islam?

The word *Islam* is derived from the Arabic root consonants of *S*, *L*, and *M* (س ل م).[46] Other words built around the same consonants include

- *salam* ("peace"),
- *tasleem* ("surrendering"),
- *salemma* ("to be saved"),
- *aslam* ("to submit"),
- *esteslam* ("to surrender"), and
- *musel* ("undisputed").

45 Sura Al Fajr (89), verses 27–30.

46 Arabic, like most Semitic languages, forms its words from combinations of three consonants; words using the same consonants have related meanings.

The common concept underlying these words is achieving peace and safety by surrendering to circumstances beyond one's control. The name Islam was given to the religion by Allah[47] when he revealed in the Quran

> Today I have perfected your religion for you, completed my favor upon you and approved Al-Islam as a Deen (*way of life for you*).[48]

The Quran also states

> Truly the [recognized] religion in the sight of Allah is Islam.[49]

There are also other references in the Quran that specify Islam to be the official title of this religion.[50]

Theologically, the word *Islam* is often interpreted as achieving peace with oneself, one's environment, and one's God by submitting to the will of the one and only God.

---

47 See chapter 1, footnote 17.

48 Sura Al-Mâ'idah (5), verse 3.

49 Sura A'l-e-'Imran (3), verse 1.

50 E.g., Surah Fussilat (41) verse 33: "Who is better in speech than one who calls *people* to Allah, does good deeds, and says 'I am a Muslim'?"

Surah A 'l-e-'Imran (3) verse 20: "So if they argue with you (*O Muhammad*), tell them: 'I have submitted myself entirely to Allah, and so have those who follow me.' Then ask those who are illiterate (*Arab pagans*): 'Will you also submit yourselves *to Allah*?' If they become Muslims they shall be rightly guided but if they turn back, *you need not worry*, because your sole responsibility is to convey the Message. All is watching all His servants *very closely*.

Sura Az-Zukhruf (43) verse 69: "*It will be said to* those who believed in Our revelations and became Muslims."

What Is a Muslim?

A Muslim is a person who is at peace with him- or herself, his surroundings and his God by submitting to the will of Allah. To become a Muslim, one must simply recite the *Shahada* ("There is no God but Allah, and Muhammad is his messenger"). A Muslim submits to the will of Allah by

- believing in the seen and unseen as described in the Quran,
- adhering to the tenets of the religion,
- obeying the commands of Allah, and
- "worshiping Allah as though you can see Him, and if you feel that you cannot see Him, then know that He can see you."[51]

Just as Islam is the title given by Allah, *Muslim* is also a title given by Allah to those who adhere to Islam. The Quran states that

> He [Allah] has chosen you and not laid upon you any hardship in the observance of your faith—the faith of your father Ibrâheem (*Abraham*). He named you Muslims before *in prior scriptures* and in this (*Qur'an*), so that the Rasool (*Muhammad*) may testify against you and you yourselves may testify against the rest of mankind.[52]

The Holy Quran

The Quran is the guiding book for Muslims. Muslims believe that the Quran was directly revealed by the archangel Gabriel (Jibril in Arabic) to the prophet Muhammad over a period of twenty-three years starting in 609 CE (thirteen years in Mecca and ten years in Medina). The Quran consists of 114 chapters (sura) of varying lengths. It addresses for Muslims all matters of human life including doctrines, social organization, and some legislation. It also provides stories from earlier history with the intent of teaching lessons from the past.

---

51 Authentic tradition of the prophet Muhammad as narrated in Al-Bukhari.

52 Sura Al-Hajj (22), verse 78.

The Quran is written in Arabic using a very poetic style. Many Arabic-speaking Muslims (and all Muslims are encouraged to learn Arabic, as Muslims believe that Allah's choice of Arabic as the language for the revelation was intentional; thus, the "true" revelation is in Arabic, and translations are considered as interpretations, thus introducing the possibility of misinterpretation and error). Muslims appreciate the Quran as the most beautiful work of Arabic ever written. The Quran challenges other authors to come up with a chapter of equivalent quality; so far, since its revelation, no other work is considered to offer a significant response to this challenge. The Quran states

> Declare: 'Even if all human beings and Jinns combined their resources to produce the like of this Qur'an, they would never be able to compose the like thereof.'[53]

Furthermore, Allah challenges nonbelievers by asking them to produce ten chapters like it:[54]

> Say *to them*: "Make up ten Sûrahs like this and call to your aid whomsoever you can, *including your gods whom you worship* besides Allah, if what you say is true." But if they fail to answer you, then you should know that this (*Qur'an*) is revealed with the knowledge of Allah and that there is none worthy of worship but He.

Later[55] Allah makes it even easier when he states

> If you are in doubt concerning that which We have sent to Our servant (*Muhammad*), then produce one Sûrah like

---

53 Sura Al-Isrâ (17), verse 88.

54 Sura Hûd (11), verses 13–14.

55 The verse cited is actually before the above-cited version in the Quran as organized. However, the chapters in the Quran are generally presented in an order according to their length, regardless of the time they were revealed. The chapter in which this verse occurs (Sura Al-Baqarah [2], verse 23) was written after Sura Hûd, containing the earlier challenge.

> this; and call your witnesses (*gods that you call upon*) beside Allah *to assist you*, if you are right *in your claim.*

The significance of this challenge is further enhanced by the context of the time when the Quran was revealed. Arabs of the seventh century CE were highly advanced in poetry and forms of verbal and written expression; they took great pride in their ability to write wonderfully expressive poetry. In such a context, Muslims consider the fact that Muhammad—a man who was illiterate and did not illustrate any poetic inclinations during the first forty years of his life—was able overnight to produce extraordinarily poetic expressions in the form of the Quran is yet another miracle and a sign of the divine nature and origin of the Quran.

The Quran has been translated into almost all of the world's major languages and is guiding people's lives in virtually every country in the world. The Quran has remained unchanged because Allah promised to protect it:

> Surely, We have revealed this reminder (*the Qur'an*); and We will surely preserve it Ourself.[56]

The text of the Quran was written down at the time of its revelation (Muhammad, being illiterate, recited it to members of his entourage who did the writing) and passed on from generation to generation. Millions of Muslims have memorized the entire Quran,[57] thereby ensuring that the text and its contents can never be lost.

In addition to the difficulties of translating poetic Arabic from the seventh century CE into modern languages, the challenge many Muslims face in interpreting the Quran is their ability to understand the history of each revelation and the intent of each verse within the context of a group of verses. For this reason, verses of the Quran are often misquoted, misrepresented, taken out of context, and otherwise inappropriately used to make certain points—particularly by those non-Muslims who aim to show Islam as a violent and deviant religion, as

---

[56] Sura Al-Hijr (15), verse 9.

[57] The word for such a person is a *hafiz*.

well as those Muslims who want to achieve certain political or religious objectives serving their own viewpoints.

The Hadith

The secondary source of guidance for Muslims (after the Quran) is the words and acts of the prophet Muhammad, also known as the *sunnah* (which translates as "the path or way of life"). These words and acts are manifested in numerous books that include compilations of *hadith* (the plural is *ahadith*, translated as "report, news, or tradition"), which also includes their train of transmission.

The Prophet Muhammad

The life of the prophet Muhammad serves as an example (as Muslims believe that Allah chose Muhammad to be the messenger because of his exemplary characteristics). The Quran states that

> You have indeed, in the life of Allah's Rasool, the 'Best Model' for him whose hope is in Allah and the Day of the Hereafter.[58]

Not only Muslims consider him to have been a great personality in history, but also many non-Muslims scholars and leaders considered Muhammad's influence and character to have been of the highest level. Appendix 1 contains a sampling of statements from these scholars and leaders.

What Is Islam Not?

Islam is certainly not a religion that was propagated by the sword that calls for believers to kill everyone who is not a Muslim. There are

---

58 Sura Al-Ahzâb (33), verse 21.

numerous verses of the Quran that support this interpretation, as we discuss below.

Muslims generally recognize that no one can be forced to convert to Islam, as Allah will guide whom he wills:

- "So keep on giving admonition, for you are an admonisher not a taskmaster over them."[59]
- "Would you [Muhammad] then compel mankind against their will to believe?"[60]
- "*O Prophet,* you cannot give guidance to whom you wish, it is Allah who gives guidance to whom He pleases."[61]

Furthermore, the Quran is very specific about the free will of the individual to choose his or her own beliefs. Verses indicating this point of view include

- "*O Prophet* proclaim: "This is the Truth from your Rabb. Now let him who will, believe in it, and him who will, deny it"[62];
- "There is no compulsion in religion"[63];
- "Now if they give you no heed *they should* know that We have not sent you, *O Muhammad*, to be their keeper. Your only duty is to convey *My message*"[64];
- "Call *people* to the Way of your Rabb with wisdom and best advice, and reason with them, *if you have to*, in the most courteous manner: for your Rabb knows best who strays from His Way and He knows best who is rightly guided"[65]; and

---

59 Sura Al-Ghâshiyah (88), verses 21–22.

60 Sura Yûnus (10), verse 99.

61 Sura Al-Qasas (28), verse 56.

62 Sura Al-Kahf (18), verse 29.

63 Sura Al-Baqarah (2), verse 256.

64 Sura Ash-Shûra (42), verse 48.

65 Sura An-Nahl (16), verse 125.

- "If it had been the will of your Rabb *that all the people of the world should be believers,* all the people of the earth would have believed!"[66]

Thus it is not for Muslims to convert someone to Islam. Even the Prophet himself was only a warner and a messenger—no more. Hence there is no need to assume that anyone has to be more than God wants him to be.

There is no place for arrogance in Islam. It is arrogance that allows us to assume that we are better than others just because we believe in a certain way. Allah says in the Quran

- "I will turn away from My signs those who are unjustly arrogant in the land, so that even if they see each and every sign they will not believe in it"[67]; and
- "Certainly He does not love the arrogant."[68]

As a matter of fact, arrogance is the characteristic of Satan, who refused to bow down to Adam (upon his creation by Allah) because he believed that he was better than Adam, as Allah had created him from fire and Adam from elements of the earth:

> When We ordered the angels: "Prostrate before Adam *in respect,*" they all prostrated except Iblees (*name of Shaitan* [Satan]) who refused in his arrogance and became a disbeliever.[69]

Also

> Behold when your Rabb said to the angels: "I am about to create a man from clay: then when I have fashioned him and breathed of My *created* spirit into him, fall down and

66 Sura Yûnus (10), verse 99.

67 Sura Al-A'rât (7), verse 146.

68 Sura An-Nahl (16), verse 23.

69 Sura Al-Baqarah (2), verse 34.

> prostrate yourselves before him." Accordingly all the angels prostrated themselves, except Iblees; he acted arrogantly and became one of the disbelievers. *Allah* said: "O Iblees (*Shaitan*)! What prevented you from prostrating yourself to the one whom I have created with My own hands? Are you too arrogant, or do you think that you are one of the exalted ones?" *Iblees* said: "I am better than he: You created me from fire while You created him from clay." *Allah* said "Get out of here: for you are accursed, and My curse shall be on you till the Day of Judgment."[70]

Thus, how can a Muslim who believes in Allah and exercises the teachings of his religion look down upon and cause harm to someone who is not a Muslim, especially out of pride or arrogance or both? Isn't arrogance the characteristic of the most despised of all creatures, namely Satan?

As for killing the innocent, the Quran says

> On account of that incident, We ordained for the Children of Israel that whoever kills a person, except as a punishment for murder or mischief in the land, it will be *written in his book of deeds* as if he had killed all the human beings and whoever shall save a life shall be regarded as if he gave life to all the human beings. Yet, even though Our Rasools came to them *one after the other* with clear revelations, it was not long before, many of them committed excesses in the land.[71]

So whether a killing is presumed to be for good cause or otherwise, when a person kills an innocent, it is irretrievably bad—equivalent to killing all of humanity.

---

70 Sura Sâd (38), verses 71–78.

71 Sura Al-Mâ'idah (5), verse 32.

A Muslim[72] who follows the teachings of his religion is therefore is *not* a person who is arrogant, condescending, ready to harm others, or even kill because they do not agree with them or do not share their belief system. Such a Muslim is a person who seeks Allah's pleasure in every breath and action of his life. These value systems are overwhelmingly similar to the value systems one finds in other religions, with the differences being in the forms of worship or practices of these religions.

Where Muslims commit atrocities, abuse people's rights, and become involved in other unacceptable activities, we should recognize that such Muslims are humans and that they commit these acts due to their weaknesses, their environment, or their upbringing, rather than by adhering to Muslim teachings and obligations. Those who commit such acts are criminals, whether they consider themselves Muslims, Christians, or atheists. Criminals plot actions and crimes out of free choice—not because Islam, Christianity, or Judaism instructs them to do so.

72 As noted above, Muslims believe that one becomes a Muslim simply by sincerely reciting the Shahada. Thus the authors consider the members of various terrorist groups that profess adherence to Islam to be Muslims—but Muslims who do not understand or live by the teachings of their religion.

Chapter 3

Islam and Political Organization

Structure of the Muslim Community as a Whole

Hold fast, all of you, to the cord of Allah, and be not divided. [73]

Islam originated in a world organized politically on a far different basis than that which we find at the beginning of the twenty-first century. The Quran does not discuss political organization, nor did Muhammad provide guidelines for the political organization of the Islamic community after his death (a source, as we discuss in chapter 5, of much controversy and many problems). Not surprisingly, Islam's ideas concerning political organization are very different that those developed in Western societies.

The Ummah and the Nation-State

Muhammad received the revelation of the Quran in the early seventh century (CE)—more than one thousand years before the emergence of the concept of the nation-state following the Treaty of Westphalia ending the Thirty Years' War in 1648. The Quran contains some sixty-two references to the *ummah* (an Arabic word meaning "nation" or "community"). It generally refers to Muslim people with a

---

73 Sura Al Emran (3), verse 103.

common ideology and culture and includes all Muslims throughout the world, regardless of location.[74] It also refers to birds,[75] animals, and other creations of God as *umam* (plural of *ummah*), so that *ummah* means all species that share common ways of life and common interests.

Throughout most of their history, Muslims organized themselves politically under arrangements that reflected mostly tribal or geographic demarcations. The authority and, thus, reach of a sultan (a political, rather than a religious, leader) depended on his ability to collect taxes, ensure the safety and welfare of the population, and if needed, address rebellions effectively. While Muslims may have accepted the political authority of a leader, on a local level, their primary allegiance was generally to their tribe or clan. Nonetheless, most Muslims held a sentimental and religious attachment to the ummah, understood as the global Islamic community, and Muslim political leaders would occasionally appeal to the leaders of other Muslim communities to assist them in resisting non-Muslim incursions (e.g., the Ottomans appealing to Muslims from as far as Morocco and India for assistance during World War I).[76]

While Europe divided into nation-states during the seventeenth through nineteenth centuries, the nation-state arrived along with colonialism in the Muslim world in the late nineteenth century and even more in the twentieth, with the Muslim world being divided into independent nation-states generally after World War II.

> The ideology of [the] nation-state has had no equivalent either in the early Islamic thinking or practice. It's [sic] introduction in the Muslim world, as elsewhere, was related to Western colonialism. Moreover, the retreating colonial powers put in place a nation-state structure in the notionally free political entities of the Muslim world. Nonetheless, the nation-state system did not acquire an ideological legitimacy from the populace in the Muslim world. Its acceptance or tolerance by the Muslim world on the *Realpolitik* grounds

74 http://en.wikipedia.org/wiki/Ummah.

75 Surah Al An'âm (6), verse38.

76 http://www.newislamicdirections.com/nid/articles/reflections_on_the_ummah_nation_state_divide.

> should not be treated as tantamount to ideational or intellectual conformity. In fact, on spiritual and ethical foundations of Islam, it would be a difficult proposition to rationalize/legitimize it in the context of the Muslim World [sic]. At best, it enjoys an ambiguous legitimacy as its viable alternative in any concrete form, is found wanting in the present period . . . [I]n the contemporary world, it is increasingly perceived, particularly by Muslims, that the nation-state order dismembers the *Umma(h)* because territorial delimitation is the hallmark of a nation-state, whereas *Ummah* [sic] overrides territoriality and holds its adherents together by a common bond of faith. In fact, it divided the *Umma(h)*, and for the West it became easier to exploit one national Muslim state with another, as the establishment of the Muslim *Umma(h)* poses the greatest threat to their interests.[77]

Most Muslims consider the borders of these nation-states as arbitrary and an imposition by Western powers; often such state border lines were created with full understanding and intention to create geographic and national conflict points by dividing natural boundaries between various countries to ensure continued disagreements and divisions. For example (and there are others), the Kurds were divided between Iran, Iraq, Turkey, and Syria; Kashmiris were split between Indian and Pakistani Kashmir; the Pashtuns were divided between Pakistan and Afghanistan. Indeed, many Muslims suspect a more or less conscious effort by Western nations to use the nation-state system to prevent Muslim unity and the emergence of a single Muslim political unit.

---

[77] Basu, Rumki, *Globalization and the Changing Role of the State* (Sterling Publishers Pvt. Ltd., 2008), pp. 68–9, found in https://books.google.com/books?id = jtHCyMaQ3ngC&pg = PA60&lpg = PA60&dq = dar + al + sulh + diplomatic + relations&source = bl&ots = MgICRsbJUP&sig = xUMTexOSFFXPMTIa3NqigkefZ1g&hl = en&sa = X&ei = suM7VemTBsXesAW57oDADQ&ved = 0CD4Q6AEwBw#v = onepage&q = dar%20al%20sulh%20diplomatic%20relations&f = false.

> One of the most profound developments in the modern history of Islam has been the emergence of the Nation-state in Europe and its subsequent imposition on the Muslim world. Its profundity is illustrated by the fact that it has come to capture the imagination of all politically active Muslims. In the process, it became one of the principal means for consolidating the destruction of a viable Islamic civilization by introducing into the Muslim world an institutional and conceptual framework that helped to hasten the disappearance of the institutions and organizations that gave Muslim societies their unique character and identity.[78]

"Houses" in Islam

Although not based in the Quran and with questionable roots in the ahadith[79], Islamic jurisprudence has traditionally divided the world into three main spheres, also called *dar,* or house. *Dar al-Islam* (the house of Islam, where peace and tranquility reign), *dar al-harb* (the house of war)—also known as *dar al-kufr* (the house of disbelief)—and *dar al-ahd* (the house of truce), also known as *dar al-sulh* (the house of peace, conciliation, or treaty). The distinction is legal, rather than theological;[80] the determination is based upon the government, the legal system, and behavior as well as treaties and agreements in place. Even though also practiced in the time of the Prophet, as in the example of Mecca before its conquest by Muslims (629 CE), these terms were coined much later. Thus a Muslim-minority or non-Muslim country not ruled by Islamic law is either *dar al-harb or dar al-sulh,* while a Muslim-majority country observing Islamic law is *dar al-Islam.*

Dar al-harb is a nation that is in active war with a Muslim-majority country or *dar al-Islam.* There are no peace treaties in place; there is

---

78 http://www.newislamicdirections.com/nid/articles/reflections_on_the_ummah_nation_state_divide.

79 See, e.g., http://en.wikipedia.org/wiki/Divisions_of_the_world_in_Islam (no basis in the *ahadith*) and http://www.khilafah.com/clarifying-the-meaning-of-dar-al-kufr-a-dar-al-islam/ (arguing for such a basis).

80 http://atheism.about.com/od/islamicextremism/a/daralharb.htm.

no exchange of embassies, and there is an active military confrontation in progress. In the world of the twenty-first century, with extensive relationships between Muslim-majority and Non-Muslim-majority countries, few countries (perhaps Israel), if any, would fall into the *dar al-harb* category—and even for them, civilians are not to be victimized.

Dar al-ahd (the house of truce) or *dar al-sulh* (the house of conciliation or treaty)[81] refers to non-Muslim-majority territories that have concluded an armistice with a Muslim-majority government and agreed to protect Muslims within their boundaries. Whereas the term was also used before, the Ottoman Empire used the term primarily to describe its relations with the Christian territories that it administered (and which paid tribute to it). The Ottomans also extended the concept to cover countries with which the sultan had concluded a truce; such countries could not be attacked, and their inhabitants could not be enslaved as prisoners of war or killed. It is generally accepted in contemporary Islam that the establishment of diplomatic relations (and the installation of an embassy or consulate) with another country constitutes a political treaty of respect and adherence to mutual friendship, thereby allowing such non-Muslim-majority countries to benefit from this status.[82]

The Notion of an Islamic Country

The term *Islamic* (or *Muslim*) *country* is often used to refer to countries with a majority Muslim population. However, this description is just as misleading as to consider the United States, Germany, France, or Brazil as Christian countries. It is true that certain countries have a historical affiliation with the Christian or Islamic religion and that the majority of the citizens profess that religion, and that some of their laws are influenced by the religious beliefs of their majority Christian or Muslim population. However, it would be wrong to suggest that every law and every aspect of the political life in these countries are directly linked to or affected by the religious teachings of these countries. Consequently, many Muslim historians, scholars, and others engaged with the situation of the Muslim world prefer to call Muslim-majority

---

81 http://en.wikipedia.org/wiki/Divisions_of_the_world_in_Islam.

82 http://islamicus.org/dar-al-sulh/.

countries as such (as we will as well). They make no reference whatsoever to the Islamic nature of their system of government or their adherence to Islamic teachings.

In fact, there have been studies that show that all Muslim-majority countries are significantly distanced from the Islamic teachings for good governance, care for various groups of population, and for economic, political, and social development. In an article titled "How Islamic Are Islamic Countries?" published in 2010 in the *Global Economy Journal*,[83] all countries of the world are evaluated based on the norms that make up an Islamic system of governance. Utilizing Islamic teachings from the Quran and the sunnah, the authors have developed an Islamicity index, based on which they rate various countries based upon how well they implement the teachings of Islam. Appendix 2 contains excerpts from the article.

> The article attempt[s] to discern if Islamic principles are conducive to (a) free markets and strong economic performance, (b) good government governance and rule of law, (c) societies with well formed human and civil rights and equality, and (d) cordial relations and meaningful contributions to the global community, or are they, in fact, a deterrent.[84]

Their conclusion is that the teachings of Islam are conducive to achieving these goals—but that it is Western countries that are doing a far better job of following and implementing Islamic teachings in their economy and society than Muslim-majority countries. To provide confirmation for this finding, they evaluate each of 208 countries on 113 measurable variables that they believe represent proxies for meeting the above criteria.

The results are surprising. The top 17 (i.e., the countries that best implement the teachings of Islam) are all developed countries (New Zealand is number 1, followed by Luxembourg and Ireland). The first developing country is the Bahamas, at 18. The United States is 25 (also

---

83 Rehman, Scheherazade S. and Hossein Askari, "How Islamic Are Islamic Countries?" *Global Economy Journal* 10, no. 2 (2010), article 2.

84 Ibid.

the average for members of the Organization for Economic Cooperation and Development), preceded by Barbados and followed by Slovenia. The first Muslim-majority country is Malaysia at 38. Saudi Arabia is 131; the Islamic Republic of Iran is 163. The average for the member states of the Organization of Islamic Countries is 139. A complete list of the rankings is provided in appendix 2.

Hence, it is clear that there is no such thing as an Islamic country, which would imply full or at least significant adherence to the principles and rules of the Quran and sunnah in their system of governance. At most we can talk about countries whose inhabitants are predominantly Muslim, even if such countries choose to declare their system of government as Islamic or claim that their laws are Islamic.

Chapter 4

War and Violence in Islam: The Question of Jihad

There Is No Such Thing as a Holy War in Islam

I became more than ever convinced that it was not the sword that won a place for Islam in those days in the scheme of life.

—Mahatma Gandhi[85]

Recent events in the Middle East and attacks on non-Muslims (both in the Middle East and in the West) have created a widespread impression—particularly among non-Muslims—that Islam is a religion preaching violence and forced conversion ("by the sword"). Moreover, today no word creates more fear—and leads to more misunderstanding—than *jihad.* Yet for the great majority of Muslims, their religion is one of peace that can coexist perfectly and seamlessly with non-Muslims. Jihad, properly understood, is a duty that Islam places upon all Muslims; it rejects violence in all but the most exceptional circumstances. A good Muslim exercises jihad every day in ways that raise no threat whatsoever to his or her non-Muslim—or Muslim—neighbors.

---

85 http://www.goodreads.com/quotes/936395-i-wanted-to-know-the-best-of-the-life-of.

Verses in the Quran

Islam does not condone war, but it allows war as a last resort to eliminate suppression and injustice and allow people to freely exercise their religions.

> Fighting has been made obligatory for you, much to your dislike. It is quite possible that something which you do not like is good for you and that something that you love is bad for you. Allah knows, and you do not know.[86]
>
> Fight against them until there is not more disorder and Allah's supremacy is established. If they desist, let there be no hostility except against the oppressors.[87]

While allowing war as a last resort, Islam can legitimately claim to be among the first religions (if not *the* first) to advocate rules for conducting war and limitations on the violence associated with it—more than 1,300 years before the Geneva Conventions.

Both the Quran and the ahadith provide many restrictions on war and violence.

> Islam as a religion of peace discourages aggression and made war a legitimate phenomenon only when it becomes necessary. Even in cases where Islam approves war as a legitimate option and allows Muslims to participate in the hostilities, it has at the same time provided for rules to regulate the prosecution of the war. One among the rules and principles set out by Islam for the purpose of regulating conduct of hostilities hundreds of years back is the basic need to distinguish between combatant and civilian and between civilian objects and military objectives, and accordingly, military operations shall only be directed against military objectives.[88]

---

86 Sura Al-Baqarah (2), Verse 216.

87 Sura Al-Baqarah (2), Verse 193.

88 http://www.ijhssnet.com/journals/Vol_4_No_5_1_March_2014/27.pdf.

The Quran places significant emphasis on the value of human life, whether Muslim or non-Muslim. It forbids absolutely the taking of innocent life unjustly. The Quran equates such a crime with the killing of all humanity:

> We ordained for the Children of Israel that whoever kills a person, except as a punishment for murder or mischief in the land, it will be *written in his book of deeds* as if he had killed all of the human beings and whoever will save a life shall be regarded as if he gave life to all the human beings.[89]

The Quran clearly rejects war in all but exceptional circumstances, stating

> Fight in the cause of Allah those who fight against you, but do not exceed the limits. Allah does not like transgressors.[90]

Peace is the ultimate objective of every Muslim, even if the believer has doubts as to the integrity or intention of the adversary:

> If the enemy is inclined toward peace, do make peace with them, and put your trust in Allah. He is the One Who hears all, knows all.[91]

A Muslim's duty extends beyond prohibiting aggression and safeguarding rights. Islam commands its believers to deal kindly and compassionately with all those who seek to live in peace and harmony:

> Allah does not forbid you to be kind and equitable to those who had neither fought against your faith nor driven you out of your homes. In fact, Allah loves the equitable.[92]

---

89 Sura Al-Mâ'idah (5), verse 32.

90 Sura Al-Baqarah (2), verse 190.

91 Sura Al-Anfâl (8), verse 61.

92 Sura Al-Mumtahanah (60), verse 8.

Moreover, Muslims must respect the property, wealth, family, and dignity of all individuals. Violating these rights and accumulating wealth and power are forbidden:

> Be good to others as Allah has been good to you, and do not seek mischief in the land, for Allah does not love the mischief mongers.[93]

Declarations of the Prophet and His Followers

The Prophet clarified appropriate conduct during times of war, forbidding the killing of noncombatants:

> Whoever has killed a person having a treaty with the Muslims shall not smell the fragrance of Paradise, though its fragrance is found for a span of forty years.[94]

He further prohibited Muslim soldiers from killing women, children, and the elderly, saying

> Do not betray, do not be excessive, do not kill a newborn child.[95]

Such offenses are extremely serious. Next to denying the oneness and supremacy of Allah, killing is the second major sin of Islam:

> The first cases to be adjudicated between people on the Day of Judgment will be those of bloodshed.[96]

---

93 Sura Al-Qasas (28), verse 77.

94 http://www.islam-guide.com/ch3-11.htm.

95 http://www.islam-guide.com/ch3-11.htm.

96 http://www.islam-guide.com/ch3-11.htm.

This promise covers not only Muslims but also non-Muslims who choose to live in peace with Muslims; they are to be protected:

> Truly your blood, your property and your honor are inviolable.[97]

This treatment extends to all of God's creations:

> There is a reward for kindness shown to every living animal or human.[98]

The followers of Muhammad followed a similar line. Abu Bakr, the first caliph after the death of the Prophet, instructed his general Yazid when confronting the Byzantine armies to abide by the basic tenets of Islamic warfare, ordering

> I advise you ten things: do not kill women or children or an aged, infirm person. Do not cut down fruit-bearing trees. Do not destroy an inhabited place. Do not slaughter sheep or camels except for food. Do not burn bees and do not scatter them. Do not steal from the booty, and do not be cowardly.[99]

Jihad

The word *jihad* comes from the Arabic root word *jahada*, meaning "to strive, to struggle, or to exert." Almost since its first use in the Quran, it has been the subject of much controversy and discussion—both within the world of Islam and without.

---

97 http://www.islam-guide.com/ch3-11.htm.

98 http://www.islam-guide.com/ch3-11.htm.

99 http://www.searchtruth.com/book_display.php?book = 21&translator = 4&start = 10&number = 21.3.10.

Jihad in the Quran

A "familiar"[100] idea is that the term *jihad*, when used in the Quran (some thirty-six times) means internal effort or striving "in the way of Allah";[101] when the Quran directs Muslims to fight, the word used is not *jihad* but *qital* or words built from a similar root. Islam insists that the real struggle is the one that aims to achieve "peace of heart."[102] It is the third dimension of the soul, namely the soul at peace with itself, its God, and His creations.[103] The Quran clarifies this idea on numerous occasions, including

> By the soul and He Who perfected it and inspired it with knowledge of what is wrong for it and what is right for it; indeed successful will be the one who purifies it, and indeed unsuccessful is the one who corrupts it![104]

Islam considers life to be a "test of balance for men who are capable of inducing both the best and the worst from themselves."[105]

> Tension [within man] is natural and the conflict of the inward is properly human. Moreover, man proceeds and realizes himself by the effort that he furnishes in order to give force and presence to the inclination of his least violent, irascible and aggressive being. He struggles daily against the most negative forces of his being, as he knows that his humanity will be the price of their mastery. This inward effort and this struggle against the "postulations" of interiority is the most appropriate (literal and figurative) translation of the word *Jihad*.

---

100 Johnson, James Turner, *The Holy War Idea in Western and Islamic Traditions* (The University Park, PA: Pennsylvania State University Press), 1997, p. 35.

101 Sura Al-Hajj (22), verse 78.

102 *Islam, the West and Challenges of Modernity* by Tariq Ramadan, p. 60.

103 Sura Al Fajr (89), verses 27–29.

104 Sura Ahs-Shams (91), verses 7–10.

105 *Islam, the West and the Challenges of Modernity* by Tariq Ramadan, p. 61.

> It is not a question here of reducing *Jihad* to a personal dimension (*Jihad Al-nafs*), but rather returning to its most immediate reality. *Jihad* is to a man's humanity what instinct is to an animal's behavior. To be, for man, is to be responsible and such responsibility is linked to a choice, which always seeks to express the goodness and respect of oneself and others. Choosing, in the reality of inward conflict, is to have a resolve for peace of heart.[106]

A faithful Muslim is in a continuous state of effort to master him- or herself. "This tension toward the mastery of the self is conveyed in Arabic by the word *jihad*."[107]

Islam is fully clear about God's intention to create human beings in many nations and tribes and to create differences in their belief systems and their cultures. So engaging in war and armed conflict against people because of differences in belief systems cannot and must not be because of their religious beliefs, but rather because of our innate nature to seek justice and equality for all and to defend ourselves against aggression and oppression. The Quran is very clear in many instances that it is not Allah's will to forcefully convert people to Islam, but rather to accept and appreciate the differences with which He has created all and that jointly enrich our world.

> O mankind, indeed We created you from a single *pair of a* male and female, and made you into nations and tribes that you might get to know one another.[108]
>
> If Allah wanted, He could have made all of you a single nation. But He willed otherwise in order to test you in what He has given you; therefore, try to excel one another in good deeds. *Ultimately* you all shall return to Allah; then He will tell you the truth of those matters in which you dispute."[109]

---

106 Ibid., p. 61

107 *Islam, the West and Challenges of Modernity* by Tariq Ramadan, p. 62.

108 Sura Al-Hujurât (49), verse 13.

109 Sura Al-Mâ'idah (5), verse 48.

> If it had been the will of your Rabb *that all the people of the world should be believers*, all the people of the earth would have believed! Would you then compel mankind against their will to believe?[110]
>
> O believers! Be steadfast for the sake of Allah and bear true witness and let not the enmity of a people incite you to do injustice; do justice; that is nearer to piety. Fear Allah, surely, Allah is fully aware of all your actions.[111]

It is clear that God's only desire in commanding jihad is to help us live a more God-conscious life:

> Fighting in the path of God means mobilizing all our human forces, directing all our efforts giving of our properties and of our own persons in order to overcome all adversities whether they be injustice, poverty, illiteracy, delinquency or exclusion.[112]
>
> The true believers are those who believe in Allah and his Rasool, then never doubt; and make Jihâd with their wealth and their persons in the cause of Allah. They are the ones who are truthful *in their claim to be the believers.*[113]

The Quran offers such latitude in the interpretation of the word *jihad;* this notion appears in its first revelation:

> Do not yield to the unbelievers, and make Jihad (*strive*) against them with this Qur'an a mighty Jihad (*strenuous striving*).[114]

---

110 Sura Yûnus (10), verse 99.

111 Sura Al-Mâ'idah (5), verse 8.

112 *Islam, the West and Challenges of Modernity*, by Tariq Ramadan, p. 67.

113 Sura Al-Hujurât (49), verse 15. As noted before, the sura in the Quran are not in chronological order, but rather (generally) in order of their length.

114 Sura Al-Furqân (25), verse 52.

There is here mention of a struggle (*jihad* and *jihadan*) that is of a learned and scientific nature, one that relies on dialogue, discussion and debate.[115]

> Nowadays, our enemies, in the path of God, are hunger, unemployment, exploitation, delinquency, and drug addiction. They require intense effort, a continuous fight and a complete Jihad, which needs each and everyone's participation.[116]

Clearly, qital or armed conflict is also authorized and called for in the Quran, which is only one form of jihad. Many of such fighting references involve a defensive reaction. We have already seen the injunction in Sura Al-Baqarah (2), verse 190, but other examples are

> Will you not fight against those people who have broken their oaths, conspired to expel the Rasool and were the first to attack you? Do you fear them?[117]
>
> You will find other *hypocrites* who wish to be safe from you as well as from their own people; but who would plunge into mischief whenever they get an opportunity. Therefore, if they do not keep distance from you and neither offer you peace, nor cease their hostilities against you, seize them and kill them wherever you find them. In their case, We give you clear authority.[118]

A number of verses, however, authorize offensive fighting (while always using the word *qital*):

> *O believers,* fight them until there is no more oppression and until the whole Deen (*way of life*) is for Allah Alone; but if they cease oppression, then surely, Allah is All-Seer of

115 *Islam, the West and Challenges of Modernity*, by Tariq Ramadan, pp. 67–68.

116 *Ibid.*, p. 68.

117 Sura At-Tauba (9), verse 13.

118 Sura An-Nisâ (4), verse 91.

> what they do. If they give no heed, then you should know that Allah is your protector. He is the best to protect and the best to help.[119]
>
> Fight those people of the Book (*Jews and Christians*) who do not believe in Allah and the Last Day, do not refrain from what has been prohibited by Allah and his Rasool and do not embrace the religion of truth (*Al-Islam*), until they pay Jizyah (*protection tax*) with their own hands and feel themselves subdued.[120]

Even in the case of offensive fighting, the point is to reduce the unbelievers into submission to Islamic order and not to convert them to Islam, as is often stated by the opponents of Islam. The fact that for hundreds of years all of Spain was clearly under Muslim rule and there were still a majority Christians and Jews living in peace under Islamic rule is clear evidence of this lack of compulsion to convert that Muslims exercised.[121]

Post-Quranic Usage

The sense of the word *jihad* has evolved significantly since its use in the Quran. Early on, jihad began to associate the ideas not only of inner struggle but also of war.

> Jihad, as signifying the waging of war, is a post-Koranic usage, and . . . in the Koran it is used classically and literally in its natural sense.[122]

The Prophet spoke of "greater jihad" (the struggle to purify oneself and submit to the will of Allah) and "lesser jihad" (warfare). Classical Islamic jurists described four types of jihad:

---

119 Sura Al-Anfâl (8), verses 39–40.

120 Sura At-Tauba (9), verse 29.

121 Johnson, op. cit., p. 62.

122 Ali, Moulavi Cheragh, cited in Johnson, op. cit., p. 36.

- Jihad of the heart (faith).
- Jihad of the tongue (right speech).
- Jihad of the hand (good works).
- Jihad of the sword (warfare).[123]

When jihad as warfare occurs, it must occur

- within the context of *dar al-Islam* versus *dar al-harb*;
- as the collective duty of the community, with specific categories of who should fight and who should perform other duties;
- after issuing an appeal for the opponents to accept Islamic rule (the *da'wah*); and
- according to strict rules of engagement and within defined limits.[124]

Qital or armed jihad is the lesser jihad because it is part of the continuum, namely part of the all-inclusive effort to secure peace and justice for all. Even during armed conflict, Muslims are required to observe all the behavior requirements of being just, controlling anger, avoiding harm to civilians, and avoiding harm to fruit trees, houses, places of worship, etc. Muslims are required to ensure that they remember that Allah is witness to their actions even in the most critical time of their life, namely while fighting for their lives, their loved ones, and their property. But then those are also required at other times, and they do not end when armed conflict ends. Hence, the responsibility of jihad to seek justice and behave in a self-disciplined manner starts before the war, continues during the war, and does not end when the war ends. For this reason, jihad in its unarmed method is the greater jihad, because it is there before the war, during the war, and long after the war, while the qital or armed jihad is there only for a short period to achieve the objectives of fighting against oppression and corruption. Hence, the description of the greater jihad, or the struggle against one's inner self or ego, starts with the end of the lesser jihad, namely qital or armed resistance.

---

123 Johnson, op. cit., p. 61.

124 http://www.scu.edu/ethics/publications/submitted/heit/whatisjihad.html.

In summary, Islam is a religion that emphasizes peaceful coexistence between people and societies and prohibits war and destruction to gain wealth, power, and influence. It urges its followers to seek peace and to respond to peace with peace. Islam does not encourage the presenting of "the other cheek" when struck on one, but it clearly encourages forgiveness when wrong is done to a person. Such forgiveness is encouraged to be from a position of strength rather than one of weakness.

Islam also encourages a proactive approach to fighting evil. The prophet Muhammad is quoted as saying

> When you encounter evil, fix it with you hand (or action), if you cannot, then with your words (advise and urge the offender to stop it) and if you can't, then hate it in your heart and this is a sign of the weakest faith (Iman).

Silence or indifference in the face of evil is, therefore, not acceptable, while action has to clearly follow the norms and guidelines of Islam's teachings for fairness, judicial interaction, and peaceful coexistence. People preaching hate and indiscriminate warfare are, therefore, in clear and direct violation of the Islamic code of conduct.

Chapter 5

The Diversity of Islam

Islam Is Not a Monolithic Religion

If thy Lord had so willed, He could have made mankind One People: but they will not cease to be diverse.[125]

While it is common parlance in the West to speak of "the Muslim world," in fact Islam shows a remarkable degree of diversity—and is anything but monolithic.

A religion may be termed monolithic when

- it is clearly defined;
- it is self-contained (i.e., where one person or institution defines what the religion believes or practices; for example, the Catholic Church[126] is by our definition self-contained, as the pope's decrees define its official positions); and
- all of its followers have the same or similar backgrounds.

125 Sura Hûd (11), verse 118.

126 We speak here only of the Roman Catholic Church as narrowly defined. The Christian community includes not only Catholics and Protestants but also the Orthodoxy, Maronites, Copts, and other denominations—a diversity arguably equal to that within Islam.

How could Islam or Muslims be monolithic with more than 1.625 billion followers and almost 1,400 years of history?

Islam's guiding principles are set forth in its holy scripture, the Quran, as well as the life and advice of the prophet Muhammad transmitted in the works of the ahadith. Islam does not recognize any single individual who, after Muhammad's death in 632 CE, can have binding authority to guide or even explain or clarify any theological issues or questions. Under generally accepted Islamic teachings, Allah has made the (final) revelation available to all believers; each believer is charged with understanding and implementing in their daily life directly, without further intermediation.

Thus Islam is (unlike, for example, Roman Catholicism) a non-hierarchical religion. Islam is similar to Judaism and Protestantism—and distinct from Roman Catholicism—in that it does not have a central figure that can issue religious decrees and can provide guidance or specific doctrines or policies that are binding on believers. Each Muslim is responsible for understanding Allah's revelation as set forth in the Quran and interpreted by the ahadith—and incorporating and implementing its lessons in the life they lead.

Of course, individual Muslims can find assistance from scholars and other interpreters of the Quran at any given time. These scholars are generally learned people who have studied and thought about the scriptures for long periods of time. They have, by virtue of their knowledge and experience, gained more or less widespread popular followings and acceptance and thus are best positioned to exert the authority to guide believers. Such interpreters, however, number in the hundreds of thousands at any one time and, not surprisingly, do not reach a consensus on how to apply the teachings of Islam to a multiplying variety of contexts in an increasingly complicated world.

While Islamic scholars may issue fatwas,[127] they have no binding authority and are effective only to the extent that their reasoning is convincing and within the regional context, the prevailing circumstances and the time of the fatwa. Anyone with an educational background in Islam may issue such a nonbinding decree. Moreover, consistent with the teaching mentioned above concerning the responsibility of understanding the Quran, any Muslim when confronted with a new situation is allowed (indeed, expected) to use their personal judgment (in Arabic, *ijtehad*) for guidance as to how to think and behave. For a fatwa to be convincing, the person issuing the decree must be knowledgeable

- in the subject area concerning the ruling (e.g., financial matters, family law, health questions);
- concerning the regional context in which the seeker of the ruling will apply it (so that a legal scholar in Saudi Arabia cannot issue a fatwa concerning Muslims in the United States); and
- about the circumstances giving rise to the request for the fatwa (so that a scholar can only speak to a specific situation and not issue "across the board" fatwa*s*).

This open and dynamic procedure for religious rulings means that religious practices and value systems have been continuously changing over time. Interpretations of the Quran and the traditions of the Prophet may be different from one part of the world to another; different persons

---

127 A fatwa is an Islamic legal pronouncement, issued by an expert in Muslim religious law, pertaining to specific issues, usually at the request of an individual or a judge to help resolve an issue where Islamic jurisprudence is unclear. Typically such questions occur concerning new technologies or societal evolution. While a fatwa can be analogized to a court ruling and is (at least theoretically) applicable to all members of the worldwide Muslim community (the ummah), it is specifically not binding; each individual has the right (and the responsibility of deciding whether) to follow the decision contained in the fatwa.

http://www.islamicsupremecouncil.org/understanding-islam/legal-rulings/44-what-is-a-fatwa.html.

may legitimately interpret the same verses of the Quran and the ahadith differently. Islam is thus more of a kaleidoscope than a monolith.

As a result, Islam as understood and practiced in Africa is often very different from the way it is lived in Asia, Europe, or the United States. These differences have added significant richness to the religion but have made it challenging to determine what the teachings of Islam are at any one time. Clearly there is a basic consensus as to the main core of the belief system, which is fairly straightforward and unambiguous, shared by all Muslims in every part of the world. However, differences exist in the way those beliefs are exercised and lived in conjunction with other teachings of the religion focusing on Muslim daily life.

Throughout its history, Islam has never been disconnected from politics. Kings, presidents, caliphs, emirs, sultans, and other leaders have always been intimately connected with their religion and guided by its teachings. Not all leaders of Muslims have always been honest, decent, fair, and judicious; rather, many leaders, especially in the more recent past, have been more or less corrupt and unjust. When Islamic teachings sometimes went contrary to their interests, the leaders either suppressed the population that raised its voice against them or assigned muftis[128] the task of ensuring that their actions were justified by Islamic teachings. For centuries Muslim leaders have systematically persecuted Islamic scholars and destroyed their works if such works did not reflect the leaders' official positions or if the works criticized their actions.

An example of corrupted scholars supporting the formal position of their governments and mistranslating and interpreting text of the Quran to fit their preferences is the Saudi government's translation of the Quran into English language. Dr. Khaled Abul Fadl, analyzes this interpretation in chapter 57 ("Corrupting God's Book") of his book titled *Conference of the Books* (set forth in appendix 3). In this chapter, he shows how, by translating the Quran into English in such a way as to support their Wahhabi (see chapter 8) interpretation of the Quran (while deviating significantly from a literal translation of the original Arabic text), the Saudi government seeks to impose a particular interpretation (requiring very strict restrictions on women's dress and behavior) on Muslim women throughout the world. If these types of deviations from the original text to fit one's political preferences are

128 An Islamic scholar who is interpreter or expounder of Islamic law.

possible in the twenty-first century with the Internet and access to other technologies that allow verification of sources and origins, one can only imagine how interpretations of the original text were deviated from and misrepresented by "scholars" in service of corrupt leaders over more than one thousand years of often-unchallenged rule in those countries.

Ever since the revelations in the seventh century CE, Muslims have sought to adapt the teachings of Islam to the cultures—which in many cases predate the Quran—in which they live. These teachings have been integrated into many of these cultures—to varying degrees—in many cases to such a great extent that often the boundaries within these cultures between religion and nonreligious aspects of the culture have faded. Thus, an Egyptian Muslim living in rural Asyut considers female circumcision to be a Muslim religious act, while her Coptic Christian sister nearby considers the practice as part of her own religious tradition—but objectively neither of the two religions prescribes this practice.

The history of the Muslim religion over 1,400 years has had an impact on people—and the practitioners of the faith have affected the religion. In all religions, the believers' ways of life impacts the belief system and, by extension, their value system; Islam is no exception. While the original text of the Quran has remained unchanged since its original notation in the seventh century CE, the narrations from the words and the life of the prophet Muhammad may have been affected by history. As a result, Muslims have become selective in which traditions and words of the Prophet and which instructions of the Quran they choose to emphasize and to allow the greatest impact on their lives.

Similarly, while all Muslims recognize the authority of the Quran and the ahadith, the ways in which they practice their religion and implement its teachings are anything but monolithic. Muslim religious teachings vary based upon

- who interprets the scriptures;
- the geographic and cultural setting; and
- the believer's

    - educational status
    - wealth
    - family status.

Rural Muslims tend to interpret Islam very differently than urban believers; Muslims in Karachi, Pakistan, will practice their religion differently than their colleagues in New York, London, or Istanbul. Better-educated Muslims experience their religion quite differently than those who are un- or marginally educated; wealthy Muslims will live their religion in another fashion than that experienced by poorer Muslims. In Western societies, a first-generation immigrant is unlikely to view his life and religion in the same way as his children or grandchildren. Within the United States, African-American Muslims will have practices that differ from those of Hispanic, Caucasian, and Asian Muslims—and in all of these areas, the diversity is growing rather than decreasing.

In the next chapter, we will examine the current major communities within the Muslim world and describe how they differ from one another.

Chapter 6

The Communities of Islam

The Sunni, the Shi'a, and Everything Else

O mankind! We created you from a single pair of a male and female, and made you into nations and tribes that you might get to know one another. Surely, the noblest of you in the sight of Allah, is he who is the most righteous. Allah is All-knowledgeable, All-Aware.[129]

While all Muslims accept Muhammad as the Prophet and the Quran as the revelation of Allah, unity within the community of Islamic believers (the ummah) did not last long after the Prophet's death in 632 CE. We outline the main communities within Islam that evolved since that time.

Sunnis, Shi'as, and Sufis

The three main groups (although there are numerous smaller offshoots, as discussed below) are Sunnis, Shi'as, and Sufis.

The term *Sunni* derives from an Arabic word that means "adherence to sunnah" (i.e., the customary practices of the Prophet). *Shi'a* comes from an Arabic word meaning "following a sect." Sufism (Arabic تصوف, *taṣawwuf*, practitioners are known as Sufis) is a concept defined as the

[129] Sura Al-Hujurât (49), verse 13.

inner, mystical dimension of Islam;[130] all Sufi orders trace their origins from the Shi'a branch of Islam, with the significant exception of the Sunni *Naqshbandi*, who trace their origins to the first caliph, Abu Bakr.

While both Sunnis and Shi'as recognize the Quran as the sole holy scripture of Islam and the ahadith as the principal source of interpretation for the Quran, they do not agree as to the identity and importance of the stories and sayings constituting the ahadith. For example:

- The Shi'a reject any transmission of ahadith by people who were involved in the governments of Mu'awiyah[131] and Yazid.
- Shi'as lay great significance on the transmission of sayings of Ali, called *Nahj Al-Balagha*. While Sunnis also consider *Nahj Al-Balagha* important, they do not view Ali's sayings as a critical source of guidance for Muslims.
- Shi'as believe in the *Fiqh Al Jaafaria* (*jaafaria,* "jurisprudence"), which was founded by Imam Jaafar ibn Muhamad Al Sadiq (705–750 CE). The teachings of Imam Jaafar were compiled by his students as 400 *usul* (foundations) that consisted of ahadith, Islamic philosophy, theology, Quran commentary, literature, and ethics[132]. Over time, these 400 *usul* were categorized into three books, which are the main source of ahadith for the Shi'as:

    - o *Usul al-Kafi* by al-Kulayni (died 329AH[133])
    - o *Man La Yahduruh al-Faqih* by al-Saduq (d. 381AH)
    - o *Il-Tahdib* and *al-Istibsar* by al-Tusi (d. 460AH)

---

130 http://en.wikipedia.org/wiki/Sufism.

131 The founder of the Umayyad dynasty (663–747 CE) and its first caliph; Yazid, his son, was the second caliph of the Umayyad dynasty.

132 http://www.al-islam.org/inquiries-about-shia-islam-sayyid-moustafa-al-qazwini/five-schools-islamic-thought.

133 The Muslims use a lunar calendar—the *Hijri* calendar, abbreviated AH—of 354 days, which determines the proper dates for Muslim to observe certain holidays and festivals. The *Hijri* calendar starts in 622 CE, the date when Muhammad emigrated from Mecca to Medina. In the Gregorian calendar year 2016, we are mostly in AH 1437, which runs from October 12, 2015, through October 1, 2016.

Scholars generally hold that the split is based upon differences as to who was to have leadership over the Muslim community—the ummah—after the death of the Prophet. Sunnis believe that Muhammad did not appoint a successor to lead the Muslim community and that, after an initial period of confusion, a group of his most prominent companions elected Abu Bakr as the first caliph (the ruler of the ummah) of Islam. Muslims who accepted Abu Bakr as the first caliph became known as "the people of tradition and unification" to distinguish them from the Shi'a, who rejected Abu Bakr in favor of Ali, the Prophet's cousin and son-in-law. Sunnis recognize Ali as the fourth caliph (after Abu Bakr, Umar, and Uthman); the Shi'a recognize Ali as the first caliph. It should be noted that Ali himself also recognized the first three caliphs.[134]

One Islamic scholar distinguishes the three currents in Islam as follows:[135]

Shia Islam

> The followers of Ali were known as the *Shia* (partisans) of Ali. Although they began as a political group, the Shia, or Shia Muslims, became a sect with specific theological and doctrinal positions. A key event in the history of the Shia and for all Muslims was the tragic death at Karbala of Husayn, the son of Ali, and Muhammad's daughter Fatima. Husayn had refused to recognize the legitimacy of the rule of the Umayyad Yazid, the son of Mu'awiyah, and was on his way to rally support for his cause in Kufah. His plans were exposed before he arrived at Kufah, however, and a large Umayyad army met him and 70 members of his family at the outskirts of the city. The Umayyads offered Husayn the choice between a humiliating submission to their rule or a battle and definite death. Husayn chose to fight, and he and all of the members of his family with him were massacred.

134 https://en.wikipedia.org/wiki/Caliphate.

135 Extracts from chapter 2 of "Philosophy of Religion" from Dr. Philip A. Pecorino, http://www.qcc.cuny.edu/SocialSciences/ppecorino/PHIL_of_RELIGION_TEXT/CHAPTER_2_RELIGIONS/Islam.htm.

The incident was of little significance from a military point of view, but it was a defining moment in the history of Shia Islam. Although not all Muslims are Shia Muslims, all Muslims view Husayn as a martyr for living up to his principles even to death.

Sunni Islam

Sunni Islam was defined during the early Abbasid period (beginning in AD 750), and it included the followers of four legal schools (the Malikis, Hanafis, Shafi'is and Hanbalis). In contrast to the Shias, the Sunnis believed that leadership was in the hands of the Muslim community at large. The consensus of historical communities, not the decisions of political authorities, led to the establishment of the four legal schools. In theory a Muslim could choose whichever school of Islamic thought he or she wished to follow and could change this choice at will. The respect and popularity that the religious scholars enjoyed made them the effective brokers of social power and pitched them against the political authorities.

After the first four caliphs, the religious and political authorities in Islam were never again united under one institution. Their usual coexistence was underscored by a mutual recognition of their separate spheres of influence and their respective duties and responsibilities. Often, however, the two powers collided, and invariably any social opposition to the elite political order had religious undertones.

Sufism

An ascetic tradition called Sufism, which emphasized personal piety and mysticism and contributed to Islamic cultural diversity, further enriched the Muslim cultural heritage. In contrast to the legal-minded approach to Islam,

Sufis emphasized spirituality as a way of knowing God. During the 9th century Sufism developed into a mystical doctrine, with direct communion or even ecstatic union with God as its ideal. One of the vehicles for this experience is the ecstatic dance of the Sufi whirling dervishes. Eventually Sufism later developed into a complex popular movement and was institutionalized in the form of collective, hierarchical Sufi orders.

The Sufi emphasis on intuitive knowledge and the love of God increased the appeal of Islam to the masses and largely made possible its extension beyond the Middle East into Africa and East Asia. Sufi brotherhoods multiplied rapidly from the Atlantic coast to Indonesia; some spanned the entire Islamic world, others were regional or local. The tremendous success of these fraternities was due primarily to the abilities and humanitarianism of their founders and leaders, who not only ministered to the spiritual needs of their followers but also helped the poor of all faiths and frequently served as intermediaries between the people and the government."

The Four Sunni Schools

Neither the Sunni nor the Shi'a are themselves monolithic groups. The Sunnis have four main schools of thought (dating back over one thousand years)—the Hanafi, Shafi'i, Maliki and Hanbali[136].

1. *Hanafi.* The Hanafi school of thought originates with the Afghan scholar Imam Abu Hanifa al-Nu'man ibn Thabit (CE 699–767). This school is the oldest school and is practiced by majority of Muslims of the world mostly residing in Southeast and Central Asia, Turkey, and the Balkans. The Hanafi school

---

136 http://islamic-laws.com/articles/sunnischools.htm. The order listed in the text is that described in the sections on each school (although the article does not present the schools in that order).

of thought is known to be a mostly lenient school because of a significant amount of *ijtihad* and *qias* (analogy) used by its founder. Other schools were founded in late eighth and ninth centuries and are mostly reliant on collection of ahadith as supplemental sources of religious understanding.

2. *Shafi'i.* The Shafi'i school of thought originates from Abu Abdullah Muhammad Ibn Idris al-Shafi'i (CE 767–820). He was a collector of ahadith and a leading scholar of religious sciences. The Shafi'i school of thought is mostly practiced in the Middle East. This school, after consulting the Quran and the ahadith, looks first to the consensus of the companions of the Prophet as a source of religious law. They do not consider (unlike the Hanafis) *ishtihan* (the personal opinions of Muslim legal scholars) as acceptable source of law, as that would allow "human legislation" of Islamic law.[137]
3. *Maliki.* The Maliki school of thought originates from Malik Bin Anas (CE 711–795) and is mostly practiced in parts of the Arabian Gulf countries and in North Africa. The Maliki school relies on the Quran and ahadith as primary sources. Unlike other Islamic *fiqh*s, Maliki *fiqh* also considers the consensus of the people of Medina to be a valid source of Islamic law.[138]
4. *Hanbali.* The Hanbali school of thought originates from Imam Ahmad Ibn Hanbal (CE 780–855) and is today practiced in parts of Saudi Arabia, Iraq, Qatar, and Syria. The Hanbali school of thought is a very strict interpretation of Islam.

The fact that each school is practiced in geographically different areas of the world is a sign that the understandings of the religion in different parts of the world are different, and hence their interpretation by the scholars of that area affected the Islamic jurisprudence of that area. This difference is yet another indication of the fact that geographical diversity of Muslims contributes to the diversity of understanding of Islam, which cannot be a monolithic religion. Each of these schools has numerous trends and movements, creating some thousands of different groups among Sunni Muslims.

---

137 https://en.wikipedia.org/wiki/Shafi%27i.

138 https://en.wikipedia.org/wiki/Maliki.

The Ahmadiyya

The group, officially called the Ahmadiyya Muslim Community, is a heterodox Sunni sect founded in British India near the end of the nineteenth century (CE) by Mirza Ghulam Ahmad (1835–1908 CE). Mirza Ghulam Ahmad claimed to have fulfilled the prophecies of the world's reformer during the end of times—that he was the *Mujaddid* (divine reformer) of the fourteenth Islamic century, the promised Mahdi awaited by the Muslims. Similar to Muhammad ibn Abd al-Wahhab, the founder of Wahhabism (discussed in chapter 8), Mirza Ghulam Ahmad considered himself a reformer who had come to rid Islam of fanatical innovative beliefs and practices and to reinforce Islam's true and essential teaching as practiced by prophet Muhammad and the early Islamic community (the *Salaf*—see chapter 8).

The Ahmadiyya believe that Ahmad appeared in the likeness of Jesus to end religious wars, condemn bloodshed, and reinstitute morality, justice, and peace. Since Ahmad's death in 1908, the community has been led by a number of caliphs and has expanded into over two hundred countries. The Ahmadiyya were among the earliest Muslim communities to arrive in Britain and other Western countries. The current Ahmadiyya caliph, Mirza Masroor Ahmad, leads a community estimated at around 10–20 million followers and is, unlike other Muslim communities, relatively monolithic.

Shi'a Variants

> The Shi'a are also divided into numerous subgroups. The three main subgroups are

Twelvers

> The Twelvers compose the majority of the populations in Iran, Iraq, Azerbaijan, and Bahrain. According to Dr. Philip Pecorino,
>
> The Twelver Shia, or *Ithna-'Ashariyya*, is the largest of the Shia Muslim sects. They believe that legitimate

Islamic leadership is vested in a line of descent starting with Muhammad's cousin and son-in-law, Ali, through Ali's two sons, Hasen and Husayn, and then through Husayn's descendants. These were the first 12 imams, or leaders of the Shia Muslim community. The Shia Muslims believe that Muhammad designated all 12 successors by name and that they inherited a special knowledge of the true meaning of the scriptures that was passed from father to son, beginning with the Prophet himself. This family, along with its loyal followers and representatives, has political authority over the Shia Muslims.

Isma'ilis[139] *(Seveners)*

Isma'ilis (located mainly in Pakistan, India, and Afghanistan) accept Isma'il bin Jafar, whom the Twelvers (who accept Isma'il's younger brother Musa al-Kadhim) reject. They concentrate on a deeper, more esoteric meaning of Islam (Twelvers being more literalistic).

Zaydis[140] *(Fivers)*

Zaydis are named after Zayd ibn 'Ali, the grandson of Husayn (killed at Karbala as mentioned above). They are the closest to the Sunnis and do not believe in the infallibility of the imams after Husayn. They are located principally in Yemen; the Houthi rebels are mostly Zaydis.

---

139 http://en.wikipedia.org/wiki/Ismailism.

140 http://en.wikipedia.org/wiki/Zaydi.

Among the other Shia Muslims sects are:

Alawites[141]

Alawites, meaning "followers of Ali," are a branch of Twelver Muslims founded in the ninth century (CE) by Ibn Nusayr. They revere Ali ibn Abi Talib, the cousin of the Prophet and fourth caliph (according to the Sunni way of counting caliphs). They are based mainly in northwestern and coastal Syria, where they represent 12% of the population, and count approximately 4 million followers worldwide.

Alawites have historically kept their beliefs secret from outsiders and noninitiates, so their belief system is not well-known, although they incorporate Gnostic, neo-Platonic, Christian, and other nontraditionally Muslim elements. The establishment of the French Mandate in Syria after World War I caused Alawites to be recruited into the French Army and led to the establishment of an Alawite-controlled state in Syria. While the Alawite state was later dismantled, Alawites continued to play a significant role in the Syrian Army, with Hafez al-Assad taking power in Syria in 1970; his son, Bashar, remains in control of Syria (as of April 2016).

Alevis[142]

Alevis are a religious group within Shi'ism that combines elements of Sufism. Some 10–20 million Muslims consider themselves Alevis, overwhelmingly in Turkey.

Over time, the differences between the Sunni and Shi'a traditions have increased. In recent times (and in particular as an unintended consequence of the US invasion of Iraq in 2003), the differences have reached levels where some radical

141 http://en.wikipedia.org/wiki/Alawites.

142 http://en.wikipedia.org/wiki/Alevi.

Sunni Muslims consider the Shi'a as outside the Islamic faith; some doctrinaire Shi'a harbor the same feelings toward Sunni Muslims.

Druze

The Druze (who refer to themselves as the *al-Muwahhideen*—the believers in one God) are located almost entirely in rural, mountainous Lebanon (east and south of Beirut), where they constitute some 5% of the population, numbering about 250,000. The Tanukhids inaugurated the Druze community in the eleventh century (CE), due to their leadership's close ties with the Fatimid ruler al-Hakim bin-Amr Allah.

The diagram below[143] shows the various branches of Muslim communities, their geographic location, and their share of the population.

[143] David McCandless at *www.informationisbeauttiful.net*

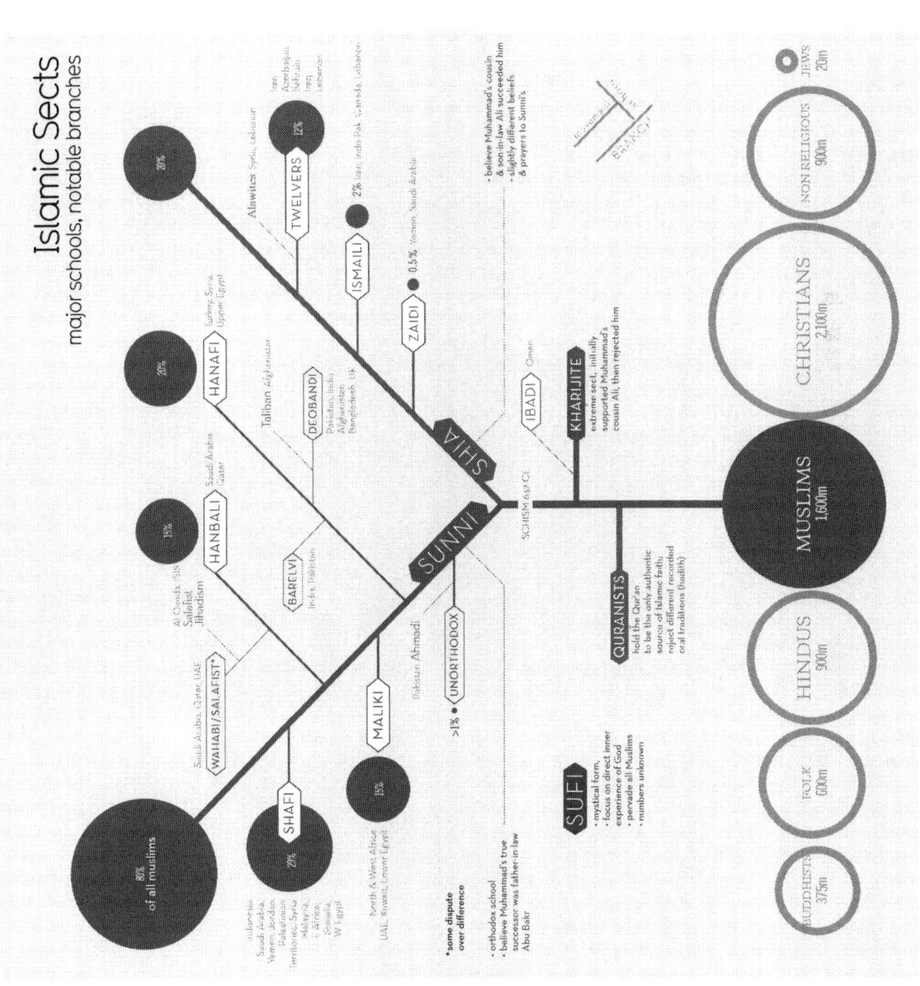
Islamic Sects
major schools, notable branches
80%
of all muslims
SUNNI
SHIA
SHAFI
29%
WAHABI/SALAFIST*
HANBALI
15%
HANAFI
20%
MALIKI
15%
North & West Africa
UAE, Kuwait, Lower Egypt
Al Qaeda, ISIS
Salafist
Jihadism
BARELVI
India, Pakistan
DEOBANDI
Pakistan, India
Afghanistan
Bangladesh, UK
Taliban Afghanistan
Turkey, Syria,
Upper Egypt
Saudi Arabia
Qatar
TWELVERS
12%
Iran
Azerbaijan
Iraq
Lebanon
Alawites Syria, Lebanon
ISMAILI
2%
ZAIDI
0.5%
20%
UNORTHODOX
Pakistan Ahmadi
>1%
* some dispute
over difference
· orthodox school
· believe Muhammad's true
successor was father-in-law
Abu Bakr
· believe Muhammad's cousin
& son-in-law Ali succeeded him
· slightly different beliefs
& prayers to Sunni's
SCHISM 632 CE
IBADI
Oman
KHARIJITE
extreme sect, initially
supported Muhammad's
cousin Ali, then rejected him
QURANISTS
hold the Qur'an
to be the only authentic
source of Islamic faith;
reject different recorded
oral traditions (hadith)
SUFI
· mystical form,
· focus on direct inner
experience of God
· pervade all Muslims
· numbers unknown
BRANCH
BUDDHISTS
375m
FOLK
600m
HINDUS
900m
MUSLIMS
1,600m
CHRISTIANS
2,100m
NON RELIGIOUS
900m
JEWS
20m

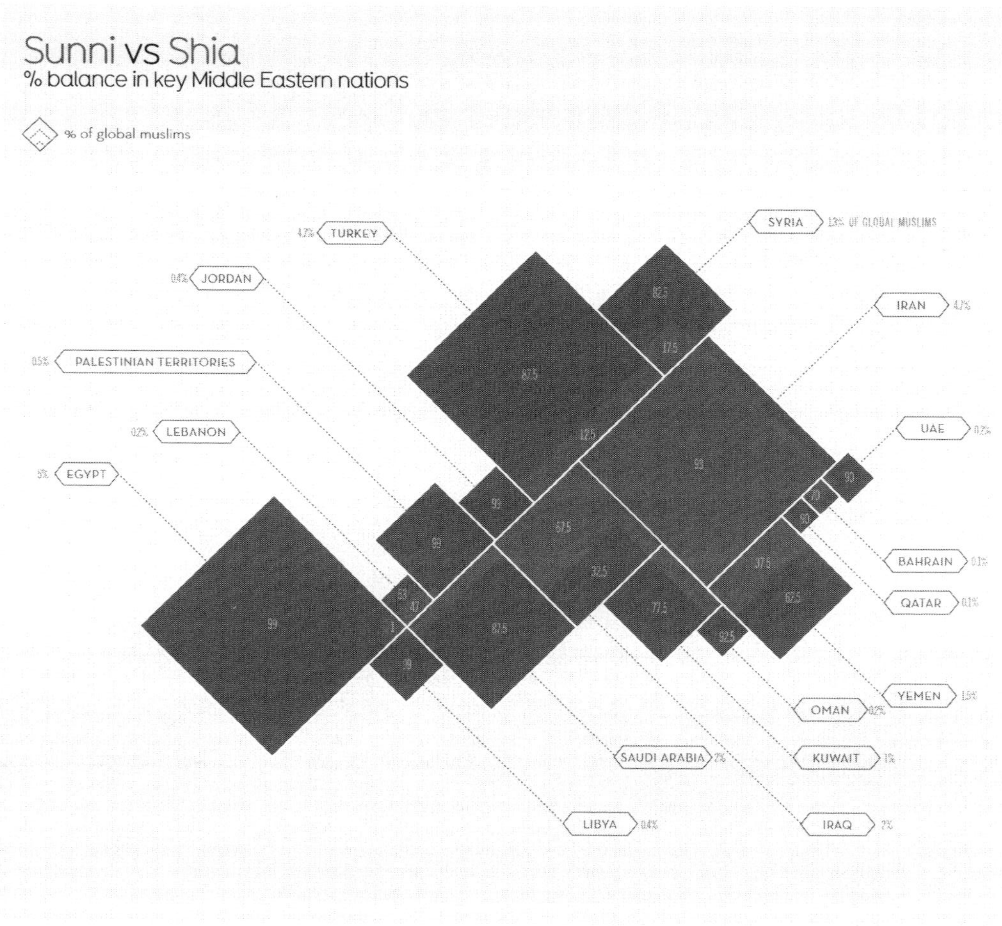
Sunni vs Shia
% balance in key Middle Eastern nations
% of global muslims
TURKEY 4.7%
JORDAN 0.4%
PALESTINIAN TERRITORIES 0.5%
LEBANON 0.2%
EGYPT 5%
SYRIA 13% OF GLOBAL MUSLIMS
IRAN 4.7%
UAE 0.2%
BAHRAIN 0.1%
QATAR 0.1%
YEMEN 1.5%
OMAN 0.2%
KUWAIT 1%
SAUDI ARABIA 2%
IRAQ 2%
LIBYA 0.4%

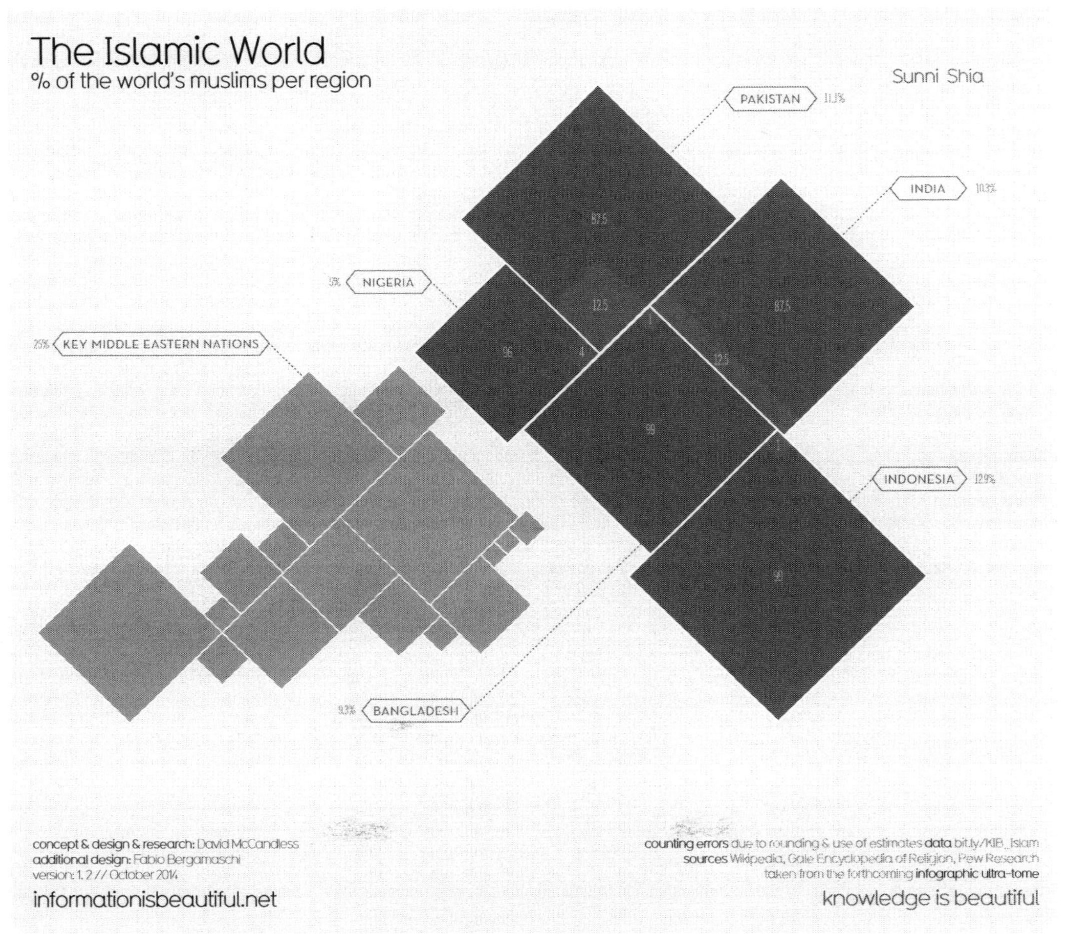
The Islamic World
% of the world's muslims per region
Sunni Shia
PAKISTAN 11.1%
INDIA 10.3%
NIGERIA 5%
KEY MIDDLE EASTERN NATIONS 25%
INDONESIA 12.9%
BANGLADESH 9.3%
87.5
12.5
87.5
12.5
96
4
99
1
90
concept & design & research: David McCandless
additional design: Fabio Bergamaschi
version: 1.2 // October 2014
informationisbeautiful.net
counting errors due to rounding & use of estimates data bit.ly/KIB_Islam
sources Wikipedia, Gale Encyclopedia of Religion, Pew Research
taken from the forthcoming infographic ultra-tome
knowledge is beautiful

While secular Muslims and Western Muslims do not represent distinct communities, such as the Sunni or Shi'a, in the view of the authors, they differ sufficiently in their outlook and practice from other Muslims (particularly in Muslim-majority countries) so as to merit separate mention.

Secularism in the Muslim World

Just as there are Muslims who believe in the inseparability of religion from politics, there are also significant numbers of Muslims throughout the world who believe in their separation. The so-called secularist movement began in Turkey in the 1920s with the leadership of Kemal Ataturk and gained widespread strength in other Muslim-majority countries in the 1960s and 1970s. Today, significant numbers of Muslims throughout the world adhere to the secular school of thought. While practicing Islam in their daily lives and believing in Allah, they consider Islam best served if the religion is separated from government.

In his book *Islam and the Secular State*, Abdullah an-Na'im writes, "In order to be a Muslim by conviction and free choice, which is the only way to be a Muslim, I need a secular state."[144] Brian Whitaker, discussing an-Naim's writing, further elaborates:

> The object of state neutrality, an-Na'im says, is to facilitate "the possibility of religious piety out of honest conviction" and allow individuals in their communities the freedom "to accept, object to, or modify any view of religious doctrine or principle." States that take sides in such matters become an obstacle to religious freedom.[145]

However, An-Na'im's view is not universal: "Maulana Maududi, founder of Jamat-e-Islami-e-Hind, had said while leaving for Pakistan in 1948 that those who participated in secular politics were raising the

---

144 Cited in http://www.theguardian.com/commentisfree/belief/2009/apr/14/religion-islam-secularism.

145 http://www.theguardian.com/commentisfree/belief/2009/apr/14/religion-islam-secularism.

flag of revolt against Allah and his Messenger."[146] Even a non-Muslim such as Mahatma Gandhi is quoted to have said, "Those who thought that religion could be separate from politics understand neither religion nor politics."[147]

Thus the discussion, both inside and outside Islam, on the question concerning Islam and secularism (whose answer is so self-evident to Westerners) is as ongoing and as spirited as ever. Whereas over the past two decades the idea of a strong connection between Islam and politics seems to be gaining the upper hand (to the dismay of at least one of the authors), very significant numbers of Muslims in every country still believe that Islam should be separated from politics.

There are considerable variations in the thinking and approaches of secular Muslims, each current believing that they have found the true message of Islam and the essence of Islam's understanding of the participation of religion in political life. At the same time, some Muslims have gone to the extreme of completely removing Islam from their lives by following laicism. In contrast to secularism, which has a positive connotation (namely being contemporary), laicism is negatively viewed by most Muslims as being neither religious nor atheistic. Laicism means that religion can exert no influence on the organization or functioning of the state or the interpretation of the law. Laicism occurs primarily in Turkey, but it is also prevalent in other countries, both where Muslims are a majority and a minority.

---

146 http://andromeda.rutgers.edu/~rtavakol/engineer/secular.htm.

147 Mahatma Gandhi, cited in Hashemi 2008 (https://books.google.com/books?id = vYO_AAAAQBAJ&pg = PA213&lpg = PA213&dq = Those + who + thought + that + religion + could + be + separate + from + politics + understand + neither + religion + nor + politics&source = bl&ots = 6BeEbonnrv&sig = kZ_HQqHhBqfIcFFU-IIvdsSF6yg&hl = en&sa = X&ved = 0CB4Q6AEwAGoVChMImcjj7IOLyAIVAhaSCh3qpQNZ#v = onepage&q = Those%20who%20thought%20that%20religion%20could%20be%20separate%20from%20politics%20understand%20neither%20religion%20nor%20politics&f = false).

Muslims in the West

Similarly, as Western Muslims are in many ways distinct from their coreligionists in Muslim-majority countries, we believe that they deserve separate discussion. Since Muslims living in the West originate from all countries of the world, they bring with them their own culturally nuanced understanding of Islam. Additionally, their level of education, economic standing, and social position also contribute to their diversity. Significant differences occur, particularly between first-generation Muslim immigrants and second- and third-generation Muslims.

In the United States, where the society has been described as either a "melting pot" or (as the authors prefer) a "salad bowl,"[148] the integration of Muslims (and of people of other religions) of different backgrounds has been relatively seamless. Because of American culture and having the US Constitution as its primary "cement" (and the litigious nature that goes along with it), Muslims have easier access to resources and opportunities and are able to exercise their religion freely. According to a Pew Research study,[149] Muslims in America have a higher educational level and earn more than the average American. They have higher levels of US citizenship than any other group of first-generation immigrants,[150] thereby suggesting a higher degree of integration into US society. This place in the mainstream of US society does not, however, mean that US Muslims are any less diverse or nonmonolithic than Muslims anywhere else in the world.

Whereas most Muslims coming to the United States did so out of political necessity or came to occupy well-paying jobs, bringing with them a high level of education, most Muslims migrating to Europe came after World War II as guest workers doing types of work that "native" Europeans did not want or were not willing to do. European Muslim immigrants typically were laborers with less education, with rural origins. Muslims in Germany and the Netherlands came mostly

148 The "melting pot" metaphor implies that immigrants give up their culture and become part of a homogenous American society; the "salad bowl" implies that the various immigrant communities retain at least some of their particular aspects while becoming part of a more variegated American society.

149 http://www.people-press.org/files/2011/08/muslim-american-report.pdf.

150 http://www.pewsocialtrends.org/2013/02/07/second-generation-americans/.

from Turkey and Morocco, whereas Muslims in France came from the Maghreb (Morocco, Algeria, and Tunisia) or former French colonies such as Senegal, Mali, Niger, and Cote d'Ivoire. In Britain, most Muslims emigrated from Pakistan, India, and Bangladesh. In all of these cases, such emigrants were among the less-educated populations of these countries, so that their education levels were considerably below those of the average of the populations in the countries where they arrived.

Moreover, the new home countries of these Muslim immigrants have deep-rooted cultures with longstanding traditions. Unlike the United States, with its proud welcoming of immigrants (a tradition that appears to the authors to be increasingly controversial), these countries do not have substantial prior immigrant populations or a tradition of accepting foreign influences into their culture; indeed, they often reject such outside influences. As a result, Muslims have had more difficulty in integrating into European societies. In many of these European countries, the (Judeo-) Christian religion is part of this national identity, making it difficult for not only first-generation but also second- and sometimes third-generation Muslims to integrate into the societies of their new home countries. This lack of integration means that Muslims retain a corresponding higher degree of distance from their local cultures, rather than blending in to a greater degree as they have in the United States.

Chapter 7

The Golden and the Dark Ages of Islam

It Wasn't All So Bad All the Time

An era of stunning intellectual and cultural achievements.[151]

Many observers speak of the "Golden Age of Islam"—generally to contrast it with the Dark Ages[152] that Europe was going through at much the same time. The years from 622 CE (the *Hegira*) and 1258 (the Sack of Baghdad and overthrow of the Abbasid Dynasty by Hulagu Khan) are considered the Golden Age of Islam;[153] some consider the

---

151 http://worldofthislam.weebly.com/.

152 The term "Dark Ages" as applied to Western civilization has no specific dates attached to it. It is generally considered to be that period between the decline of the western Roman Empire (as distinct from the Byzantine Empire) and the return of urbanization and learning during the Middle Ages. For the authors, the dates of 325 CE (the founding of Constantinople) and 1073 CE (the beginning of the papacy of Gregory VII, leading to the Investiture Crisis) seem as good as any—although we leave the precise definition to scholars of that period.

153 See, e.g., http://islamichistory.org/islamic-golden-age/ and http://regentsprep.org/regents/global/themes/goldenages/islam.cfm.

period since 1258 through current times, despite the growth in the number of followers, the Dark Age of Islam.[154]

The Golden Age of Islam

The rapid spread of Islamic teachings began during the life of the Prophet but continued apace after his death. Under the Umayyad Dynasty (founded in 661 CE), this spread extended the areas under Muslim control from Spain to Pakistan. By the year 750 CE (less than 120 years after the Prophet's death, and the date generally given as the beginning of the Abbasid Dynasty), Islam was already the dominant religion in the Middle East and Central Asia, as well as parts of today's India, China, Europe, and North Africa. The Islamic world was, by that date, already a superpower of its time. During Islam's early years, it experienced significant gains in the territories peopled by its believers and underwent considerable intellectual and social development.

This Golden Age was a period of considerable scientific advancement. As Barack Obama said in his 2009 speech in Cairo:

> It was Islam that carried the light of learning through so many centuries, paving the way for Europe's Renaissance and Enlightenment. It was innovation in Muslim communities that developed the order of algebra; our magnetic compass and tools of navigation; our mastery of pens and printing; our understanding of how disease spreads and how it can be healed.[155]

Muslim science was the most advanced in the world until about the thirteenth century.[156] This premodern science, however, is not identical in approach with the scientific research of today; premodern science sought knowledge primarily to understand philosophical questions

---

154 See, e.g., http://www.abc.net.au/religion/articles/2013/06/17/3783568.htm and http://www.patheos.com/blogs/tonyjones/2013/05/25/islams-dark-ages/.

155 Cited in http://www.thenewatlantis.com/publications/why-the-arabic-world-turned-away-from-science.

156 Ibid.

concerned with meaning, being, and what is good. Indeed, the word *science* was first used in the nineteenth century; the closest word in Arabic (*ilm*) means "knowledge"—and is not limited to knowledge of the natural world,[157] although it encompasses such knowledge. However, many of the inventions and discoveries of early Muslims were very significant, even according to today's definition of science. What made the difference was not so much that science was the objective, but that it was seen as a tool to appreciate and understand God and his creations.

Why did science thrive during the Golden Age? The centralized Abbasid state (headquartered in Baghdad) was theologically and ethnically diverse. The removal of political barriers meant that scholars from different backgrounds could travel and interact with one another; moreover, the use of Arabic as a lingua franca facilitated communications throughout this diverse community. As the Abbasid Empire spread, it came into contact with ancient Chinese, Egyptian, Greek, Indian, and Persian civilizations, whose learning it readily incorporated (it is worth noting that the Abbasids found little of interest in the West—and for good reason, as the West was going through its own Dark Age during most of this period). Philosophical and scientific activity enjoyed a wide range of political and cultural support and became a self-perpetuating enterprise supported by the entire elite of Abbasid society. Early Muslims' understanding of their religion and the essence of God's command to think when observing His creation on the earth and in the heavens was the guiding motive for Muslims. It was in following this command that Muslims sought to understand the essence of God's creation and with it explore science, technology, medicine, astronomy, and other blessings of God.

> Surely, in the heavens and the earth there are signs for the *true* believers; in your own creation and that of animals which are scattered through *the earth*, there are signs for those who are firm in faith; in the alternation of night and day, in the sustenance that Allah sends down from heaven with which He revives the earth after its death and in the changing of the winds, there are signs for those who use their common sense. These are the revelations of Allah which We

[157] Ibid.

> are reciting to you in all truth. Then, in what report after Allah and His revelations, will they believe?[158]

The pro-science movement, which was given an additional boost under the second Abbasid caliph al-Mansur, reached its culmination under the caliph al-Mamun in the early ninth century CE. Al-Mamun tried to undermine Muslim scholars that believed in a stagnant religion by actively sponsoring Mu'tazilism, a doctrine that promoted rationalism, particularly based upon Aristotelianism. *Mu'tazila* is an Arabic term meaning "abandoning or departing from" and is specifically used by Wasil Ben Ata al-Ghazal, who chose to depart from the class of a major scholar of the second century of Islam (Hassan al-Basri), because he disagreed with his notion that intellect is subservient to religious teachings.

The essence of Ben Ata al-Ghazal and other scholars of the Mu'tazila school and their theory was the question *"Why?"* They examined everything that they confronted with this question, using logic, science, technology, philosophy, and other techniques to find convincing answers to their "why" questions. They were vehement about their desire to explore God's creation and find answers to their questions. They relied on hundreds of verses from the Quran that called upon them to use their intellect, to think, to ponder, to comprehend, and similar statements. Some of these verses triggering scientific research are listed below:

> Surely, in the creation of the heavens and the earth, in the alternation of the night and the day, in the sailing of the ships through the ocean for the profit of mankind, in the rain which Allah sends down from the skies, with which He revives the earth after its death and spreads in it all kinds of animals, in the change of the winds and the clouds between the sky and the earth that are made subservient, there are signs for rational people.[159]

> It is He Who sends down rainwater from the sky and therewith produces vegetation of all kinds: He brings forth green *crops* producing grain piled up *in the ear*, palm-trees

158 Sura Al-Jâthiya (45), verses 3–6.

159 Sura Al-Baqarah (2), verse 164.

laden with clusters of dates within reach, gardens of grapes, olives, and pomegranates; though their fruit resembles in kind yet is different in variety. Look at their fruits as they yield and ripen. Behold! In these things are signs for true believers.[160]

The example of this worldly life (*which you love so much that you have even become neglectful of Our signs*) is like the water which We send down from the sky; it mingles *with the soil* and produces vegetation which becomes the food for men and animals. Then, at the very time when the crops are ripened and the land looks attractive, the people to whom it belongs think that they are able to cultivate it, these comes Our scourge upon it, by night or in broad day, and We mow it down thoroughly as if nothing existed there yesterday! Thus do We spell out Our signs for those who are thoughtful.[161]

In the earth there are tracts side by side: gardens of grapes, crops and palm trees growing singly or in cluster. They are all watered with the same water, yet, We make some of them excel *in taste* as food. Surely in this, there are signs for people who use their common sense.[162]

O mankind! If you doubt about the life after death, remember that We first created you from dust, then from a sperm, then from a leech-like mass, then from a morsel of flesh, some formed and some unformed, so that We may manifest to you *Our power*. We cause to remain in the womb whom We wish for an appointed term, and then We bring you forth as infants; then We *nourish you so that* you may reach your age of full strength. There are some of you who die young and some who lie on to their abject old age when all that they once knew they know no more. You sometimes see the land dry and barren; but no sooner do We pour down rain upon it then it begins to stir and swell, putting forth

160 Sura Al-An'âm (6), verse 99.

161 Sura Yûnus (10), verse 24.

162 Sura Ar-Ra'd (13), verse 4.

> every kind of beautiful growth. This is because Allah is the Ultimate Truth: it is He Who gives life to the dead and it is He Who has power over everything, and that the Hour of Doom is sure to come—there is no doubt about it; and that Allah will raise up those who are in their graves. Yet, there are, among people, others who wrangle about Allah, though they neither have knowledge or guidance, nor an enlightening Book, twisting his neck *in arrogance* to lead others astray from the Path of Allah—for such people there is disgrace in this life, and on the Day of Resurrection we shall make them taste the punishment of burning fire.[163]

> O assembly of jinn and men! If you have power to pass beyond the zones of the heavens and the earth, then pass beyond (them)! But you will never be able to pass them, except with authority (from Allah)! Then which of the Blessings of your Lord will you both (jinn and men) deny?[164]

The Mu'tazilist scholars knew that without the authority from God they would not be able to know about God's creation, but then God had not shown them the limits of what they could learn, so they went out to explore and reach the limits of what they could know. The question *"Why?"* led them on their path to discovering God and His creation.

This spirit of openness and exploration extended to other areas of society as well, such as law, social interaction, political recourse, economic development, and the like. This period saw the flourishing of *ijtihad*, or independent judgment and critical thinking, in every aspect of their life, including in worship and in social interaction within a society.

This spirit was not limited to the Mu'tazilism school but was prevalent from the onset of Islamic education at the time of the Prophet and his immediate companions. However, with the strong push for Mu'tazilism, the sky became the limit, resulting in some people venturing in extreme analysis and verging on questioning some of the essentials of the Islamic belief system, such as the superiority in the sight of God of the prophets and placing the scholars of science and other knowledge above the

---

163 Sura Al-Hajj (22), verses 5–9.

164 Sura Ar Rahman (55), verses 33–34.

prophets. This trend became excessive for quite a few Muslim thinkers and triggered opposition to the Mu'tazila school of thought.

While innovation began to decline in the later Abbasid period—a decline that accelerated after the 1258 Mongol conquest—such a decline is the rule in history, rather than the exception.[165]

The Ash'ari School and the Coming of the Dark Age

The opposition to Mu'tazilism was led by the antirationalist Ash'ari school and its associated subdivisions such as the Athari (Literalist) school and the eponymous Maturidi school. Whereas the Maturidi school believed that if one does not understand an Islamic context, one can venture into trying to comprehend it and explain to the general population to enhance their understanding, the Athari school insisted on believing and accepting even without understanding. For example, when the Quran speaks of *yad Allah*, or "Allah's hand," the Maturidi explain that by *Allah's hand*, the power and influence of Allah is intended and not physically the hand of Allah. The Athari school on the other hand chose to limit themselves to a literal understanding of Islam and would hence use the same reference to say "Allah says it is His hand and we do not understand what He means with it. Hence, we will accept it as such without further explanations or clarification." This concept is called *tafweed*, which basically means that whatever the Quran and the Prophet say stands without further clarification and does not warrant pondering over it.

The rise of the Ash'ari school and its submovements created an environment that was increasingly opposed to original scholarship and any scientific inquiry that did not aid in the religious regulation of all aspects of life.

> While the Mu'tazilites had contended that the Koran was *created* and so God's purpose for man must be interpreted through reason, the Ash'arites believed the Koran to be coeval with God — and therefore unchallengeable. At the

---

165 http://www.thenewatlantis.com/publications/why-the-arabic-world-turned-away-from-science.

> heart of Ash'ari metaphysics is the idea of occasionalism, a doctrine that denies natural causality. Put simply, it suggests natural necessity cannot exist because God's will is completely free. Ash'arites believed that God is the only cause, so that the world is a series of discrete physical events each willed by God.[166]

The Ash'arites contended that everything that is to be known is already known about the religion and there is no value in looking for new knowledge. Hence, all one has to do is to exercise the religion and not reinvent it with passage of time.

Among the Ash'aris there were people who were balanced and recognized the importance of scholarship with an open mind, and there were radicals who were literalists and insisted on a zero-compromise way of evaluating religious teachings. Anything above and beyond what was absolutely clear has to be taken into consideration with a philosophy "to err on the safe side," namely not to engage with the matter, lest one venture into the forbidden zone. As is the case in virtually every situation and every culture, in the absence of strong and fair leadership, the fanatics always gain an upper hand because they choose the hardline, simplistic path compared to the moderates. The Islamic leadership of the time had been corrupted and engaged in policies and habits that were contrary to the teachings of Islam; their way of ensuring their totalitarian rule was with the support of radicals, fanatics, and scholars with a nonflexible interpretation of the religion. In this jungle of ignorance, even the more balanced Ash'aris were often sidelined for the more hardline approach to interpreting Islamic teachings.

Thanks to the extremists within the Mu'tazila school, who allowed themselves all freedoms to question every aspect of their faith, the backlash against the new Mu'tazilism doctrine was not long in coming—and was very successful. Al-Mamun initiated an inquisition punishing those who refused to profess their allegiance to the new doctrine of Mu'tazilism, but the resistance was such that by 885 CE

---

166 http://www.thenewatlantis.com/publications/why-the-arabic-world-turned-away-from-science.

(half a century after al-Mamun's death), it had become a crime to copy books on philosophy.

In contrast to the Mu'tazilism school of thought that raised the *why* question, the essence of the Ash'ari school of thought was to ask *how*. The implication of the *how* question is a description of what needs to be done rather than why one is doing a particular thing.

With the *how* question, the science of *fiqh* (Islamic jurisprudence) was to become the key to religious inquiry. Fiqh, as exercised in those days and in most Muslim-majority countries even today, enabled scholars to spend half of their lives memorizing texts—and the other half repeating the same text to others without thinking about the implications of the circumstances surrounding their actions and the deep-rooted reasons for their practices. Fiqh, as they understood it, is about form—not substance or essence.

The most influential voice of the Ash'arites was Abu Hamid Muhammad ibn Muhammad al-Ghazali (1058–1111 CE). Al-Ghazali argued that when people were influenced by philosophical arguments, they came to trust philosophers on matters of religion, making them less-pious Muslims. Reason was the enemy; by assuming necessity in nature, philosophy was incompatible with Islamic teaching, which explains that nature is entirely subject to God's will.

> By the end of the eleventh century, discordant ideas were increasingly seen as a problem, and autocratic rulers worried about dissent—so the "gates of *ijtihad*" were closed for Sunni Muslims: *ijtihad* was seen as no longer necessary, since all important legal questions were regarded as already answered. New readings of Islamic revelation became a crime. All that was left to do was to submit to the instructions of religious authorities; to understand morality, one needed only to read legal decrees. Thinkers who resisted the closing came to be seen as nefarious dissidents. (Averroës, for example, was banished for heresy and his books were burned.)[167]

This de-Hellenization process continued until the movement was completely marginalized by the twelfth and thirteenth centuries (CE).

---

167 Ibid.

Al-Ghazali's views increasingly prevailed in the Sunni community so that opposition to philosophy became entrenched, with independent inquiry becoming tainted, even to the point of becoming criminal. Muslim contributions to science became increasingly rare as the antirationalist views prevailed.

The demise of the Mu'tazilite school of thought was the beginning of the end of Islam's Golden Age. With the complete takeover by the Asha'arite school of thought, a new Islamic system had taken control—a system that rejected change and adapting to changing times, a system that was contrary to the life and teachings of the Prophet, and a violation of the spirit as well as the text of the Quran.

The Muslim Dark Age

As noted above, the spirit of discovery and openness that characterized the first centuries of the Abbasid Dynasty was declining by the beginning of the twelfth century CE. Some observers date the beginning of the Muslim Dark Age to the fall of Baghdad to Hulagu Khan and the end of the Abbasid Dynasty in 1258 CE.[168] From this time, Islam entered into a period of political decline (despite the brief emergence of Timur and of the Ottoman Empire, already in decline little more than a century after its founding in 1453[169]). The decline in learning was even more dramatic; the "List of Muslim Scientists" in Wikipedia of some seventy noted Islamic astronomers, chemists, social scientists, and economists shows some 85% living before the end of the thirteenth century, none in the sixteenth through nineteenth centuries, and only with a few names beginning to emerge toward the end of the twentieth century.[170]

However, with the emergence of Muslim communities in the West (most notably in the United States but also in Europe), there is reason for hope that the Muslim Dark Age, as we discuss in concluding chapter of this book, may be coming to an end.

168 See, e.g., https://books.google.com/books?id = 3qwuhK3BBH8C&pg = PA215#v = onepage&q&f = false.

169 http://www.turizm.net/turkey/history/ottoman3.html.

170 https://en.wikipedia.org/wiki/List_of_Muslim_scientists.

Chapter 8

Wahhabis and Salafis

The Modern-Day Reformation

Salafis are evangelicals who wish to convert Muslims and others to their "purer" form of Islam.[171]

While the Wahhabi and Salafi movements started at different times and with different objectives, they merged during the 1980s and 1990s into a single movement, Salafi pan-Islamism, which is even stronger today. It is this movement that is currently causing much of the havoc throughout the Muslim world.

The Wahhabi Movement

The Wahhabi movement was launched by a Hanbali scholar, Muhammad ibn Abd al-Wahhab, in the eighteenth century in the Najd region of what is today Saudi Arabia. Followers of his school of thought are called "Wahhabis"; Wahhabism is the official school or fiqh of the Saudi royal family.

The Wahhabi movement was a revivalist reform effort advocating a purging of practices such as the popular worship of Islamic "saints" and

---

171 Ed Husain, the author of the quote, is an adjunct senior fellow at the Council on Foreign Relations and a senior adviser to the Tony Blair Faith Foundation.

shrine and tomb visitations, which al-Wahhab considered as idolatry, impurities, and innovations that had little or nothing to do with the traditions of the Prophet[172]. He claimed that the downfall and miserable state of the Muslim world was due to foreign influences (*bida'a*—Arabic for "innovation") that had crept into Islam over hundreds of years, either from European modernism or from preexisting traditions of peoples in different parts of the world that had converted to Islam. Al-Wahhab believed that these influences were foreign to the original Najdi[173] traditions and needed to be eliminated from the practice of Islam. He also placed particular emphasis on *tawhid* (monotheism), considering most Islamic traditions as anti-Islamic and deviations leading to *shirk* (polytheism). He wanted to purge such (in his view) polytheistic traditions, giving jihad, which he mostly defined as "armed struggle," a heretofore unusual level of prominence.

The Salafi Movement

The Oxford Dictionary of Islam defines Salafism as

> Name (derived from salaf, "pious ancestors") given to a reform movement led by Jamal al-Din al-Afghani and Muhammad Abduh at the turn of the twentieth century. Emphasized restoration of Islamic doctrines to pure form, adherence to the Quran and Sunnah, rejection of the authority of later interpretations, and maintenance of the unity of ummah. Prime objectives were to rid the Muslim ummah of the centuries-long mentality of taqlid (unquestioning imitation of precedent) and stagnation and to reform the moral, cultural, and political conditions of Muslims. Essentially intellectual and modernist in nature. Worked to assert the validity of Islam in modern times, prove its compatibility with reason and science, and legitimize the acquisition of Western scientific and technological achievements. Sought reforms of Islamic law, education,

172 http://en.wikipedia.org/wiki/Wahhabism.

173 Today's Saudi Arabia.

> and Arabic language. Viewed political reform as an essential requirement for revitalization of the Muslim community. Its influence spread to Algeria, Morocco, Tunisia, Syria, India, Indonesia, and Egypt in particular. The most influential movements inspired by Salafi were the Muslim Brotherhood of Egypt and Jamaat-i Islami of Pakistan. In the late twentieth century, the term came to refer to traditionalist reformers.[174]

In seeking these founding principles, Sayyid Jamal al-Din al-Afghani, Mohammad Abduh, Hassan al-Banna, and many other Muslims placed particular emphasis on the *Salaf*, the original followers of Islam, using an open-minded and critical approach to understanding Islam based upon that period of time from the beginnings of the revelations through the third generation of Muslims. A hadith quoting Muhammad saying "The people of my own generation are the best, then those who come after them, and then those of the next generation" is seen by some as an injunction to follow the example of these first three generations, known collectively as the Salaf or Pious Predecessors (*as-Salaf as-Saleh*).

While Wahhabism rejected modernity and went back to the origins of the Islamic religion, the Salafi movement also proposed reform, but through slow and gradual social changes, primarily through education.

> The early Salafis admired the technological and social advancement of Europe's Enlightenment, and tried to reconcile it with the belief that their own society was the heir to a divinely guided Golden Age of Islam that had followed the Prophet Muhammad's Revelations.[175]

This movement was later further refined by Sayed Qutb and his brother Muhammad Qutb, as well as by Hassan al-Banna; these three are now considered the intellectual fathers of the Muslim Brotherhood.

---

174 http://www.oxfordislamicstudies.com/article/opr/t125/e2072.

175 Understanding the Origins of Wahhabism and Salafism, Trevor Stanley, http://www.jamestown.org/programs/tm/single/?tx_ttnews%5Btt_news%5D = 528&#.VOe7M7PF920.

> The name Salafi comes from as-salaf as-saliheen, the 'pious predecessors' of the early Muslim community, although some Salafis extend the Salaf to include selected later scholars. The Salafis held that the early Muslims had understood and practiced Islam correctly, but true understanding of Islam had gradually drifted, just as the people of previous Prophets (including Moses and Jesus) had strayed and gone into decline. The Salafis set out to rationally reinterpret early Islam with the expectation of rediscovering a more 'modern' religion.[176]

Because the Salafis were believers in modern science and technology, while seeking to return to the origins of their religion as it was lived by the Prophet and the first three generations, their message was attractive to highly educated professionals in virtually every field, including, e.g., engineering, medicine, science, technology, literature, and philosophy. Early members of the Salafi movement were thus members of Muslim society's intellectual elite.

However, other members of intellectual elites, who happened to be Muslims but were often not religious, were uncritically impressed with Western culture and the Western way of life. Such persons were often wealthy and also belonged to the political elite. They frequently despised the religious approach of Salafi intellectuals and, because of the significant public support of Salafi religious ideals, considered them as a threat to their power and their way of life. Such sentiments often gave rise to the suppression of the rights of the Salafis, the persecution of the Muslim Brotherhood as the vocal representatives of the original Salafi movement, and similar political conflicts, particularly in countries such as Egypt and Tunisia.

The Salafis were quite conscious of the opposition of the Western-oriented elites in power. Over time and with continued suppression of their rights, they considered these power-holding elites as a threat to their way of practicing their religion and the lifestyles of these elites as a deviation from their understanding of religious observance. The original idea of freedom of expression and right of choice as defined by Sayyid Jamal al-Din al-Afghani and Mohammad Abduh were soon

---

176 Ibid.

forgotten and often replaced with hatred for the oppressive colonial powers and their installed cronies. Their reaction was severe—a rejection of everything the power-holding elite represented. The Salafis were also reacting to the colonial rule of the British, French, and Italians in the Middle East. As a result, they rejected any elements of Western culture, even if such elements were desirable and brought tangible advantages to Middle Eastern societies.

Even though the original leaders of the Salafi movement such as Muhammad Abduh, Hassan al-Banna, Muhammad Qutb, Sayed Qutb, Abul Ala Mawdudi, and others were open-minded and willing to consider anything that could be positive for Islam, even if it represented an innovation, their later followers were not so flexible. These followers were not able to forget the atrocities committed by the colonial powers—or their unthinking followers in their post–colonial era countries. Hence, by the 1960s and 1970s the Salafi approach often had become rejectionist and confrontational, angry and full of grudges, very much in violation of the teachings of Islam and the personality of the Prophet. For this reason, the authors consider this movement as a reactionary fundamentalist movement, because they shaped themselves as a movement that eventually became reactionary to an existing political system, rather than maintaining their original proactive approach to achieving slow and sustained change at the grassroots level.

The Merging of Salafism and Wahhabism

In his efforts to modernize, during the late 1960s and 1970s, the Saudi ruler, King Faisal Bin Abdul-Aziz, invited many scholars associated with the Muslim Brotherhood in Egypt to Saudi Arabia to teach. Over time, the Salafis of the Muslim Brotherhood were able to provide modern-day structures to the Wahhabi movement and make it viable for growth. Furthermore, some were attracted to the uncompromising nature of the Wahhabi school and basically helped to merge the Wahhabi and Salafi schools of thought into a single Wahhabi-Salafi school. This new school was also based upon a return to Islamic fundamentals but coupled with a complete and utter rejection of modernism, Western science and technology—as well as an emphasis on jihad to spread their "return to fundamentals" approach. This merged school relied on the life of the Salaf ("predecessors"), but in a very literal sense, and redefined the Salaf as the immediate companions of the Prophet and not the first four centuries of Islam, as it had been previously defined, and excluding modernity from its teachings while laying significant emphasis on jihad.

The Salafis were a blessing to Wahhabism, which heretofore had been confined mainly to Bedouin populations within Islam and not at all intellectually supported. With the help of the Salafi scholars, the Wahhabis were finally able to instrumentalize Wahhabi thought and make it ripe for further propagation beyond the borders of Saudi Arabia. The result was a Wahhabi-Salafi fusion that was neither modern nor fundamentalist—but instead radical, angry, and aggressive.

Thus, over the years the Salafi movement has split into two distinct tendencies—the followers of the intellectually elite Muslim Brotherhood, who have been somewhat marginalized in some parts of the world, and the more radical, aggressive, and fanatic Wahhabi-Salafi tendency, which has received substantial (particularly Saudi) financial support and has been the fastest growing arm of the movement.

Thus today any differences between Wahhabism and Salafism are nonexistent, and the Islamic Brotherhood is gradually distancing itself from Wahhabism-Salafism. Even among the Wahhabi-Salafi current of Islam, there are groups that are more Wahhabi than Salafi (and vice versa); there are also *takfiri* (deniers of the faith) groups that are more radical and ready to "excommunicate" other Muslims (i.e., deny that they are followers of Islam).

Many of the Muslim world's current struggles, including those in Afghanistan, Libya, Iraq, Syria, Nigeria, and others have been funded and otherwise politically supported by the Wahhabi-Salafi movement in Saudi Arabia and the Persian Gulf; this movement is generally denigrated by the majority of Muslims throughout the world.

Chapter 9

The Three Directions of Islam

The Bigger Picture of How Muslims Are Categorized

People evolve and it's important to not stop evolving just because you've reached adulthood.

—J. K. Simmons[177]

In reviewing the evolution of Islam's 1,400 years since the revelations of the Quran, the authors have discerned three directions—evolutions around which groups of Muslims seem to find more or less common ground. These directions tend to some extent to overlap and, at times, to contradict one another. Each of the three directions has been affected by historical, geographic, political, and intellectual circumstances that gave them shape, but together they comprise the "salad bowl" that forms contemporary Islam and makes it interesting and so often surprising.

Conservative, Traditionalistic Islam

Practitioners of the conservative, traditionalist direction of Islam are the direct inheritors of the Ash'ari movement. After 1,200 years of Ash'ari thought and more than eight hundred years of its absolute

177 http://www.brainyquote.com/quotes/authors/j/j_k_simmons.html.

domination, the principal concerns of this direction are rituals and external appearance—how to dress, how long a beard should be, where to hold your hands while standing for prayer, with which hand to eat—and other trivial matters. The essence of why these acts are performed and the roots of the thought behind these actions are left untouched. Believers who dare to question these acts and their practitioners are scorned, punished, or even categorized as *kafirs*—rejecters of the faith.

Among the current representatives of the conservative, traditionalistic direction of Islam are the Taliban and similar movements in Afghanistan, Pakistan, and other non-Arab and non-Arab countries, as well as movements in North Africa. The Taliban-like rules in Afghanistan and elsewhere were a manifestation of this conservative direction that considered it an obligation to limit learning to Islamic knowledge, to force women to wear the burqa[178] and men to grow beards measured by the glass of kerosene lamps, and to prohibit women to leave their homes without a first-degree male relative.

> Mohammed Yusuf, the late leader of a group called the Nigerian Taliban, explained why "Western education is a sin" by explaining its view on rain: "We believe it is a creation of God rather than an evaporation caused by the sun that condenses and becomes rain." The Ash'ari view is also evident when Islamic leaders attribute natural disasters to God's vengeance, as they did when they said that the 2010 eruption of Iceland's Eyjafjallajökull volcano was the result of God's anger at immodestly dressed women in Europe. Such inferences sound crazy to Western ears, but given their frequency in the Muslim world, they must sound at least a little less crazy to Muslims. As Robert R. Reilly argues in The Closing of the Muslim Mind (2010), "the fatal disconnect between the creator and the mind of his creature is the source of Sunni Islam's most profound woes."[179]

---

178 A loose outer garment (usually black or light blue) worn by Muslim women that covers the head and face and sometimes the entire body. http://www.thefreedictionary.com/burqa.

179 Ibid.

This Taliban mentality still persists in many parts of the Muslim world and has sometimes joined with convoluted forms of Wahhabism to create truly frightening armed movements such as the Islamic State of Iraq and Sham (ISIS).

Islamic Revival—the Modernist/fundamentalist Direction

The fundamentalist direction within Islam is in reaction to both the Ash'ari-based traditionalists as well as the Western colonial powers that controlled the Muslim world during the nineteenth and early twentieth century (CE). Sayyid Jamal al-Din al-Afghani, a nineteenth century ideologue of the reactionary movement and an influential figure in contemporary pan-Islamism (as well as the teacher of Mohammad Abduh, the founder of the Salafi movement and the godfather of Hassan al-Banna, one of the founders of the Muslim Brotherhood), said

> it is permissible . . . to ask oneself why Arab civilization, after having thrown such a live light on the world, suddenly became extinguished; why this torch has not been relit since; and why the Arab world still remains buried in profound darkness.[180]

Al-Afghani's response was simple: Islam must return to its initial founding principles, embracing modernity to the extent it is built upon such principles, and recreate the lost religion.

The reactionary fundamentalist movement was spearheaded by an Egyptian schoolteacher, Hassan al-Banna (1906–1949 CE). In 1928 he founded the Muslim Brotherhood

> to promote implementing of traditional Islamic sharia law and a social renewal based on an Islamic ethos of altruism and civic duty, in opposition to political and social injustice and to British imperial rule. The organisation initially focused on educational and charitable work, but

---

180 Quoted in http://www.thenewatlantis.com/publications/why-the-arabic-world-turned-away-from-science.

> quickly grew to become a major political force as well, by championing the cause of disenfranchised classes, playing a prominent role in the Egyptian nationalist movement, and promoting a conception of Islam that attempted to restore broken links between tradition and modernity.[181]

The Muslim Brotherhood was persecuted in Egypt, but it spread to other countries and soon grew into a formidable global movement that combined a modern understanding of Islam with an emphasis on the fundamentals of the religion—a movement that became known as the Salafis. However (as discussed above), even the Salafis were initially not reactionary but eventually evolved into a reactionary movement when they were confronted with political persecution and oppression under uncritical followers of Western culture and lifestyle by the political elite of their respective countries.

Liberal, Modernist Islam

Starting during the 1970s and continuing to this day, Muslim intellectuals (many of them following the original Salafi school of thought as taught by Sayyid Jamal al-Din al-Afghani and Mohammad Abduh), either established in their careers or just beginning, including doctors, engineers, and scientists, were increasingly dissatisfied with their treatment and the possibilities in their home countries and chose to migrate to Europe and the United States. They brought with them clear minds and consciences, as well as a deep understanding of their religion. They found in their new countries open societies that allowed an unfettered exercise of their Muslim religion; an environment that provided access to information, knowledge, and resources in a wide variety of fields; and the possibility to develop in cultures that were

181 Mura, Andrea (2012). "A genealogical inquiry into early Islamism: the discourse of Hasan al-Banna."

Journal of Political Ideologies **17** (1): 61–85. doi:10.1080/13569317.2012.644986, cited in http://en.wikipedia.org/wiki/History_of_the_Muslim_Brotherhood_in_Egypt.

deeply analytical and encouraged analysis of complex systems. These transplanted Muslim elites found the opportunity not only to live rich, satisfying lives but also to write books, build mosques, and establish advocacy and exploratory organizations.

This movement, strikingly similar to that of Islamic traders entering Southeast Asia in the eighth and ninth centuries (CE), attracted positive attention to Islam through their character and experience—both in Muslim and non-Muslim communities. These Muslim elites established families, raised their children with their own value systems, and intermarried with local Christians and Jews. Soon, a new community began to emerge comprised of highly educated first-generation immigrants, the second-generation children of these immigrants benefiting from the best of the traditions of their parents and the possibilities in their (new for their parents) homes, and converts to Islam attracted by the resulting intellectual ferment.

Today, Europe and America are home to a range of Islamic scholars, including, by way of example:

- United States
    - Fethullah Guelen
    - Zaid Shakir
    - Muzamil Siddiqui
    - Suhaib Webb
    - Hamza Yusuf
- Canada
    - Jamal Badawi
    - Khaled Abou El-Fadl
- United Kingdom
    - Yusuf Islam
    - Hakim Murad
    - Muhammad Akram Nadawi

- Germany
    - Ahmad von Denffer
    - Sven Muhammad Kalisch
    - Muhammad Rassul
- Europe
    - Adnan Ibrahim (Austria)
    - Tariq Ramadan (Switzerland)

They give lectures, write books, and lead humanitarian and educational institutes, think tanks, and similar organizations. We discuss some of their thinking about the current and future direction of Islam in the coming chapters. It is they who will play the dominant role in determining the evolution of Islam.

Chapter 10

Terrorism

What Do Islam and Muslims Say about It?

One man's terrorist is another man's freedom fighter.[182]

Terrorism is hardly new—and hardly Islamic. Rather, it has its origins early in recorded human existence and has occurred in many different cultural and historical contexts.

Terrorism Defined

No generally accepted definition of terrorism exists.[183] Like with a US Supreme Court justice's definition of obscenity—"I know it when I see it"[184]—observers struggle to find a sufficiently broad—but nevertheless useful—description that can distinguish terrorism from

---

182 This quote is attributed to Gerald Seymour in his 1975 book *Harry's Game.*

http://www.answers.com/Q/Who_said_one_man's_terrorist_is_another_man's_revolutionary.

183 See, e.g., http://abcnews.go.com/US/story?id = 92340.

184 Supreme Court justice Potter Stewart in Jacobellis v. Ohio (378 US 184, 1964), cited in http://blogs.wsj.com/law/2007/09/27/the-origins-of-justice-stewarts-i-know-it-when-i-see-it/.

other types of political behavior (and indeed, some observers question whether terrorism must have a political motive). That said,

> the use of violence and threats to intimidate or coerce, especially for political purposes[185]

seems to the authors to provide as good a definition as one is likely to find.

Some other official definitions of terrorism are

- The Oxford English Dictionary

> The use of violence and intimidation in the pursuit of political aims.[186]

- Title 22 of the US Code, section 2656f(d)

> Premeditated, politically motivated violence perpetrated against noncombatant targets by subnational groups or clandestine agents, usually intended to influence an audience.[187]

- The US Federal Bureau of Investigation

> The unlawful use of force or violence against persons or property to intimidate or coerce a government, the civilian population, or any segment thereof, in furtherance of political or social objectives. [188]

---

185 http://dictionary.reference.com/browse/terrorism.

186 http://www.oxforddictionaries.com/us/definition/american_english/terrorism.

187 US Department of State, Office of the Coordinator for Counterterrorism, Country Reports on Terrorism, April 30, 2007.

188 http://www.fbi.gov/about-us/investigate/terrorism/terrorism-definition.

Whichever definition is chosen, the targets of terrorism are always civilians or noncombatants; the intent is mass destruction, assassination, and kidnapping.

Such terrorist acts are equivocally and clearly rejected by Islam in all of its critical scriptures and clearly violate the life and spirit of the prophet Muhammad.

A Brief History of Terrorism

Terrorism as a political tool predates Islam; perhaps the first example in history is the Sicarii,[189] a Jewish group that used armed attacks to try to overturn Roman control in Judea during the first century of the common era. The al-Hashshashin (whence our word *assassin*) were a secret order of Nizari Isma'ilis (and thus Shi'a Muslims) founded in the late eleventh century (CE) who used murder to achieve the goals of the order.[190]

Modern terrorism is generally deemed to have started with the Reign of Terror during the French Revolution (1793–95); sources in English in 1798 speak of "the systematic use of terror as a policy."[191] One of the first terrorist organizations in the United States was the Fenian Brotherhood, founded in 1858, which organized a series of attacks in the United States and Canada, as well as in Ireland, in the 1860s and 1870s.[192] Narodnaya Volya successfully assassinated Czar Alexander II in 1881 and conducted terrorist operations in late nineteenth-century Russia; Vladimir Lenin's older brother, Alexander Ulyanov, was a member.[193]

Terrorist attacks became an unfortunate feature of late nineteenth- and early twentieth-century American life, starting with John Brown's assault on Harper's Ferry in 1859, and including the anarchist

---

189 http://terrorism.about.com/od/groupsleader1/p/Sicarii.htm. The term *sicarii* comes from the Latin word for *dagger*.

190 http://en.wikipedia.org/wiki/Assassins.

191 http://en.wikipedia.org/wiki/History_of_terrorism.

192 http://en.wikipedia.org/wiki/Fenian_Brotherhood.

193 http://en.wikipedia.org/wiki/Narodnaya_Volya.

Haymarket riots in 1886[194] and the assassination of President William McKinley in 1901.[195]

The most widespread and famous terrorist organization during this period of American history was the Ku Klux Klan. The KKK in its original incarnation was founded in 1865 but died out soon afterward; it was revived in 1915 and became a major political organization in a number of Southern and Midwestern states, with a membership estimated in the millions at its zenith in the mid-1920s.[196]

Terrorist violence continued to grow in the early twentieth century, with perhaps the most famous incident being the assassination of Archduke Franz Ferdinand in 1914 by the Serbian Black Hand anarchist group, leading to the outbreak of the First World War.[197] Terrorism was a major feature of the Irish independence movement from 1916 to 1923.[198] Both the Zionist and Muslim sides used terrorism extensively during the period between the First World War and the declaration of the State of Israel in 1948.[199] Indeed, Menachem Begin, who acted as a terrorist (by our definition) during the struggle to create Israel, subsequently became Israel's prime minister.

While terrorism was never absent from the United States, it became a more permanent and prominent feature of American life during the Cold War period, particularly starting in the 1960s. Unrest from organizations such as Students for a Democratic Society, the Black Panthers, the Weather Underground, and the Symbionese Liberation Army became part of the American political debate. Terrorism became a tactic for such varied groups as white supremacists, antigovernment groups (most notably the 1995 attack on the Oklahoma City Federal Building, leaving 168 dead), Christian extremists, Jewish extremists, and black and leftist militant organizations.

Terrorism (non-Muslim) also became part of the European political dialogue during the Cold War period. None of the major European

---

194 http://www.history.com/topics/haymarket-riot.

195 http://en.wikipedia.org/wiki/Leon_Czolgosz.

196 http://en.wikipedia.org/wiki/Ku_Klux_Klan.

197 http://en.wikipedia.org/wiki/History_of_terrorism.

198 Ibid.

199 Ibid.

countries escaped the phenomenon—the United Kingdom (the Irish Republican Army), France (*Action Directe*), Germany (the Baader-Meinhof Gang), Italy (*Brigate Rosse*) and Spain (Basque separatists such as the ETA).

Terrorism in the Muslim World

While certain fringe groups of Muslims choose a selective interpretation of the Quran and ahadith, taking verses out of context and bending the language to misinterpret Islamic values to their own personal and political agendas, an absolute and overwhelming majority of Islamic scholars in all parts of the world denounce terrorism as a grave deviation from the text and spirit of Islam.

As the quotations in chapter 4 show, the Quran and ahadith clearly reject anything that aims to cause harm to innocent people not involved in violence, even though the Quran and ahadith were created long before terrorism became part of the conversation. Muslim scholars in America, Europe, and throughout the world have been fairly vocal in their rejection of terrorist attacks aimed at civilian population. They have categorically and with a united voice expressed their clear rejection of any association of terrorism with Islamic teachings or Islamic way of life. Even early Islamic scholars rejected what would today be considered terrorist attacks:

> Classical Muslim jurists . . . were uncompromisingly harsh toward rebels who used what the jurists described as stealth attacks and, as a result, spread terror. Muslim jurists considered terrorist attacks against unsuspecting and defenseless victims as heinous and immoral crimes, and treated the perpetrators as the worst type of criminals. Under the category of crimes of terror, the classical jurists included abductions, poisoning of water wells, arson, attacks against wayfarers and travelers, assaults under the cover of night and rape. For these crimes, regardless of the religious or political convictions of the perpetrators, Muslim jurists demanded the harshest penalties, including death. Most important,

> Muslim jurists held that the penalties are the same whether the perpetrator or victim is Muslim or non-Muslim.[200]

Modern Islamic scholars hold similar views. Hamza Yusuf, a founder of Zaytuna College (the first Muslim liberal arts college in the United States), has described terrorism as strictly a secular phenomenon, offering the following views:

- "Suicide is *haram* in Islam. It's prohibited, like a mortal sin. And murder is *haram*. And to kill civilians is murder."
- "The Prophet also said that there are people who kill in the name of Islam and go to hell. And when he was asked why, he said 'Because they weren't fighting truly for God.'"
- "Terrorism to *jihad* is what adultery is to marriage."[201]

In a similar vein, the Islamic Society of North America adopted the following resolutions:

> [1] All acts of terrorism, including those targeting the life and property of civilians, whether perpetrated by suicidal or any other form of attacks, are haram (forbidden) in Islam.
>
> [2] It is haram for a Muslim to cooperate with any individual or group that is involved in any act of terrorism or prohibited violence.
>
> [3] It is the civic and religious duty of Muslims to undertake full measures to protect the lives of all civilians, and ensure the security and well-being of fellow citizens.[202]

Even scholars associated with the Muslim Brotherhood and other Islamist organizations whom some Westerners would regard as "radical clerics" reject terrorism as a violation of Islamic law and principles. Yusuf

---

200 El Fadi, Khaled Abou, *The Search for Beauty in Islam: A Conference of the Books* (Lanham: Rowman & Littlefield, 2006), ISBN-13: 978-0761820819.

201 https://www.abc.se/home/m9783/ir/ez/isl/Islam-hijacked.html.

202 http://www.isna.net/isnas-position-on-terrorism-and-religious-extremism.html.

al-Qaradawi, the Egyptian head of the International Union of Muslim Scholars (associated with the Muslim Brotherhood), said:

> Islam, the religion of tolerance, holds the human soul in high esteem, and considers the attack against innocent human beings a grave sin, this is backed by the Qur'anic verse which reads: 'Whosoever kills a human being [as punishment] for [crimes] other than manslaughter or [sowing] corruption in the earth, it shall be as if he has killed all mankind, and who so ever saves the life of one, it shall be as if he had saved the life of all mankind' (Al-Ma'idah:32).[203]

Rached Ghannouchi, the head of Tunisia's (Islamist) Ennahda party (which is part of the Tunisian ruling coalition), has said

> such destruction can only be condemned by any Muslim, however resentful one may be of America's biased policies supporting occupation in Palestine, as an unacceptable attack on thousands of innocent people having no relation to American policies. Anyone familiar with Islam has no doubt about its rejection of collective punishment, based on the well-known Quranic principle that "no bearer of burdens can bear the burden of another."[204]

Among the keys to eliminating the association between Islam and terrorism are dialogue and education. In a conference on terrorism in the holy city of Mecca, Ahmed al-Tayib, head of al-Azhar University of Egypt (perhaps the most respected university in the Muslim world), called for educational reforms as an important tool to contain the spread of religious extremism. He reportedly linked Muslim extremism to bad interpretations of the Quran and the sunnah, blaming an accumulation of extreme trends in Islam as the main culprit for terrorism, causing some people to embrace a misguided form of Islam. He stated that

---

[203] http://kurzman.unc.edu/islamic-statements-against-terrorism/.

[204] Ibid.

> the only hope for the Muslim nation to recover unity is to tackle in our schools and universities this tendency to accuse Muslims of being unbelievers.[205]

Islam and Education Systems in Muslim-Majority Countries

Scholars and governments as well as educated Muslims have been stressing the need to revisit the education system of their respective countries as an important step to curb terrorism. The education system in most Muslim-majority countries is structured in such a manner that upon completion of high school, the top student achievers are enrolled in medical and engineering fields, followed by the lower achieving students into other fields such as law, economics, pharmacy, sciences, humanities, and other related fields. The least performing students then are directed toward pedagogy and religious studies. The outcome is that those with the least bright minds are often tasked to educate Muslim children and to teach them about their religion.

Dr. Yusuf Qadhi of the Maghrib Institute, a famous Islamic scholar with a doctorate in the sciences, is quoted as having said that he needed ten times more intellectual knowledge to learn his religion than to learn the sciences that he was tasked with. In Muslim-majority countries, unfortunately, the realities are very different. People with far inferior intellectual abilities than those studying the sciences are being charged with learning and teaching Islam. This lack of qualified religious students leads to a downward spiral that only serves to hurt generations of Muslims in their quest to learn their religion. Muslims produce teachers with only superficial knowledge of the teachings of their religion, limiting their capability to understand fully the overall philosophy and spirit of Islam as lived by the Prophet. As a result, they engage in repetitive "analysis" of their faith and teach their students to memorize texts without critically looking at their viability in a twenty-first century context. When questioned about their teaching method or their analysis of Islamic teachings, they often defend their own limited knowledge by interpreting the critic's intention as an attack on

205 http://www.theguardian.com/world/2015/feb/23/top-muslim-cleric-ahmed-al-tayeb-urges-education-reform-to-counter-extremism.

Islamic teachings. This hostility to dialogue creates an environment of suppression of expression and choking of analysis resulting in continued misinterpretation of religious texts. This cycle of mismatch to the Quran's text and the Prophet's spirit and life has gone on for generations and still continues in most Muslim-majority countries. Unless systemic change to the education system in these countries is made, this cycle of ignorance supported by ignorance will not end.

What Does the Quran Say?

While terrorism as we know it was not an issue when the Quran was revealed, the Quran has many references that show that terrorism is not remotely Islamic.

In addition to human life, the property, wealth, family, and dignity of all individuals in society are also sacred and to be respected and protected. Transgression against these rights and those that sow corruption on earth incur the wrath of God:

> And do not seek mischief in the land, for Allah does not love the mischief mongers.[206]

Beyond prohibiting oppression and safeguarding rights, Islam also commands its faithful to deal kindly and compassionately with all those who seek to live in peace and harmony.

> God does not forbid you from showing kindness and dealing justly with those who have not fought you about religion and have not driven you out of your homes, that you should show them kindness and deal justly with them. God loves just dealers.[207]

God forbids an aggressive war:

---

[206] Sura Al-Qasas (28), verse 77.

[207] Sura Al-Mumtahanah (60), verse 8.

> Fight in the cause of God against those who fight you, but do not begin aggression, for God loves not aggressors.[208]

Peace is the ultimate objective of every Muslim, even if there are doubts in one's mind about the integrity of intention of the foe.

> If the enemy is inclined toward peace, do make peace with them, and put your trust in Allah. He is the One Who hears all, knows all.[209]

Even in times of extreme anger and hatred, a Muslim is commanded to adhere to the religion's true value and ensure justice, avoiding transgression.

> O believers! Be steadfast for the sake of Allah and bear true witness and let not the enmity of a people incite you to do injustice; do justice; that is nearer to piety. Fear Allah, surely, Allah is fully aware of all your actions.[210]

There are no Robin Hoods in Islam. If the objective is good, the method to achieve the objective must also be sound. Therefore, the Quran says

> the recompense for an injury is an injury proportionate to it; but if a person forgives and makes reconciliation, he shall be rewarded by Allah; He does not like the wrongdoers.[211]

Clearly Islam differentiates between the good and the evil. Under no circumstance can evil be justified because it is for a "good" cause.

> Good deeds are not equal to the evil ones. Repel *other's* evil deeds with *your* good deeds. You will see that he with

---

208 Sura Al-Baqarah (2), verse 190.

209 Sura Al-Anfâl (8), verse 61.

210 Sura Al-Mâ'idah (5), verse 8.

211 Sura Ash-Shûra (42), verse 40.

> whom you had enmity, will become as if he were your close friend.[212]

The Prophet clarified the code of conduct in times of war more than 1,300 years before the drafting of the Geneva Conventions. He forbade the killing of women, children, and elderly in war. The Prophet warned that

> whoever has killed a person having a treaty with the Muslims shall not smell the fragrance of Paradise, though its fragrance is found for a span of forty years.[213]

It is generally established that where there is a representation of a country within a Muslim-majority country in the form of an embassy or a consulate, the Muslim-majority country has a political treaty of respect and adherence to mutual friendship. Thus such a government is a government with a treaty with Muslims of that country.

The Prophet prohibited Muslim soldiers from killing women, children, and the elderly or cutting palm trees, and he advised them,

> do not betray, do not be excessive, do not kill a newborn child.[214]

---

212 Sura Fussilât (41), verse 34.

213 https://books.google.com/books?id = 9C91XMVN53sC&pg = PA60&lpg = PA60&dq = Whoever + has + killed + a + person + having + a + treaty + with + the + Muslims + shall + not + smell + the + fragrance + of + Paradise, + though + its + fragrance + is + found + for + a + span + of + forty + years.&source = bl&ots = svyNYcFvfb&sig = iKqoYMcI9UVVBv9wtz-XF4ZH25I&hl = en&sa = X&ved = 0CDQQ6AEwBGoVChMI5-iM5PvRxwIVUX-SCh3BMQxq#v = onepage&q = Whoever%20has%20killed%20a%20person%20having%20a%20treaty%20with%20the%20Muslims%20shall%20not%20smell%20the%20fragrance%20of%20Paradise%2C%20though%20its%20fragrance%20is%20found%20for%20a%20span%20of%20forty%20years.&f = false.

214 https://en.wikiquote.org/wiki/Muhammad.

He has also made it very clear that

> the first cases to be adjudicated between people on the Day of Judgment will be those of bloodshed.[215]

Next to assigning partners with God, killing is the second major sin in Islam.

The Prophet's promise to Muslims and non-Muslims alike that choose to live in peace with the Muslims is that of the sanctity of blood, property, and honor. In his statement to the Jews and Christians of Medina, the Prophet states

> truly your blood, your property, and your honor are inviolable.[216]

The treatment of God's creatures with kindness and compassion is not just limited to humans but encompasses God's creation. The Prophet indicates

> there is a reward for kindness shown to every living animal or human.[217]

Not only did the Prophet adhere to highest respect for life, honor, and property of people, but also his followers insisted on the same. When confronting the Roman armies, Abu Bakr, the first caliph, instructed his general, Yazid, to abide by the basic tenets of Islamic warfare (as we discussed in chapter 4).

Thus an overwhelming body of evidence from both the Quran and the ahadith suggest that terrorism is completely at odds with the teaching of Islam. But the Islamic State and Boko Haram, among others, claim that their killings and destruction of historic sites are justified by Islam. In the next chapter, we examine the (feeble) arguments that they use to try to justify their terrible behavior.

---

215 http://www.islam-guide.com/ch3-11.htm.

216 http://www.islam-guide.com/ch3-12.htm.

217 http://www.islam-guide.com/ch3-11.htm.

Chapter 11

How Do Terrorists Justify Their Actions?

When Taking Teachings Out of Context, One Can Justify Anything

Kill them all and let God sort them out.[218]

Terrorists and those who sympathize with them use verses from the Quran and quotations from the ahadith outside their context to justify violent acts against Muslims and non-Muslims. They select passages as part of a wider deliberation that includes political circumstances, historical references, citations of political injustice, misleading fatwa by historical scholars as well as emotional appeals to make a case that, to achieve their political objectives, exhorts potential adherents to extreme violence.

Donald Holbrook analyzes what he calls the "Jihadi-Salafist narrative" through an empirical approach focusing on prominent extremist articles written in English by cause sympathizers. In an article "Using the Qur'an to Justify Terrorist Violence," he writes that

> militant Islamist ideologues and propagandists seek to supplement their message with references to the Holy Book of Islam, framing the narrative in a religious setting and

218 The quotation dates from the Albigensian (anti-Cathar) Crusades and is attributed to Arnaud Amalric (speaking in French), the representative of Pope Innocent III, at the Beziers Massacre on July 22, 1209.

> adding perceived religious purpose and legitimacy to the prescribed campaign of jihadist militancy.[219]

Holbrook argues that terrorism justifiers select only those Quranic verses that fit their message, citing them out of context and often omitting following passages that significantly change the quoted phrases. They ignore both the

> original context and also the variety of historical differences among committed Muslims about how to apply their dicta . . . [and collapse] the broad spectrum of Qur'anic teaching into a double requirement: first to believe and then to fight.

He concludes that the Islamists rely on

> a Qur'an a la carte based on cherry-picked passages . . . the propagandists of jihad violate the Salafists' own demands for doctrinal purity in terms of adherence to the Qur'an. In other words—they tend to be dishonest and hypocritical.[220]

For Holbrook the basic argument stems from the verse

> o believers, do not hold Jews and Christians as your allies. They are allies of one another; and anyone who makes them his friends is surely one of them.[221]

He notes that for Ayman al-Zawahiri (the current head of al-Qaida), this verse is the fundamental principle that all Muslims should follow: to respect the division of *al-Wala wa-i-Bara* (loyalty and disavowal—the exclusion of all enemies and the cohesion of the righteous ummah)—despite the numerous references in the Quran to People of the Book, the respect due these religions, and that such people should not be

219 http://www.terrorismanalysts.com/pt/index.php/pot/article/view/104/html.

220 Ibid.

221 Sura Al Maida (5), verse 51.

converted against their will. Other verses that support this line of argument include:

> Say: "O people of the Book! Let us get together on what is common between us and you: that we shall worship none but Allah; that we shall not associate any partners with Him; that we shall not take from among ourselves any lords beside Allah." If they reject your invitation then tell them: "Bear witness that we are Muslims (*who have surrendered to Allah*)."[222]

and

> Do not argue with the People of the Book except in good manner—except with those who are wicked among them—and say: "We believe in that which is sent down to you; our God and your God is the same One God (*Allah*), to him we submit *as Muslims*."[223]

Terrorists ignore such verses or interpret them in their own peculiarly self-serving way. They then promote the value of martyrdom in Islam and exhort such voluntary acts outside the context of a just war that is defensive in nature, citing, among other verses,

> Never think that those who are killed in the way of Allah are dead.[224]

Once the terrorists have succeeded in defining Jews and Christians as the enemy and establishing that martyrdom is desirable for believers (and that martyrs do not die but live in the company of Allah—a very desirable outcome!), they go on to emphasize, again out of context, those verses of the Quran that relate to violence to justify its use against their chosen enemies. Such verses include

---

222 Sura Â'l-e-'Imrân (3), verse 64.

223 Sura Al-'Ankabût (29), verse 46.

224 Sura Al Baqarah (2), verse 154.

> Fight them; Allah will punish them by your hands and will humiliate them. He will grant you victory over them and soothe the hearts of believing people. He will take away all rancor from their hearts. Allah accepts the repentance of whom He pleases; and Allah is All-Knowledgeable, All-Wise.[225]

The terrorists also do not hesitate to use parts of a single verse to justify their intentions to spread terror. For example, Holbrook cites:

> Muster against them all the military strength and cavalry that you can afford so that you may strike terror into the hearts of your enemy and the enemy of Allah, and others besides them who are unknown to you but known to Allah. *Remember* that whatever you spend in the cause of Allah, shall be paid back to you in full and you shall not be treated unjustly.[226]

Holbrook notes that many commentators use this verse to justify violent jihad. It also provides the justification for "praiseworthy terrorism,"[227] as the act of violence committed in the service of Allah, since it commands believers to "strike terror" against the enemies of Islam. He goes on to argue that the terrorists ignore the subsequent verse, which qualifies and limits the nature of the violence authorized in the preceding verse, saying

> If the enemy is inclined toward peace, do make peace with them, and put your trust in Allah. He is the One who hears all, knows all.[228]

---

225 Sura At-Tauba (9), verses 14–15.

226 Sura Al-Anfâl (8), verse 60.

227 The phrase used by Osama bin Laden in his audio message of December 13, 2001 to justify the 9/11 bombings, as cited in the Holbrook article, op cit.

228 Sura Al-Anfâl (8), verse 61.

The terrorists argue that it is worthy to continue to fight forever if necessary because they will always win, whether they succeed in killing or are killed themselves:

> *O believers,* fight them until there is no more oppression and until the whole Deen (*way of life*) is for Allah Alone; but if they cease oppression, then surely, Allah is All-Seer of what they do.[229]

and

> Indeed, Allah has purchased from the believers their persons and their wealth, in return has *promised* them paradise; they fight in the cause of Allah and slay and are slain. This is a true promise which is binding upon Him mentioned in Tawrât (*Torah*), the Injeel (*Gospel*) and the Qur'an, and who is more true in fulfilling his promise than Allah? Rejoice, therefore in the bargain which you have made and that is a mighty achievement.[230]

Terrorists also justify the killing of Muslims who don't agree with them. They consider their views as evil and a deviation of the "true" teachings of Quran, as presented by themselves. They first demonize them, then make them into unbelievers and finally into targets worthy of being fought and killed. In making this argument, they cite:

> There are some people who say: "We believe in Allah and the Last Day;" yet, they are not *true* believers. They *try* to deceive Allah and the believers. However, they deceive none except themselves; yet, they do not realize it. In their hearts is a disease (*of hypocrisy, and because of their misbehavior*) Allah has increased their disease and they shall have a painful punishment for the lies they have told. When it is said to them "Do not make mischief on earth," they say: "We make peace." Beware! They are the ones who make

[229] Sura Al-Anfâl (8), verse 39.

[230] Sura Al-Tauba (9), verse 111.

> mischief but do not realize it. When they are told: "Believe as others believe," they *sarcastically* ask: "Should we believe like fools?" Be aware! They themselves are the fools, if only they could understand. When they meet the believers they say: "We are believers," but when they are alone with their shaitâns, they say: "We are really with you; we were only mocking *the believers*." Allah will throw back their mockery on them and leave them alone in their trespasses; so they wander to and fro like the blind. These are the people who barter guidance for error; but their bargain is profitless and they are not going to be guided.[231]

and

> Those who are believers, fight in the cause of Allah and those who are unbelievers fight in the cause of Tâghoot (*false deities—Shaitân*); so fight against the helpers of Shaitân; surely, Shaitân's crafty schemes are very weak.[232]

Thus Muslim soldiers and civilians that work under the leadership of non-Muslims or "satanic" rulers are just as guilty as the unbelievers and satanic leaders and are, therefore, "legitimate" targets for attack.

Terrorists tell their followers that there must be something wrong with them if they do not take action against the enemies of Islam. They threaten them with the wrath of Allah if they refuse to fight the unbelievers and their Muslim allies. They reference verses such as:

> O believers! What is the matter with you that when you are asked to march forth in the way of Allah, you cling to the earth? Do you prefer the life of this world to the life of the hereafter? The comfort of this life is so little compared to that of the life of the hereafter. If you do not march forth, He will inflict on you a painful punishment and replace

---

231 Sura Al-Baqarah (2), verses 8–15.

232 Sura An-Nisâ (4), verse 76.

> you with other people, and you cannot harm Him at all, for Allah has power over everything.[233]

The terrorists also use misquoted ahadith to further justify their objectives and to convince their mostly religiously illiterate (or minimally literate) audience to become radicalized and then to become violent. They use both the Quranic verses and the ahadith out of context, sometimes using only a portion of a verse to justify their hatred and their efforts to destroy, kill, and terrorize their enemies, whether Muslim or non-Muslim. In these ways they are able to garner growing support among a marginally literate population throughout the world.

Clearly the terrorists propagate hatred, destruction, and murder, knowing that they are violating the teachings and the spirit of the Quran and the traditions of the Prophet. However, they are either intent on abusing every tool to achieve their political objectives or are blinded by their hatred for their enemy, so that they intentionally ignore the objections of the Quran and sunnah to their behavior. They explain the killing of innocent people in the midst of their violence as unavoidable collateral damage. They justify it as God's will. If the innocent are truly innocent, they will enter paradise, which is in any event a desired outcome for all, as the life of this world is a temporary condition in preparation for the hereafter. They follow the misguided principle cited at the beginning of this chapter: "Kill them all and let God sort them out."

233 Sura At-Tauba (9), verses 38–39.

Chapter 12

Using Religion for Political Ends

The Example of the Protestant Reformation

Cuius region, eius religio.[234]

Islam continued to remain stagnant all the way to the early twentieth century. Most Muslims were somewhat resigned to the presence of the Ottoman Caliphate as their mouthpiece while continuing to adhere to their traditionally established ways of life and government. After the demise of the Ottoman Caliphate following World War I, Muslims found themselves in a vacuum of identity and representation. They looked toward Egypt and Saudi Arabia for leadership but failed to see any significant capabilities. Hence they resigned themselves to the fate.

Shortly after the demise of the Ottoman Caliphate with the Treaty of Sevres in 1920,[235] the Muslim Brotherhood was established in Egypt in 1928, which initially did not have any political ambitions but later became more politicized. However, given the nature of the organization and the strong resistance from the pro-Western elites that were in charge of the governments in most Muslim-majority countries, the Brotherhood remained a politically persecuted and weakened organization.

---

234 "Whose realm, his religion." https://en.wikipedia.org/wiki/Cuius_regio,_eius_religio.

235 http://www.nzhistory.net.nz/war/ottoman-empire/collapse.

In 1947, Pakistan was created as the only nation ever established with Islam as an ideology, including two widely separated and ethnically and culturally distinct regions, West and East Pakistan (which separated from West Pakistan to become Bangladesh in 1971). Pakistan's creation coincided with that of Israel, the only nation created with Judaism as its religious motivation. Both were created with the active participation and support of the British Empire, which was heretofore in control of these territories. For Muslims of South Asia, the creation of Pakistan was an opportunity to revive the spirit of Islam within a government setting, as Pakistan's establishment was based on the Islamic ideology of its founders. Whereas Israel's creation immediately generated some level of global support, Pakistan received very limited recognition and support from other Muslims of the world and had to wait until the Soviet invasion of Afghanistan to appreciate fully the value of its Islamic origination as a political asset.

On the other hand, Saudi Arabia, which was the home of Islam's two holiest sites in Mecca and Medina, was going through its own reformation, which took the shape of the modern Wahhabi state run by the al-Saud family. The relationship between the al-Saud family and the Wahhabis dates to the eighteenth century, when the Saud family adopted Muhammad al-Wahhab when he was forced to flee Medina.[236] The relationship continued to develop through the nineteenth and early twentieth centuries. In the 1920s, Abd al-Aziz ibn al-Saud relied increasingly on the Wahhabi school *ulema* to provide credibility for the political regime he was seeking to create. In 1932 Abd al-Aziz ibn al-Saud united the Arabian peninsula into the Kingdom of Saudi Arabia and proclaimed Wahhabism as the state system of jurisprudence for the kingdom, founding a government that was based on a clear-cut combination of hatred for anything that was modern with the religious zeal of the Wahhabis, imposing a conservative, narrowly-defined religious rule over the Arabian peninsula. However, because of the extreme nature of Wahhabism coupled with the limited access of Saudi Arabia to sophisticated scholars, it did not find any significant support in the rest of the Muslim world.

By the 1970s, however, financed by the oil revenues from the 1973 oil boycott and the growing role of the Organization of Petroleum

---

[236] http://www.fsmitha.com/h2/ch17arab.html.

Exporting Countries, Saudi Arabia achieved significant riches in a short period. With these newly earned riches, King Faisal of Saudi Arabia invited Muslim Brotherhood scholars and experts in various sectors to help in establishing schools and universities in various parts of the country. Within less than ten years, the Wahhabi school of thought was structured as a potentially credible albeit very hardline alternative to existing schools of jurisprudence. Soon thereafter, Saudi Arabia started gradually to export this new school of jurisprudence to other Muslim countries by financing and founding mosques and madrassas throughout the Muslim world (perhaps most notably in Pakistan and Afghanistan). With the combination of strong funding and religious education backed by the credibility of caretakers of Islam's holy sites in Mecca and Medina, the already traditionally motivated and uneducated population of the areas around the madrassas and mosques were brainwashed into believing that the Wahhabi school was the best alternative to their existing condition. They believed that only hardline Islam, with the aim of achieving paradise at any cost, would be the appropriate response to the corruption and oppression of their leaders and masters, the United States and Europe.

By late 1970s two significant incidents occurred that triggered a major shift for the Wahhabi school of thought under the Saudi royal family's leadership, namely (1) the invasion of Afghanistan by the Soviet Union and the resistance of Afghans in the name of Islam and (2) the successful toppling of the Persian shah and the installation of Ayatollah Ruhollah Khomeini as the supreme leader of the Islamic Republic of Iran. Whereas the former was a majority-Sunni country, the latter was a revolution in an overwhelmingly Shi'a country.

During the 1980s, the mujahideen (Afghan resistance fighters), with help from the United States, Western Europe, and most Muslim-majority countries, were able to force the Soviet Union to withdraw from Afghanistan. The Soviet withdrawal eventually contributed to the downfall of the Soviet Union and the ultimate defeat of communism at the hands of the Muslims in Afghanistan.

During the same decade, Saddam Hussein of Iraq chose to invade Iran and was supported financially and militarily by the United States, the Soviet Union, all of Europe, and most Arab countries. In spite of this major force and support, Iran, which fought with an Islamic mind-set and in the name of Islam against the secular Saddam, eventually prevailed.

By the 1990s the value of religion as a tool to gain political advantage and achieve political goals and power among Muslims was already undeniable, and the Saudi government, with its oil dollars, pursued with full force its policy to ensure that the Wahhabi school of thought was a significant contributor to movements in almost every part of the Muslim world aiming to gain political power.

The Christian Reformation—an Analogy to Wahhabism-Salafism as a Use of Religion for Political Ends

This recent development within the Muslim world was little different from the use of religion by European princes in the sixteenth century to gain wealth and prominence and to consolidate their power bases.

While the Reformation is commonly agreed to have begun on October 31, 1517, with Martin Luther posting his Ninety-Five Theses on the doors of the church in Wittenburg (now eastern Germany), Luther was not a political figure and saw himself as a reformer within the established Catholic Church. However, as Luther's ideas began to take hold more widely in Europe, particularly in its northern regions, many of the ruling kings and princes saw "Lutheranism" as a tool for gaining political power, land, and taxes within their realms.

Whether German princes, Swedish royals, or British kings and queens, all the leaders cited below used the essence of religious emancipation as a tool to gain political prominence, wealth, or other advantages.

- In 1527, Gustavus I of Sweden, who had no religious convictions but had significant financial needs, used

> Lutheran arguments (plus a threat of abdication) to persuade a diet at Västerås to authorize his appropriation of

church property—amounting perhaps to a quarter of all the land in the kingdom.[237]

- In the same year, Philip of Hesse (Germany), under the pretext of the Reformation, closed down the monasteries in his principality and used the proceeds to educate Lutheran clergy and to found a university in Marburg.[238]
- In 1543, Maurice of Saxony (Germany) confiscated ecclesiastical lands and used the proceeds to establish the University of Leipzig and three new schools to provide free education.[239]
- In 1536 in England, Henry VIII also had no religious convictions but used the Reformation movement purely as a political strategy to appropriate church wealth.[240]
- In 1536, Christian III of Denmark, Norway, and Iceland, who was a committed Lutheran, confiscated the wealth of all Catholic monasteries, and with it, "vast funds flowed into the royal exchequer."[241]

In every one of the cases mentioned above, in addition to in Norway, Iceland, and other countries of central and northern Europe, the vast riches of the Catholic Church had always been a thorn in the side of the rulers, who had to compete with the Catholic Church for taxes and power. Because of the overwhelming strength of the Catholic Church, manifested by its unified leadership in the Vatican, for hundreds of years, the European princes had no chance at success.

During the early years of Reformation, the faith of the population of a country or region was fully handed over to the rulers of the region, who in turn, after the signing of the Peace of Augsburg in 1555, chose the religion of their subjects. Thus, German princes of

237 http://www.historyworld.net/wrldhis/PlainTextHistories.asp?ParagraphID = hoz.

238 http://www.historyworld.net/wrldhis/PlainTextHistories.asp?ParagraphID = hpo.

239 Ibid.

240 Ibid.

241 Ibid.

Lutheran persuasion as well as the kings of Denmark and Sweden had the power to impose their religion on the population. King Henry VIII of England had the same power "with his own special religion for England—Anglicanism."[242]

In every step of the way toward the dismantling of Catholicism in northern Europe (as well as in much of more southerly and easterly parts of Europe, where Catholicism ultimately prevailed), bloodshed, atrocities, and unimaginable cruelty were part and parcel of the change. The local populations suffered beheadings, torture, and being burned to death. The concept of slow fires that cause persons to burn to death in greater agony was invented during this time. Loyalties kept changing on a daily basis, and with it murders of thousands of people who believed in the wrong religion were on the agenda.

In France of 1572, Henry of Navarre, a confessed Protestant, was arrested by Catherine de' Medici and allowed to remain alive because of professing to Catholicism. However, a massacre of all of the Huguenots in Paris started that eventually extended to other towns and cities, resulting in the butchering of ten thousand to fifteen thousand Huguenots, including the famous Saint Bartholomew's Day Massacre (August 24, 1572). The French atrocities continued until 1598 with the signing of the Edict of Nantes by Henry IV, which gave Huguenots full civil rights and limited freedom of worship. Nevertheless, violence against French Protestants, leading to the emigration of many Huguenots to other European countries and to North America, continued throughout the seventeenth century.

In England, in spite of the severed ties with Rome, actual reform started only after the death of Henry VIII and the reign of his son Edward VI. Edward pushed for the reform of the Church of England in the Calvinist tradition (under the leadership of the Scot John Knox). In the process of reformation, thousands of people were beheaded, burned to death and tortured, many of them priests and other clergymen. However, after the death of Edward VI, his sister Mary I (better known as Bloody Mary), who was a Catholic, reversed the reforms. During her five-year rule, Mary I killed and tortured thousands of Protestants throughout England and caused havoc in the country.

---

242 Ibid.

Upon her death in 1558, her half-sister Elizabeth I assumed power. Elizabeth, a Protestant, soon established the Church of England (today's Anglican Church), of which she became the supreme governor. She was more moderate than her half-brother and half-sister, allowing Catholic worship in England. After her death in 1603, England eventually fell prey to the struggles of various Christian denominations including the Puritans, Calvinists, Presbyterians, Lutherans, and other groups in the English Civil War (1649–1660). It was only after the restoration of the monarchy in 1660 that the mainstream Anglican Church was re-established—although religious confrontations continued in England until the Glorious Revolution and the overthrow of King James II in 1688.

The princes and kings of Europe thus used religious figures such as Martin Luther, John Calvin, and Ulrich Zwingli and the movements they created to free themselves from the financial and political grip of the Catholic Church. Without the wealth and the military might of these princes, the leaders of the Protestant Reformation would very likely not have been able to achieve large-scale conversions in many European countries. And without the religious ideas advanced by these reformers, the kings and princess would have never been able to free themselves from the power of the Papacy and the Catholic Church. But not until the end of the seventeenth century with the Glorious Revolution, some 170 years after Martin Luther's Ninety-Five Theses, did Europe see an end to its religious wars.

The situation of present day Islam and Muslims is very similar to the struggles of Christianity of the sixteenth and seventeenth centuries. Since the fall of the Ottoman Empire in 1920, Muslims have been facing a power vacuum in terms of religious as well as political authority. The governments in Muslim-majority countries were weak and corrupt, and the Muslim community felt itself to be without a voice in the wider world.

The situation in the Arab world toward the end of the twentieth century shows a pattern the authors find similar to that of the Protestant princes during the Reformation. The combination of the merging of the Wahhabi and Salafi movements with the support of the Saudi royal family, along with the defeat of the invading Soviet forces in Afghanistan by the Afghan resistance fights (with the financial and military support of the recently strengthened Wahhabi-Salafi movement—and the

United States) has allowed local political rulers in Muslim-majority countries to impose their chosen brand of Islam on the peoples they rule—with little consultation as to the wishes of these peoples. In many cases this policy has led to support for reactionary, conservative Islam—to the exclusion of other ways of practicing Islam in these countries.

Conspiracy theorists believe that the Saudi-supported Wahhabi-Salafis are being supported by Western powers that want to see further weakening of Islam and Muslims and a defaming of the religion at the hands of these fanatics. However, Muslims in every part of the world are defending themselves against this violent movement and are struggling with the negative consequences of this merciless violence. The question is, what will the future bring to the Muslims of the world? Will the Wahhabi-Salafi movement be the predominant voice of Islam?

Chapter 13

Osama Bin Laden and the Evolution of "Islamic Terrorism"

The Origin of the Current Terrorism Wave

Even a hero falls prey to his ego.

As we've argued, terrorism is not an Islamic phenomenon; it has nothing to do with Islam and its teachings. Rather, terrorism is a form of secular expression that has become an easy tool for criminals and unscrupulous individuals to gain maximum exposure for their causes and achieve their political objectives.

Until the late twentieth century, almost no terrorist organization cited Islam as its main source of motivation. Bruce Hoffman of the RAND Institute notes that in 1980, only 2 of 64 organizations classed as terrorist had a religious motivation.[243] By 1995, however, 26 out of 56 terrorist organizations had religious ties, with a majority of them linked to Islam. But from the twelfth century al-Hashshashin until the late twentieth century, there are very few examples of Muslims anywhere in the world using terrorism to achieve political objectives.

The use of terrorism for Islamic objectives is very largely the creation of one man: Osama bin Laden. The trigger was the Saudi government's

243 http://www.rand.org/content/dam/rand/www/external/congress/terrorism/phase1/countering.pdf (page 5).

decision to allow US military bases to be established in Saudi Arabia following Saddam Hussein's invasion of Kuwait in 1990. The First Gulf War, with its civilian casualties, combined with United States and other Western support for oppressive governments in Muslim-majority countries and US behavior perceived by many Muslims as arrogant and supremacist, created a propitious climate for terrorist attacks. The Second Gulf War and the war in Afghanistan enhanced Islamic terrorism through the development of copycats, both lone wolves and organizations (e.g., Boko Haram and al-Shabaab) that self-radicalized and replicated bin Laden's actions. These copycats did not seek to align their actions with Islamic teaching but rather to surpass bin Laden with more violence, greater cruelty, and even scarier tactics.

Osama bin Laden—Life before Afghanistan

A good starting point for the story of Osama bin Laden is the arrival of his father, Muhammad Awad bin Laden, in Saudi Arabia sometime around 1930. Born in Hadramout (southern Yemen), Osama's father started life as a porter in the harbor at Jeddah. He was, however, able to develop the largest construction company in Saudi Arabia, becoming the head of the richest nonroyal family in the kingdom. Osama was born in 1957 to a Syrian mother; he was Muhammad's seventh son among some 54 children by 22 wives.[244]

Muhammad was a humble person, a devout Muslim and very generous—but a dominating personality. He kept all of the children in a single complex and enjoyed a close family life. He insisted that all of his sons manage at least one project in order better to understand the family business. He developed a deep relationship with the Saudi royal family; in the early days of the reign of King Faisal, he paid the salaries of all Saudi civil servants to compensate for a lack of funds in the royal treasury. In return, King Faisal decreed that all construction projects in the kingdom should be handled by bin Laden's company. As a result, the company was responsible for the rebuilding and major renovation of the holiest sites in Mecca and Medina and for the rebuilding of the

---

244 https://en.wikipedia.org/wiki/Mohammed_bin_Awad_bin_Laden.

al-Aqsa Mosque in Jerusalem after a fire in 1969 (although Muhammad had died in a plane crash in September 1967).

Muhammad treated his children with scrupulous equality and made sure that they received a thorough religious and moral education following strict social and moral standards. Osama had to live up to these standards and was brought up as a devout, religious Muslim. While Osama lost his father when he was ten, the strict Muslim upbringing he received stayed with him for his entire life. He married a Syrian girl at the age of 17. He studied public administration at the King Abdul Aziz University in Jeddah and never traveled outside of Saudi Arabia, Syria, Afghanistan, Pakistan, and Sudan. Through his inheritance from his father, at the time he left for Afghanistan, he had a net worth of more than $800 million.

The Soviet Invasion of Afghanistan

Osama's exposure to Islamic activism began only weeks after the Soviet invasion of Afghanistan in December 1979. He went to Pakistan and visited refugee camps, meeting with resistance (mujahideen) leaders such as Burhanuddin Rabbani and Gulbuddin Hekmatyar. He returned to Saudi Arabia determined to support the Afghan jihad with his financial resources and whatever additional support he could gather from other people in Saudi Arabia.

Bin Laden's prominence in the Afghan resistance against the Soviet Union grew rapidly. He was considered a charismatic and inspirational personality—very useful for garnering more support for the resistance. In 1982, at the age of 25, he decided to move to Pakistan to participate more actively in the jihad. The US government had by that time initiated a Central Intelligence Agency (CIA) program called Operation Cyclon, which channeled funds through Pakistan's Inter-Services Intelligence Agency (ISI) to the Afghan mujahidden. CIA operatives trained bin Laden in combat operations; he became the best-known Arab *mujahid* in the world. He developed a legendary reputation in Muslim circles by being willing to give up a life of ease as a Saudi millionaire for a simple life of service and resistance for the sake of his beliefs (recalling Saint Francis of Assisi almost eight hundred years before). He enjoyed the highest esteem—not only among Muslims—and was inspiring

Arabs and Muslims throughout the world to participate in the Afghan resistance. If Osama, a millionaire, could fight in the resistance, why couldn't others do it as well?

By 1986, bin Laden had set up structures in Pakistan and Afghanistan to receive foreign volunteers, train them, and facilitate their participation in the resistance against the Soviet-backed Afghan government. He had also set up recruiting centers throughout the world, including in Europe and the United States. He was an essential part of the resistance movement, much loved and appreciated by Muslims and the West alike.

Arab fighters did not play a major role in the outcome of the jihad in Afghanistan; at any given moment, at most some 2,000 Arab mujahaddin were present there, while Afghan resistance fighters numbered approximately 250,000. Nevertheless, the Arab presence was a great morale boost, demonstrating international support for the resistance, and bin Laden's participation significantly increased fund-raising. Bin Laden thus made a significant positive contribution to the eventual overthrow of the pro-Soviet government.

The Soviet Withdrawal and bin Laden's Return to Saudi Arabia

Faced with increasing Afghan resistance, the Soviet Union began withdrawing its troops from Afghanistan in May 1988; the withdrawal was completed by February 15, 1989. Even though the pro-Communist regime of Muhammad Najibullah was able to remain in power until April 1992, the turmoil in the Soviet Union reduced their support and participation, with all financial support disappearing after the dissolution of the Soviet Union in 1991.

Bin Laden returned to Saudi Arabia as a hero even before, in 1989, and tried to live a normal life. However, his prominence required him to speak publicly about his experiences in Afghanistan and to discuss other challenges faced by Muslims throughout the world. His speeches on conditions in Yemen, the possible invasion of Kuwait by Saddam Hussein, and other issues became increasingly contentious in conservative Saudi Arabia. The Saudis ordered bin Laden to keep a low profile; he was not always able and willing to do so.

Weeks before the Iraqi invasion of Kuwait (August 1990), bin Laden wrote a detailed personal letter to the Saudi king warning him of the imminent attack by Saddam Hussein (who at the time was on good terms with the Saudis) and discussing its implications. Within days after the invasion predicted by bin Laden, he wrote to the king again, further explaining the dangers Saddam represented for Saudi Arabia and offering to mobilize the Arab-Afghan fighters he had trained to defend Saudi Arabia. While the first reaction to his letter and offer was positive, he soon discovered that the Saudi government had chosen to seek US support to defend its territory against the potential Iraqi threat. Furious, bin Laden voiced his anger in public speeches and other forums. He chose to seek the support of Islamic scholars for the idea of a Muslim defense force for Saudi Arabia; he was able to secure a fatwa that military training was a religious duty for every Muslim. This fatwa upset the Saudi government, which now considered bin Laden a threat. Bin Laden refused to obey orders to remain silent and was placed under quasi house arrest.

By 1991, bin Laden was increasingly dissatisfied with this situation and, with the help of one of his brothers and Prince Ahmed, the Saudi Deputy Minister of the Interior, was able to leave Saudi Arabia for Pakistan and from there to Afghanistan. At that time, the Afghan mujahidden were fighting among each other and making little progress toward capturing Kabul and overthrowing Najibullah. Bin Laden instructed his followers not to get involved in the conflict; he began seeking another place of residence.

By this time, Muhammad al-Bashir had come to power in Sudan through a coup d'état. Al-Bashir was a Muslim Brotherhood ideologue who appreciated bin Laden's efforts in the Afghan jihad. Bin Laden offered to invest in Sudan's economic development and was, in return, invited to reside in Sudan. Bin Laden arrived in Sudan on a private plane and invested hundreds of millions of dollars in various construction and manufacturing projects. At the same time, he used Sudan as a platform for his verbal attacks on the Saudi royal family and the United States for their presence in the land of the two holiest Muslim sites, Mecca and Medina.

Bin Laden's New Enemy—the United States

Both the Saudi government and the United States countered bin Laden's criticism and his objections to the US presence in Saudi Arabia by demanding his deportation from Sudan and claiming that he, together with the Islamist government in Sudan, was plotting to develop chemical weapons. While bin Laden was in Sudan, three attacks against American interests occurred—in South Yemen, in Somalia, and in Riyadh (Saudi Arabia) mounted by Arabs who had fought in Afghanistan. While bin Laden was not involved in these attacks, they led to increased US pressure against both him and against the Sudanese government to have him expelled from Sudan.

By 1996, the Sudanese government asked bin Laden to leave Sudan. During his stay he had lost more than $150 million on his investments, his Saudi citizenship had been revoked, and he had nowhere to go. He approached his jihadi friends in Afghanistan; with their assistance, he was able to return to Jalalabad in eastern Nangarhar province, while the mujahideen leader, Burhanuddin Rabbani, was president of Afghanistan. At that time, the Taliban controlled Kandahar and some neighboring provinces in western Afghanistan, but control of Kabul, Nangarhar, and all of central and northern Afghanistan was still in the hands of the Rabbani government. Bin Laden received a friendly welcome and settled down in Nangarhar, later moving to Khost Province.

In June 1996, another bombing occurred in Khobar, Saudi Arabia (whose alleged perpetrator, Ahmed al-Mughassil, was arrested in August 2015). Even though bin Laden never took credit for this bombing, he was informally implicated in it. In September of that year, the Taliban captured Nangarhar and, shortly thereafter, Kabul, ousting the Rabbani government. Since many of the Taliban leaders were former mujahideen and knew bin Laden as a mujahid and supporter of jihad against the former Soviet Union, the Taliban government did not object to bin Laden's presence and granted him their hospitality. In early 1997, out of fear of imminent assassination attempts by Saudi-funded Pakistani agents, bin Laden moved to Kandahar, where he was able to receive better protection.

By then, bin Laden's involvement in open resistance to US policies in Islamic countries had increased, and he began to issue publicly anti-American statements. He gave interviews on CNN and other US and global television channels, thereby attracting significant attention. Mullah Omar, the then Taliban leader (whose death, apparently in 2013, was not announced until the summer of 2015), asked bin Laden to keep a low profile and not to engage with the media. Bin Laden generally abided by this request, but he worked under the radar to secure support from mullahs throughout Afghanistan. During this period, he developed his new strategy not only to focus on the American presence in Saudi Arabia but also to expand his reach to all areas where Muslim rights are suppressed and where the United States supports regimes that oppress Muslims. The United States was now formally his enemy.

In April 1998, bin Laden broke his silence and, in an interview with the ABC network, openly declared his intention to fight against the United States. This announcement caused significant dismay from Mullah Omar, who formally ordered him to cease all contacts with the media. Meanwhile, the US government formally demanded that the Taliban government hand over bin Laden. Such a request, however, is directly counter to the Pashtun tradition of the Taliban (Pashtuns constitute about 60 percent of Afghanistan's population), which mandates protecting the life of anyone seeking refuge with them; the Taliban thus refused.

The bombings of American targets in Kenya and Tanzania in July 1998 provoked an American retaliation against bin Laden in the form of missile attacks against a training camp in Khost province (although bin Laden was hundreds of miles away in Kandahar). The Taliban asked for evidence that bin Laden was behind the bombings; only with such evidence would they try him for these crimes. The United States refused to provide this evidence, demanding instead that he unconditionally and immediately be handed over to US authorities. The Taliban offered to have him tried in a Muslim-majority country if the United States would provide evidence of his role in the attacks, but the United States again refused, saying that they were not willing to settle for anything less than the unconditional surrender of bin Laden. Such a surrender would violate Afghan tradition and the Afghan code of honor; the Taliban's refusal should not be surprising. During this time, bin Laden was enhancing his network, revitalizing his old connections and training mercenaries to hit the United States and US interests worldwide.

The attacks of September 11, 2001, came as a surprise not only to the United States but to the Taliban as well, who had insisted that bin Laden not engage in any activities outside Afghanistan. When the United States once again demanded the handover of bin Laden, the Taliban referred to the Pakhtunwali (derived from *Pashtun*) code of conduct that requires the protection of any person seeking sanctuary from his enemies—even at the cost of the protector's own life. The Taliban's refusal triggered the US invasion of Afghanistan and the overthrow of the Taliban government. Bin Laden, however, survived.

Bin Laden after 9/11

By December 2001, the United States had launched a powerful attack on Afghanistan's Taliban regime and al-Qaida. The attacks were preceded by significant conversations and agreements with the Northern Alliance, which had been heading the government in Afghanistan and had lost power to the Taliban in 1996. Northern Alliance activity had by 2001 been limited to a small northeastern part of the country and a district in the Panjsher Valley, about one hundred kilometers north of the capital. Additionally, the US government also revitalized its contacts with other ex-mujahideen and militia groups such as those under General Dostum, Haji Qadeer, Abdul Rab Rasul Sayyaf, Ismail Khan, Hamid Karzai, and others. They were armed and funded to revitalize their armies and be the foot soldiers for the Americans. Deploying around twenty thousand soldiers, the Bush administration launched the invasion of Afghanistan, with the capture of bin Laden one of its principal objectives.

Bin Laden managed to escape and hide in the mountains and caves of Tora Bora in eastern Afghanistan for a few days and was eventually able to evade capture and escape to Pakistan. From Pakistan he continued to lead al-Qaida, although not much was seen from him from then until his death except for some video and audio messages demonstrating his defiance against America and the West. Bin Laden was avoiding capture by staying out of public view, most likely residing in Pakistan. There were many speculations about his whereabouts, mostly placing him in the Waziristan region of Pakistan bordering Afghanistan.

Numerous intelligence and indications of his whereabouts gave rise to many conspiracy theories, but bin Laden's actual whereabouts or even if he was dead or alive seemed to remain a mystery. In the meantime, al-Qaida was claiming responsibility for attacks against US interests globally. Copycats such as Abu Musab al-Zarqawi in Iraq, Anwar al-Awlaki in Yemen, and others in other parts of the world claimed association with al-Qaida. Bin Laden and his team were quick to own such movements to maintain their credibility as an organization that was still alive and kicking.

As the war in Afghanistan progressed and the United States, now under President Barack Obama's leadership, launched the surge in 2009, the influence of al-Qaida in Afghanistan shrank. With the withdrawal of US forces from Iraq, the activities of al-Qaida in Iraq also slowly ceased. Affiliates in Syria, Yemen, Libya, and other countries, however, continued to commit atrocities, while copycats in other parts of the world continued to emerge. The civil war in Syria soon provided an opportunity for competing groups such as the al-Nusra Front and others to gain upper hand and demonstrate greater cruelty and more hardline efforts to combat the United States and its allies. At the same time, al-Qaida under bin Laden's leadership was softening its stance toward civilian casualties:

> The world's most feared terrorist, at the end of his life, [was] grappling with the moral and political failure of terrorism.
>
> Among the collection, the fullest picture of Bin Laden's thinking emerges in a 44-page letter he wrote in 2010. He chastised followers who had reinterpreted *tatarrus*—an Islamic doctrine meant to excuse the unintended killing of noncombatants in unusual circumstances—to justify routine massacres of Muslim civilians. This descent into indiscriminate slaughter, he warned, had turned Muslims against the jihadi movement. Bin Laden wrote that the *tatarrus* doctrine "needs to be revisited based on the modern-day context and clear boundaries established." He asked a subordinate to draw up a jihadist code of conduct that

> would constrain military operations in order to avoid civilian casualties.[245]

This "softening" provided an opening for other groups such as Boko Haram, al-Shabaab, al-Nusra Front, ISIS (see chapter 15), and others to emerge as the leading radical organization opposed to the United States and its military intervention in different Muslim countries. Whereas al-Qaida and bin Laden were softening toward the United States, these competing organizations were demonstrating strength and significant cruelty. For example,

> he (Osama) condemned the Times Square bomber for betraying an oath of loyalty to the United States.[246]

Others were beheading Americans and encouraging Muslims in America to fight against the US government. As a result, the standing of al-Qaida with radical individuals and groups had gradually weakened and verged on insignificance.

On May 1, 2011, President Obama announced that Osama bin Laden had been killed in a raid on his compound in Abbotabad, Pakistan. According to CNN[247], the incidents directly leading to his killing were as follows:

- *2007.* US intelligence services learn the name of one of bin Laden's couriers.
- *2009.* The US ascertains where in Pakistan the courier and his brother live.
- *August 2010.* The United States identifies the home in Abbottabad where the brothers live and confirm that they have

245 http://www.slate.com/articles/news_and_politics/politics/2012/05/bin_laden_s_documents_al_qaida_letters_show_the_moral_and_political_failure_of_terrorism_.single.html.

246 http://www.slate.com/articles/news_and_politics/politics/2012/05/bin_laden_s_documents_al_qaida_letters_show_the_moral_and_political_failure_of_terrorism_.single.html.

247 http://www.cnn.com/2013/09/09/world/death-of-osama-bin-laden-fast-facts/.

no sources of income or wealth to afford such a home (worth over US$1 million).

- *September 2010.* US intelligence informs President Obama that bin Laden may be living in the Abbottabad home, based upon the extensive security arrangements observed.
- *February 2011.* Planning for an attack on the home begins.
- *March 14, 2011.* President Obama holds a National Security Council meeting to discuss an operation on the Abbottabad home to capture or kill bin Laden; five such meetings are held over the next forty-five days.
- *April 29.* A day after the last of the five meetings, President Obama gives the order to raid the Abbottabad house.
- *May 1–2.* President Obama announced the killing of Osama bin Laden (late evening in the United States, midmorning May 2 in Pakistan).
- *May 2.* Bin Laden is buried at sea off the deck of the USS *Carl Vinson* within twenty-four hours in accordance with Islamic tradition after a DNA test confirms the body is that of Osama bin Laden.

The US raid involved twenty-five Navy SEALs who arrived in two Blackhawk helicopters. The raid lasted some forty minutes and involved the killing of bin Laden, three other men (including a bin Laden son), and one woman. Bin Laden was identified by one of his wives and by facial recognition. After the raid, CIA Director Leon Panetta said that Pakistani officials either ". . . were involved or incompetent. Neither place is a good place to be."

After the death of Osama bin Laden, the Egyptian doctor, Ayman Al Zawahiri, second in command at al-Qaida, was named the head of the organization. With the demise of bin Laden, al-Qaida had lost a hero and with him much of its relevance and importance. Other organizations soon took over al-Qaida's fight, and the world was set to experience a completely new dimension of death, torture, and destruction at the hands of its copycats such as ISIS, Boko Haram and Al-Shabaab.

We next turn to a discussion of the US role in Afghanistan and Iraq before returning to the question of copycats—organizations and "lone wolves" using terror to achieve their objectives.

Chapter 14

The United States after 9/11

Interventions in Afghanistan and Iraq—the Beginning of a New Era

You can persuade an Afghan to go with you to hell but you cannot force him to go with you to heaven.

The New US Military Doctrine

With the demise of the Soviet Union, the United States found itself the sole superpower; it thus had to devise new policies and strategies to react to the changing situation, making sure that no new threat could arise against the newfound US hegemony and preventing the rise of any new superpowers. In developing this policy, one of the significant threats the United States perceived was in the Islamic world. The successes of the mujahideen in Afghanistan against the Soviet Union and of the Islamic Republic of Iran against multiple allied nations supporting Saddam Hussein of Iraq showed that Islam had the potential to become a substantial political force. Statements from Afghan mujahideen and Iranian leaders, as well as voices in many other Muslim-majority countries, exacerbated US fears that a revival of Islam was becoming imminent.

The United States began to develop the "American Army Doctrine for the Post Cold War" in 1991. The doctrine

> proceeded from a full appreciation of the strategic and operational ramifications of the fundamentally altered power situation in Europe and the freer U.S. contingency role in a world in which the retreat of Soviet power permitted more open opportunities to respond militarily to regional crises.[248]

Based on this doctrine, one focus in the new era would be the "simultaneity of fire effects"[249] and

> adaptation to sudden, radically different operational circumstances presented by sudden theater change.

The new doctrine would also ensure

> four fundamental war fighting qualities: the Army's deployability, lethality, expansibility and versatility.

Eliminating the jargon, in plain English, the new doctrine focused on small-scale threats arising in various locations simultaneously that required the military's attention at different levels. By 2015 it is clear what this new doctrine intended to achieve, namely being able to engage in multiple smaller-scale simultaneous wars in different theaters.

At present (as of April 2016), the United States is directly involved in military operations (often through the use of drones) in Afghanistan, Pakistan, Iraq, Syria, Yemen, Libya, Somalia, and other Muslim-majority countries. The doctrine was formally introduced in 1993 and used to justify actions in various Muslim-majority countries to ensure that potential threats could be dealt with using rapidly deployed military force without causing any reduction in the US military's ability to respond simultaneously to larger-scale interventions, including linear

---

248 Romjue, Don L., *American Army Doctrine for Post Cold-War* (Military History Office, United States Army Training and Doctrine Office), page 32.

249 Romjue, Don L., *American Army Doctrine for Post Cold-War* (Military History Office, United States Army Training and Doctrine Office) page 36.

warfare.[250] This doctrine has been the basis for US military actions in the pre- and post-9/11 environment and in the so-called war against terrorism.

The doctrine has, not surprisingly, evoked strong reactions in the Muslim world. Certain Muslim thinkers claim that the current world conditions and attacks against Muslims in various parts of the world, coupled with the sudden escalation of terrorist activities by Muslim organizations, are not an accident, but rather the direct outcome of the implementation of the new post–Cold War military doctrine. These thinkers often claim that actions under the doctrine are not a consequence of Islamic terrorism but have rather been an intended result of this doctrine. They argue that neoconservative strategists wanted to see a gradual degradation of Islam's reputation and Muslims in general by creating an image of an adversary that is cruel, inhumane, and willing to go to any lengths to achieve its objectives. The resulting terrorism and chaos would so defame Islam that fewer and fewer people would consider it worthy of following.

These theorists go further to suggest that the doctrine was necessitated by the unexpectedly great victory of mostly Sunni Islam in Afghanistan, which caused the downfall of the Soviet Union and could lead to a return of the medieval power base of Islam in the modern world. According to this view, the defeat of the Soviet Union in Afghanistan, coupled with the Shi'a Islamic revolution in Iran and the Iranians' ability to withstand the Saddam-led war with Iraq, created the perspective of a strong united front of different Muslim groups that constituted a significant threat to US hegemony—a threat to be countered sooner rather than later.

---

250 This term, more frequently encountered in the negative (*nonlinear warfare*), describes more conventional traditional, nonguerilla forms of warfare. Compare the linear US invasion of Iraq in the Second Gulf War with the current (nonlinear) operations of Russia in Ukraine.

Margaret Thatcher, the former British prime minister (and so-called "Iron Lady") added fuel to the fire by writing an article in 2002 entitled "Islamism[251] Is the New Bolshevism" in which she described Islamism as

> an aggressive ideology promoted by fanatical, well-armed devotees. And, like communism, it requires an all-embracing long-term strategy to defeat it.[252]

These thinkers use such arguments to propose that the West is developing a strategy for the destruction of Islam and the subjugation of Muslims.

The US Response to 9/11

The invasion of Iraq by the US-led coalition following the 1990 attack by Saddam Hussein on Kuwait was somewhat justified as legitimate because Saddam was an anti-Islamic secularist and a much-hated personality. The West justified the invasion of Afghanistan citing the 9/11 attacks, the unanimous support of the UN Security Council, and the oppressive methods of government of the Taliban. However, the Muslim world did not appreciate the aggressive language of the Bush administration labeling everyone to be either "with us or against us" and Bush's reference to the Crusades. Attacks on Muslims began to grow in the United States, in Europe, and even in Muslim-majority countries. Oppressive regimes in Muslim-majority countries were strengthened by American and European support; other regimes were coerced to work against their own national interests by pursuing anyone with an inkling of opposition to the United States and its allied regimes. Humanitarian organizations that supported legitimate (to most of the world and an increasing proportion of Americans) Muslim causes such as Palestinian resistance to Israeli occupation and aggression were demonized, and

251 This term, and the corresponding adjective *Islamist*, first appeared in English in a translation from a French-language article entitled "The Islamist Movements in Contemporary Egypt" by Gilles Kepel. See http://www.csmonitor.com/World/Middle-East/2012/0813/What-is-an-Islamist.

252 http://www.theguardian.com/world/2002/feb/12/afghanistan.politics.

Muslim scholars who dared to dissent against the prevailing policies of the United States and its allies found themselves under attack. The jihad in Afghanistan had become a liability for Arabs and other Muslims who had supported it physically, financially, or intellectually. All Muslim and Arab participants in the Afghan resistance against the Soviets were categorized as enemies of the United States and its allies. The pressure against anyone who had in any way contributed to this effort became unbearable. Many Muslims living in the United States, Europe, and other countries were terrorized by the overwhelming might of the United States threatening them directly or indirectly.

Muslims chose a variety of paths to counter this aggression and opposition. Some avoided any association with "Islamist" thought or organizations and maintained a low profile. Others engaged in dialogue to clarify the position of Muslims and Islam in this alarming situation. A third tendency voiced dismay at the attacks directed at them either verbally or through demonstrations, seeking protection for their rights and drawing attention to the injustices committed against them. A fourth group chose the nuclear option, namely to resist with force and equal or often greater or excessive aggression. This fourth group provided the long-sought forces and foot soldiers for bin Laden and al-Qaida.

The Second Gulf War

The US-led invasion of Iraq in March 2003 (with a much smaller coalition than during the First Gulf War) was viewed by most Muslims as unprovoked (unlike in 1990) and as a major injustice committed by the US government. Many if not most Muslims saw the war as a subterfuge to seek full control of Iraqi oilfields and thus to surround Iran from both east and west, at the same time creating a controlling footprint throughout the Middle East. Almost no one in the Muslim world believed the pretext of weapons of mass destruction or the "self-defense" claims of the Bush administration. Muslims viewed the concept of "preemptive war" presented by the United States as a violation of article 2, section 4 of the UN Charter[253] (requiring members to refrain

---

253 http://www.un.org/en/documents/charter/chapter1.shtml.

from the threat or use of force against the territorial integrity or political independence of any state) and an infringement of the national integrity of a Muslim-majority country. This invasion provided further incentives to potential recruits for the "nuclear option" in resisting United States and NATO aggression.

The United States exacerbated the situation by failing to use restraint in its occupation and by not making the effort to understand the cultural and religious complexities of a country with a Shi'a majority that had been repressed for decades, a Kurdish (Sunni) minority that was looked upon with suspicion by all other Iraqis, and an Arab Sunni minority jealous of its prerogatives under the Saddam regime. The United States did not have enough translators and was ill-equipped to achieve even basic communications with the local population. In addition, the United States chose to dismantle the Iraqi Army and create a vacuum of power by banning ex-Baathists (the secularist ruling party under Saddam Hussein) from public service, creating a new army that was inadequately trained and not motivated to undertake any worthwhile action. The US Army was bribing Sunni tribal elders to buy their support while threatening Shi'a leaders to subjugate them. The Kurds, who already had a quasi-government for many years prior to the US-led invasion, took advantage of the opportunity to distance themselves from other Iraqis—as well as to create significant social and economic development—in their region. However, the Kurds and their Peshmerga fighting force sought to move closer to complete independence, creating significant mistrust and suspicions from other groups in Iraq. This combination of circumstances led to ongoing tensions among the various groups and a number of violent incidents that increased the sense of lawlessness and hostile interactions throughout the country.

The banned ex-Baathist and former military personnel who were completely excluded from the government had basically two choices to survive—migrate or take up arms. Most chose to migrate to Syria and Jordan, but some preferred violent resistance and self-defense. They were willing to accept any port in a storm, and many radicals within al-Qaida were willing to offer assistance. These radicals were planning to attack the United States—and now the United States had come to their home. The US presence was a blessing—and an opportunity that could not remain unused.

Al-Qaida in Iraq soon became a prominent player in the insurgency against the United States. It used the dismay against the United States and disappointments in social and political life, providing a veneer of Islamic justification to maximize chaos and lawlessness in an already fragile environment, to achieve its goals of self-enrichment, hunger for power, and retaliation against a hated enemy. The changed situation after the fall of Saddam Hussein provided a completely new opportunity, and al-Qaida was determined to use it to its full potential. Other copycats in Iraq and elsewhere soon discovered that the situation in Iraq was a useful tool for them as well.

The Failed Afghan Invasion

Afghans at first welcomed the NATO invasion following 9/11. However, four factors soon began to create problems for the US-led experiment in nation building.

First, the United States did not understand the Afghan mentality and culture and was not willing to listen to persons with a deeper understanding of the Afghan way and view of life. A saying in Pashto goes "You can persuade an Afghan to go with you to hell, but you cannot force him to go with you to heaven." The power of persuasion can move mountains (certainly not lacking) in Afghanistan. However, an Afghan considers forcing someone to do something as equivalent to disrespecting or dishonoring him. Even if one is forcing an Afghan to do something that is good for him, he will fight against it to the death. In part for this reason, Afghanistan has always remained an unconquered land and the "graveyard of empires."

The reasons for the increasing anti-American sentiment were legion—night raids inside people's houses; entering their female quarters (which is often not even allowed for a brother); bombings of wedding parties; attacks by trigger-happy Americans on housing compounds causing the deaths of dozens of women and children; the arrests of innocent people due to incorrect intelligence reports, coupled with desecration of the dead; disrespect for the Quran; and the raising of crosses on US bases and positions—all contributed to alienate the Afghan population, which by 2004 had seen a revival of resistance against the US "invasion." In the absence of US leadership and taking responsibility for such actions, the Taliban were able to take credit for these resistance actions and put together a team capable of opposing the coalition systematically. Soon the Taliban had formally taken over the leadership of the resistance and, supported by a Pakistan that did not want to see a prosperous and successful government in Afghanistan, the war of resistance to the United States and its allies was soon in full swing.

Second, the Afghan government under Hamid Karzai turned out to be incompetent and corrupt. Karzai, forced upon the Afghan people by the US government during the Bonn Conference in December 2001, was incapable of adhering to a strategic approach to moving the country forward. After the fading of the initial excitement following the invasion and the arrival of the new government, corruption started to penetrate every aspect of people's lives and was exacerbated by inefficiency and corruption by the US military and contractors. Cash payments to the Taliban and armed gangs posing as Taliban to give a right of passage to US military convoys contributed to destroying the credibility of the entire governing system. Afghans in rural areas came to rely on the Taliban to bring justice and to provide some form of stability and accountability. The situation further enhanced insecurity and resistance throughout the country.

Third, because of the later US invasion of Iraq during the Second Gulf War and the subsequent difficulties with the security situation there, Afghans' positive feelings for the United States slowly transformed into dismay with their actions and hatred. In spite of the positive works that the United States was doing for the country in terms of health, education, and infrastructure, a significant majority of Afghans became suspicious of US intentions behind the invasion of Afghanistan, further damaging the US image and increasing resistance to their presence.

Fourth, the United States was promoting better ties with India, to Pakistan's dismay, while the Afghan government under Karzai was also seeking a stronger military and strategic partnership with India. Pakistan could not afford to sit idly by and do nothing. Thus, Pakistanis actively supported the Taliban and other groups (including those headed by Hekmatyar, Maulvi Jalaluddin Haqqani, and remnants of al-Qaida) to wage war and enhance instability and chaos. At this time the United States was putting Iran under significant pressure over their nuclear ambitions and was constantly threatening them with sanctions and military action. Iran, fighting for its survival, actively supported the Taliban and other radical groups in their struggle against the United States to divert US attention from Iran. The result was a further fueling of the conflict in Afghanistan—and the inevitable incidents considered as atrocities in the Muslim world.

All four of the above factors exacerbated the Afghan conflict and added to the hatred of the United States and its actions in a Muslim-majority country. For those Muslims who pursued violent opposition to the United States, every negative word, every story and every casualty was a new success toward recruiting disenchanted persons to join their team of killers.

Mistakes/Atrocities by US Military and Intelligence Agencies

Since the start of the Iraq war, actions considered by Muslims and many others as atrocities and war crimes committed by US military and intelligence personnel in the name of protecting the American people and pursuing the "war on terrorism" were almost daily occurrences. Whether it was torture cells in Abu Ghraib, waterboarding in Guantanamo Bay, private jails in Afghanistan, or desecration of the Quran by ideologues violently opposed to Islam such as Pastor Terry Jones, all such actions significantly harmed America's image and further reinforced the negative impression that was being propagated as the United States' global war against Islam and Muslims. Obviously, President Bush's reference to a "crusade" against terrorism did not help. The phrase continues to be heard among radical Muslims and groups such as al-Qaida to categorize US actions in Muslim-majority countries as a Christian war against the Muslim world. As a result, al-Qaida and its copycats have gained another tool for recruiting fighters in their war against the West.

Drone Attacks

The Bush administration considered drones as an effective tool to hunt down and kill terrorists anywhere in the world. The Obama administration expanded the Bush administration strategy to use drones as killing machines and has made them into a centerpiece of its national security strategy. Thus far, drone attacks have been reported being carried out in Afghanistan, Pakistan, Yemen, Iraq, Syria, and Somalia. Estimates are that some 95 percent of all targeted killings by the US military have been carried out by drones.[254] As of December 2013, more than three thousand people have been killed by drone attacks (of which at least over one-third were civilians).[255] The US use of drones has become a key tool for al-Qaida and its copycats to recruit supporters.

Using drones clearly infringes on a country's sovereignty by violating its airspace. Even if the drone strikes are carried out with the knowledge of the government of the country where the attacks occur, much of the local population feels that such strikes infringe upon their sovereignty. The sources providing intelligence for establishing targets are often questionable, leading to the frequent killing of innocent civilians or bystanders. For the United States, such deaths are unavoidable collateral damage; for the victims' families and friends, they are foreign aggression.

Drone attacks are considered by most local people as heinous, often under the cover of darkness and from thousands of feet of elevation. Many consider them equivalent to terrorist attacks. Some radical groups justify their grievous and merciless attacks against civilians with the United States' drone attacks on their people. The drone killings end up being a sort of "whack-a-mole" game, where the (often more than one) new recruits replace the dead for organizations such as al-Qaida, ISIS, and al-Shabaab.

Extraordinary Renditions and Secret Detentions

Extraordinary rendition is the transfer—without legal process—of a detainee to the custody of a foreign government for purposes of detention and interrogation, often using torture. The program was intended to protect the United States, but the outcomes have been fairly questionable. According to the Open Society Foundation,

254 http://www.propublica.org/article/everything-we-know-so-far-about-drone-strikes.

255 http://www.propublica.org/article/everything-we-know-so-far-about-drone-strikes.

> at least 136 individuals were reportedly extraordinarily rendered or secretly detained by the CIA and at least 54 governments reportedly participated in the CIA's secret detention and extraordinary rendition program; classified government documents may reveal many more.[256]

Quite a number of these detainees turned out to be innocent individuals and were citizens of Canada, Germany, the United Kingdom, and other friendly countries; a number have filed lawsuits against the US government following their release. The practice of extraordinary rendition and secret detentions has put a dark shadow on the United States' credibility as a country that promotes human rights and the rule of law; it has been used devastatingly to discredit US foreign policy and show it to be directed against Muslims and Islam. As a result, it has been an effective tool to hire more recruits for the terrorists' cause.

In summary, the United States' involvement in the Islamic world caused a blowback among those people whom the United States had trained to fight the Soviet Union in Afghanistan. The invasion of Iraq, coupled with failed strategies in Afghanistan, the lack of understanding of the (very different) cultures of both countries, the cruel and inhumane treatment of Muslims, and badly chosen rhetoric by US leaders, has contributed greatly to the so-called Islamic terrorism and caused it to gain further strength.

To expect this new phenomenon to lose momentum without the US government bringing about significant changes in its policy toward the Muslim world and toward ensuring its own security is naive. The nightmare of the terrorists that breed fear and horror in our hearts and that cause thousands of lives to be lost every year in every corner of the world cannot be fought with the same tools that caused it to be created in the first place. Fighting terrorism requires imagination and the courage to think outside the box. It takes an act of bravery to change course and look for solutions where solutions can be found.

In the absence of such an effort, we will continue to look for the problem in the wrong place. There is an old story in Afghanistan that a person was looking for something on the ground outside. He was asked

---

256 http://www.opensocietyfoundations.org/voices/20-extraordinary-facts-about-cia-extraordinary-rendition-and-secret-detention.

what he was looking for and responded that he had lost his pen. They asked him where he had lost it.

He responded, “Inside the house.”

“So why are you looking outside for your pen?” he was asked.

He responded, “Because it is dark inside the house.”

How can one expect to find his pen, even if it is bright outside, when the loss occurred elsewhere? How does the United States expect to solve the problem of terrorism if it is looking for its causes in Islam? We need to recognize that Islam is not the problem; rather, it is part of the solution. The United States needs to start looking in the right place. A significant change in United States’ foreign policy would be a good place to start.

Chapter 15

Terrorist Organizations

The Race to Outdo al-Qaida

Cooperate with each other in righteousness and piety,
and do not cooperate in sin and aggression. [257]

The "success" of al-Qaida has led to the creation of other organizations using even more gruesome tactics creating havoc in various parts of the world. The best known of these organizations are Boko Haram (based in Nigeria), al-Shabaab (centered in Somalia), and the Islamic State of Iraq and Sham[258] (ISIS, operating mainly in Syria and Iraq),[259] but similar organizations exist in such countries as the Philippines, China, Pakistan, Libya, Sierra Leone, Mali, Chad, and other countries. While

257 Sura Al-Mâ'idah (5), verse 2.

258 The word *Sham* refers to the area under the control of Damascus, which historically includes portions of Syria, Lebanon, Palestine, Israel, Jordan, Cyprus, and the Turkish Hatay Province.

https://en.wikipedia.org/wiki/Syria_(region); https://en.wikipedia.org/wiki/Sham.

259 The Islamic State is known by a number of names, including the Islamic State of Iraq and Syria (ISIS), the Islamic State of Iraq and the Levant (the historic name for the area including Syria, Jordan, Lebanon, and Palestine—ISIL) and Daesh, which is an acronym of the name in Arabic.

a significant threat, terrorist organizations are easier to manage than "lone wolves" (whom we consider in the next chapter), as they are more visible, have a geographic presence, and their tactics are relatively well-known, making it easier to develop and deploy strategies against them, although the emergence of leaderless resistance groups within these organizations is a troubling new development (discussed below).[260] It is clear, however, that this visible and measurable threat requires concrete actions to eliminate it. Nonetheless, the costs of such counterterrorism operations are high, and the cost-benefit analysis does not always provide a sufficient justification to undertake such actions. Some Muslim observers claim that the US government intentionally wants to prevent the eradication of such organizations, as their existence is a pretext for continuing the war on terrorism and robust military actions.

Al-Shabaab

The organization's official name is Harakat al-Shabaab al-Mujahidden; the short version, *al-Shabaab*, is Arabic for "the Youth." Al-Shabaab's creation dates back to the overthrow of Somali military dictator Siad Barre in 1991. Since that time, Somalia has become a "failed state," in a more or less continual state of anarchy. Competing warlords have been fighting one another and taking control of small areas of the country, with no effective central government. Over the past quarter century, numerous parties, most notably the United Nations, have sought to bring peace to the country, but all have failed. The most notable such effort was the creation of the Transitional Federal Government (TFG), consisting of various clans and militarily supported by neighboring Ethiopia. The TFG moved the capital from Mogadishu to the south-central city of Baidao but was not able to exert much influence in other areas of the country.[261]

As a reaction to the extended periods of chaos and lawlessness, neighborhoods began to create their own Sharia courts to manage

260 See, e.g., https://www.stratfor.com/weekly/countering-shapeless-terrorist-threat.

261 Wise, Rob, "Al-Shabaab," Center For Strategic and International Studies, case study 2, July 2011.

conflicts and provide some framework for the rule of law. These courts soon became centers of power for much of the country; they developed their own recruits to ensure implementation of their (often very harsh) rulings, with each court following the ideological direction of its specific leader. While the dominant tendency in Somalia is Sufi Islam (a soft, mystical, and nonradical approach to Islam), some of the courts developed harsh policies. By mid-2004, a number of these courts had joined to form the Islamic Courts Union (ICU), headed by (moderate) Sheikh Sharif Ahmad.

The ICU was able to exert significant influence and managed to expel a number of the competing warlords from the capital Mogadishu in June 2006. With the ICU managing all of Somalia, the population saw peace returning, businesses starting again, order being restored, and crime plummeting. However, these changes also brought negative implications, such as the Taliban style of government introduced by many hardline leaders. The ICU forced women to cover themselves from head to toe and banned soccer and watching television; those perceived as un-Islamic were brutally punished. One radical group within the ICU was al-Shabaab. Al-Shabaab adhered to the Wahhabi school of thought that originated in eighteenth century Saudi Arabia (see chapter 8).

In the post 9/11 environment, the United States and its Western allies considered the ICU as a new Taliban-like regime in Somalia and sought to destroy it. They encouraged Ethiopia with money and weapons to invade Somalia. Ethiopian forces entered Somalia on December 24, 2006, and disbanded the ICU. Al-Shabaab retreated to the south of Somalia and launched bloody guerilla attacks against the Ethiopians. In January 2009, the Ethiopian soldiers withdrew and were replaced by forces from the African Union Mission to Somalia; these forces limited their actions to protecting Mogadishu's airport, seaport, the presidential palace and some key Mogadishu neighborhoods. Al-Shabaab was left to operate freely in south-central Somalia and even in some neighborhoods of Mogadishu. Soon thereafter al-Shabaab began to rebrand itself as an al-Qaida affiliate and part of the global war against the West. In 2011 al-Shabaab began its attacks outside Somalia's borders, starting in Uganda and expanding to Kenya (with its large ethnic Somali population).

Today al-Shabaab is actively recruiting young Somali immigrants in the United States and Europe, encouraging them to join their war in Somalia and elsewhere. Especially in the Minneapolis-St. Paul area (with its large Somali community), the challenge of young ethnic Somalis moving to Somalia to join al-Shabaab represents a significant concern.

Boko Haram

Boko Haram is a Nigerian term meaning "Western education is forbidden." The official name of the organization is Jama'ati Ahlis Sunna Lidda'Awati Wal-Jihad, which in Arabic means "Group of the People of Sunnah for Preaching and Jihad." The organization is based in northern Nigeria but is also active in Chad, Niger, and northern Cameroon. Boko Haram is responsible for the murder of more than five thousand civilians between July 2009 and June 2014.[262] It can be considered an al-Qaida copycat concentrating on West Africa, with al-Shabaab focusing on eastern Africa.

Boko Haram was founded in 2002 by Muhammad Yusuf, a Wahhabi ideologue intensely opposed to Western influence. In July 2009, a major uprising against Boko Haram led to Yusuf's execution, following by a loss of the organization's prominence. However, in September 2010, Boko Haram regained its strength after a massive prison break and increased its brutality and sophistication. By early 2015, Boko Haram controlled an area of approximately twenty thousand square miles (over fifty thousand square kilometers—almost the size of West Virginia) in its home state of Borno. At this time they had an estimated seven thousand to ten thousand members.[263]

Boko Haram came to the West's attention through their unusually cruel and drastic actions such as the kidnapping of 276 schoolgirls in April 2014. More than 1.5 million people have fled the areas under their rule. Boko Haram is not yet known to have encouraged any activities in the United States or Europe or to be actively recruiting in these

---

262 http://www.washingtonpost.com/blogs/monkey-cage/wp/2014/10/06/the-boko-haram-insurgency-by-the-numbers/.

263 https://medium.com/war-is-boring/how-big-is-boko-haram-fac21c25807.

areas, but they are causing significant challenges for the governments of Nigeria, Niger, Chad, and Cameroon. In 2014, Boko Haram officially declared its allegiance to the self-declared caliphate of ISIS.

ISIS

Abu Musab al-Zarqawi founded what became ISIS under the name Jamaat al-Tawhid wa-i-Jihad in 1999.[264] Unlike bin Laden, who was from a wealthy family and university educated, al-Zarqawi was poorer and less educated, with a criminal past and extreme views on *takfir* (accusing another Muslim of heresy and thereby justifying his killing), which led to major friction and distrust between the two. Al-Qaida's 9/11 success led to the creation of a number of local "franchises." After the US-led invasion in 2003, al-Zarqawi became a household name in Iraq due to his personal beheadings and his campaign of suicide bombings. As a result, many foreigners sought to join al-Zarqawi's efforts, but not to be outdone by al-Zarqawi, bin Laden sought to gain control of the Iraqi jihad and pressured al-Zarqawi to join forces. In October 2004, al-Zarqawi agreed, pledging *baya* (a religious oath of allegiance) and renaming his organization al-Qaida in the Land of Two Rivers (more popularly, al-Qaida in Iraq, or AQI). This agreement provided al-Zarqawi with access to private donors, recruitment, logistics, and facilitation networks. Al-Zarqawi thus gained access to resources and the flow of foreign fighters, and particularly the allegiance of many young recruits—and thus the future generation of the jihadist movement, one of the key factors now separating ISIS from al-Qaida (whose ranks are comprised mostly of those who came of age during the Afghan resistance in the 1980s and 1990s).

Al-Zarqawi's excesses led to two stern warnings from Ayman al-Zawahiri, then al-Qaida's second in command (and now its leader). In early 2006, al-Zarqawi established the Majlis Shura al-Mujaheddin (MSM), a number of Iraqi insurgent factions with AQI at the top. Al-Zarqawi's death on June 7, 2006, accelerated the consolidation, and on October 15, 2006, a statement announced the establishment

---

264 http://www.washingtoninstitute.org/uploads/Documents/pubs/ResearchNote_20_Zelin.pdf.

of the Islamic State of Iraq with Abu Omar al-Baghdadi as its leader. While MSM had given an implied pledge of allegiance to al-Qaida (its information officer, who announced the formation of MSM, had called bin Laden "Emir") and al-Zarqawi had pledged baya to Bin-Ladin, al-Zarqawi's death invalidated that pledge. Al-Baghdadi followed the al-Zarqawi approach to takfir and his policy of beheadings and spectacular acts of violence against Muslims. He also developed a program of taking and holding territory, which al-Qaida had not done.

Al-Qaida and ISIS—the Struggle for Control of the Jihadi Movement

Over the years since inception of al-Qaida, the organization has been responsible for a significant expansion of the terrorist network throughout the world, primarily by copycats that were inspired by what al-Qaida stood for and were willing to go to any length to meet and exceed al-Qaida's work of terror. However, with the passage of time, the main source of al-Qaida doctrine, Osama bin Laden, had weakened in his resolve and had indicated a significant softening of his approach. He showed remorse for causing civilian casualties and called upon his followers to focus their attention on the United States and less on causing harm to Muslims and uninvolved civilians throughout the world. After his death in the hands of US forces on May 2, 2011, his successor, Ayman al-Zawahiri, continued this soft path. Not all of his followers in the world agreed with this soft tone and less aggressive approach, which led to a weaker network. By 2012, every al-Qaida affiliate chose to rely on themselves for their operations and avoided any significant interaction with the headquarters.

The al-Qaida affiliates in Iraq had always been extremely violent and had on various occasions been instructed by bin Laden to lessen their emphasis on violence. Upon the death of bin Laden, the organization rebranded itself as ISIS and eventually by 2013 established a territorial state. Their aggressively violent approach and ruthless beheading of Westerners, setting on fire of captives, enslavement of non-Muslims, and mass assassination of Muslim opposition created a strong current of sympathy and attraction among radical people who had already been disappointed by the softening tone of al-Qaida.

While ISIS's rise became apparent about the time it established a territorial state in 2013, it became a major focus of world concern in 2015. While the rivalry between al-Qaida and ISIS had been gradually increasing, the split between the two organizations became overt and public in 2015. Despite the efforts of Ayman al-Zawahiri to "put ISIS in its place," in Syria the conflict between the al-Nusra Front, the local al-Qaida affiliate, and ISIS spread to the battlefield, with ISIS looking like the young and stylish alternative to the increasingly old-fashioned-seeming al-Qaida.

Since 2013, ISIS has slowly emerged as a strong competitor to al-Qaida and has been successful in replacing it in numerous markets. The graph below shows the affiliation of terrorist organizations with al-Qaida and ISIS in different geographic regions:

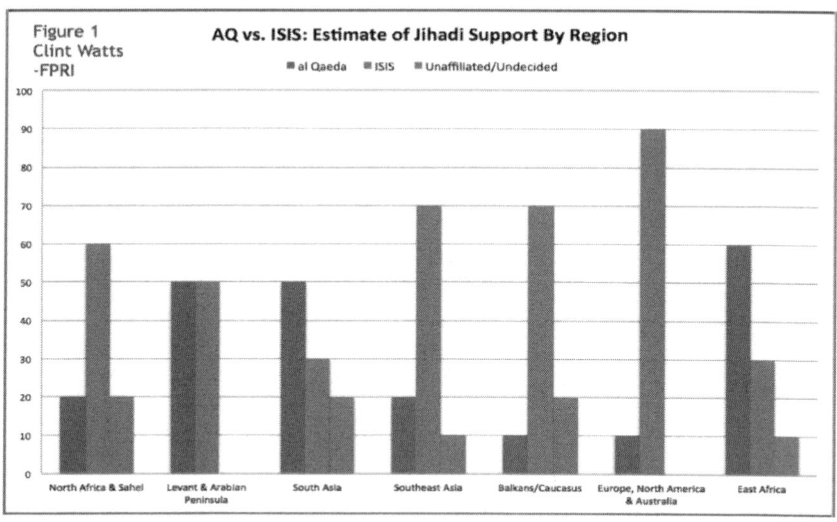

In this competition, the only swing region seems to be Yemen, where a head-to-head completion between al-Qaida and ISIS is emerging. While ISIS has garnered support from a number of Saudi foreign fighters, is the largest recipient of funds from Saudi sponsors, and has drawn the attention of Saudi authorities, Yemen remains the homeland of bin Laden. Al-Qaida in the Arabian Peninsula (AQAP) remains the strongest al-Qaida affiliate and remains the greatest obstacle to ISIS taking global control of the jihadi movement. Al-Zawahiri deftly named Nasir al-Wuhayshi, the leader of AQAP as his worldwide deputy, but whether the support of AQAP and the al-Nusra Front will be sufficient to stem the rising ISIS tide remains an open question.

Three scenarios seem possible in the struggle between ISIS and al-Qaida to dominate the worldwide jihadi movement:

- ISIS prevails over al-Qaida and becomes the de facto leader of the worldwide jihadi movement.
- Al-Qaida manages to stem the ISIS surge and remains in competition with it for movement leadership.
- The competition between the two organizations becomes a regional battle, with localized organizations such as Boko Haram and al-Shabaab maintaining only loose ties with "international" jihadi organizations and playing off the two organizations against each other.[265]

Leaderless Terrorist Organizations

Leaderless or grassroots terrorist organizations represent a new trend among radicals claiming adherence to Islam. Terrorist organization leaders, recognizing that antiterrorist authorities are very good at finding and destroying known terrorist organizations, are turning increasingly to leaderless groups, whose participants are not known to such authorities but who still have access to the organization strength and resources of known groups. While unskilled operatives in such leaderless groups often use amateurish tactics and reach out to undercover agents in antiterrorist groups, more sophisticated terrorists have shown themselves to be skillful in "hiding in the murky ambiguities of societies."[266]

While terrorist operatives are most vulnerable to detection in the preoperational phases of their operations, more sophisticated organizers often use separate organizations for surveillance, weapons making, bomb making, and launching the operation. Prevention of attacks by such organizations involves police and citizen awareness of unusual behavior; attention to small, unexplained explosions; and the presence of unexplained or unusual quantities of potentially explosive chemicals

---

265 Ibid.

266 https://www.stratfor.com/weekly/countering-shapeless-terrorist-threat.

(such as acetone, acid, peroxide and methyl alcohol, or metallic powders such as aluminum, magnesium, and ferric oxide); the presence of laboratory equipment (e.g., beakers, scales, protective gloves, and masks) in hotel rooms or residences; and evidence of the dissembling of watches or cell phones.[267]

While citizens should not become vigilantes and finding the above types of evidence is not proof of intent to commit a terrorist attack, good defense against such organization requires more eyes and ears than authorities possess and argues for education of the police and the wider population to such threats.

267 Ibid.

Chapter 16

Lone Wolves—The Problem of Individual Terrorists

From Broken Families to Fanaticism, to Radicalism and then Violence

O Believers, be steadfast for the sake of Allah and bear true witness and let not the enmity of a people incite you to do injustice. Do justice; that is nearer to piety.[268]

The problem of managing or recognizing individuals ("copycats") following the lead of al-Qaida or, increasingly, ISIS is more difficult than confronting terrorist organizations. In Muslim-majority countries, such individuals easily find a path to join a terrorist organization and thus fulfill their emotional desires. In Western countries, however, finding a vector for such individuals to vent their hidden aggressions is more difficult—but we must focus on trying to understand their motivations and paths.

268 Sura Al-Mâ'idah (5), verse 8.

Lone Wolf Characteristics

A first step is to look at individuals who join other non-Muslim terrorist groups. According to Pete Simi and Robert Futrell, coauthors of *American Swastika: Inside the White Power Movement's Hidden Spaces of Hate*, people who are radicalized, whatever their background or their religious orientation (or lack thereof), typically come from troubled and disrupted families, have had problematic and often traumatic experiences, and feel marginalized from society.[269] Educational and socioeconomic levels are not a determining factor; members come from a wide cross-section of socioeconomic backgrounds and can be "doctors, lawyers, scientists, and other highly educated folks." They often demonstrate

> certain characteristics of thinking that make a person more prone or susceptible. For instance, low tolerance for ambiguity seems to cut across most if not all extremist ideologies; this goes along with a certain type of concrete thinking where a person wants to categorize things as "black or white" rather than deal with so-called grey areas.

Such people feel lost or are looking for some easy answers.

Being part of a culture of violence is a common theme among individuals who join radical organizations.

> Some people were already violent before they ever became exposed to extremism. Some were exposed to violence in the home as children or were already getting into fights at school or in their neighborhood.[270]

Radical movements are continuously on the lookout for such personalities and offer them an oversimplified version of a highly complicated world. Simi and Futrell note

---

269 http://www.splcenter.org/get-informed/intelligence-report/browse-all-issues/2014/spring/Why-They-Join.

270 *Ibid.*

> That's a powerful thing to offer people, especially those who feel lost or are looking for some easy answers.

Not all persons sympathizing with, wanting to join, or joining radical organizations are violent. However, they may transition to violence because

> becoming immersed in a world of extremism definitely encourages additional violence. Violence is a central part of the culture . . . violence brings status and respect amongst your peers and frankly gives you a sense of power.

According to Simi and Futrell, ideology is less important than the sense of belonging and inclusion that membership provides:

> Ideology is important but it's not necessarily the initial attraction that draws the person to the group. The ideology is often there early on, but it's very crystallized—it's like there may be bits and pieces of the ideology that are attractive early, but rarely do you have someone who has a full appreciation for the ideology and then seeks out the group. Over time, ideology becomes more important as the person becomes more familiar with the ideas . . . But it's not necessarily a smooth process where each member becomes a full convert to the same extent.

While Simi and Futrell's analysis concentrates primarily on the radicalization of white supremacists, the same forces are at work with the radicalization of Muslims in Western countries—as with extremists espousing anarchist, antigovernment, animal rights, environmental, black separatist, anti-abortion, and similar causes.

Most Muslims that have carried out or planned to carry out violent acts in the United States or other Western countries are categorized as lone wolves or, to use the phrase of Jerome P. Bjelopera, "a form of leaderless resistance"[271] (discussed in the previous chapter). Bjelopera believes that "lone wolves can hew to broader ideological causes and use them to justify their actions." The advantages of leaderless resistance movements were first articulated in the 1980s and '90s by the white supremacist Louis Beam, who defined *leaderless resistance* as involving "militant, underground, ideologically motivated cells or individuals (lone wolves) [that] engage in movement-related illegal activity without any centralized direction or control from an organization." He described this approach as "a means of avoiding law enforcement infiltration."

The Muslim terrorist motivated by radical groups such as al-Qaida, Al-Shabaab, or ISIS followed a rather similar path to that of the radicalized white supremacists described by Simi and Futrell and Bjelopera. Almost all came from troubled circumstances and had major personality issues making membership in or sympathy with such organizations attractive. They felt marginalized and were longing for a community with which they could identify themselves and which would provide meaning to their lives. They were angry young men (almost exclusively) who saw the world in black-and-white. Their financial and educational backgrounds varied, but they shared a common hatred for the injustice being committed against Muslims in the world and the system producing such injustice. Some had a history of violence (such as the Copenhagen shooter in February 2015, who was a known gang member who had spent a year in jail for stabbing someone in a commuter train). Others did not have such a history of violence but chose to escalate into becoming violent criminals. Yet others were coerced and entrapped by undercover FBI agents into becoming violent.[272], [273], [274]

---

271 Bjelopera, Jerome P., "The Domestic Terrorist Threat: Background and Issues for Congress," January 17, 2013, https://www.fas.org/sgp/crs/terror/R42536.pdf.

272 http://www.nytimes.com/2012/04/29/opinion/sunday/terrorist-plots-helped-along-by-the-fbi.html?_r = 0.

273 http://www.rollingstone.com/politics/news/how-fbi-entrapment-is-inventing-terrorists-and-letting-bad-guys-off-the-hook-20120515.

274 http://news.yahoo.com/fbi-pushed-muslims-plot-terrorist-attacks-rights-report-160325158.html.

Organizations Marketing to Lone Wolves

Muslim organizations are not the only ones seeking such individuals. According to Bjelopera,

> in the counterterrorism world, there has been much concern regarding violent jihadist use of the Internet. However, domestic terrorists also are computer savvy and active online. One count suggested that 657 U.S.-based hate websites existed in 2010. A Web presence may help extremist groups—sometimes relatively small, with rosters in the 100s or fewer—educate their existing membership and forge a group identity. Also, in many instances they can use websites to focus on outsiders to propagandize, socialize, and recruit new adherents. A few domestic terrorists also have exploited the Web to harm their targets.

Terrorist organizations based in Muslim-majority countries are learning their lessons from white supremacists and are also using the Internet to communicate their hate-filled messages to audiences that are predisposed to welcome their ideas. Such organizations also use traditional Western media to supplement their messages and connect their victims to their websites and other messaging tools. Among their methods are initiating theatrical and dramatic actions such as beheadings, setting people on fire, suicide bombings, and kidnappings targeted against civilians (both non-Muslims and Muslims alike). The attackers create dramatic scenes that ensure widespread media coverage and attention. For weeks following each incident, Western media repeat over and over the scenes of killing and torture; experts talk about them and analyze their actions until there is nothing left to be analyzed. They provide a new video, commit a new atrocity, and create more destruction for Western audiences, keeping them hooked to their televisions and listening to their talk shows. Television networks show men in beards and turbans riding on horses or driving brand-new Toyota Land Cruisers across the deserts of Iraq and Syria. Reporters mention $500 monthly stipends (with all expenses covered), young women wanting to join them to marry these fighters, a life full of excitement and camaraderie, of successes on the battlefield and other previously unimaginable adventures. Men committing atrocities are presented as devout Muslims doing what their religion commands them to do, while Christians killing elementary schoolchildren or moviegoers are considered mentally ill and thus not accountable for their actions. The potential Muslim radical feels that he will be seen by the world not as a mentally ill person but rather as a martyr for the cause of Allah.

The disturbed mind of a young man who is distraught and disconnected from the society he lives in, a young mind that can only think in black-and-white and is ready to take anything different from his current situation, watches the news and wants to be part of this "wonderful" group. Such young men (and, increasingly, women) search these organizations on Google and find information that is like music to their ears; they watch videos on YouTube and wish they were there. Their imagination runs rampant, and before they know it, they are planning to be part of the bunch. They want to be legends, motivations for others just as they are motivated by the figures they see. They do not see the radicalization process and that they are about to commit the greatest atrocities. And without a conscious decision, they have become a radical willing to engage in horrific violence.

Chapter 17

The Role of Western Media

Sensation Mongering Promotes Terrorism

If you tell a lie big enough and keep repeating it,
people will eventually come to believe it.[275]

Individuals and organizations resort to terror because they do not have the political power and influence, either organizationally or financially, to wage a full-fledged war or to achieve their objectives through other means. The terrorists have only limited resources to propagate their message to their audience and little access to the tools to raise funds and recruit members. Thus, they resort to activities that are so shocking and dramatic that they generate sufficient media interest to keep them in the public's consciousness.

The media[276] are an important tool for terrorists and their organizations. Terrorists use the media to communicate their message and recruit new members to a wide audience. They seek media attention to raise funds, create coalitions, and encourage copycats to join their criminal cause.

---

275 Joseph Goebbels (Nazi Germany) https://www.jewishvirtuallibrary.org/jsource/Holocaust/goebbelslie.html.

276 By the term *media* we are including traditional media such as print journalism, radio, television, and news websites. We are not here discussing social media.

Securing media attention depends on a number of factors, including the agenda of the terrorist, the intensity and level of the violence, the number of casualties from the attack, the origin of the terrorists, whether the attack reinforces commonly held prejudices, and the association of the message of the terrorists with other relevant and current issues of interest.

The terrorists' ability to garner media attention is also directly affected by the ability of the terrorist organization to plan the attack in an efficient and publicity-generating manner. Some terrorist attacks generate very little publicity, while others create a great deal. For example, the burning of an Ohio mosque by a white racist named Randolph Linn[277] generated almost no publicity outside a limited local area, while a shooting spree in Copenhagen, Denmark, committed by a gang member and convicted (for a train stabbing) criminal generated widespread media attention—because the attacker was Muslim and had expressed support for ISIS on his Facebook page.[278] Indeed, the Linn arson was not even reported as terrorism, even though the attacker had been "riled up by Fox News" against Muslims prior to his attack. Such behavior of the media, which many observers—both Muslim and non-Muslim and including the authors—consider to be hypocrisy, is used by terrorist organizations to show that the West is an enemy of Islam and Muslims and that all good Muslims need to join hands to revenge their hatred against them.

James Igoe Walsh has studied the conditions under which terrorist attacks draw media attention.[279] His research shows that

> attacks receive more coverage when they harm or kill victims, involve hijackings or aircraft, have known perpetrators and select targets associated with Western countries . . . attacks that inflict injuries are twice as likely

---

277 http://www.toledoblade.com/Courts/2012/12/20/Man-pleads-guilty-to-3-counts-in-Islamic-Center-mosque-fire.html.

278 See, e.g., https://en.wikipedia.org/wiki/2015_Copenhagen_shootings, http://www.theguardian.com/world/2015/feb/14/copenhagen-cartoonist-charlie-hebdo-style-attack.

279 "Media Attention to Terrorist Attacks: Causes and Consequences," http://www.jamesigoewalsh.com/ihss.pdf.

> to attract media attention as those that do not; attacks in which the perpetrators can be identified are 4 times as likely to be reported in newspaper and 10 times as likely to be reported on television; attacks in the Middle East and Europe are twice as likely to receive media attention as attacks perpetrated in Latin America . . . Very similar factors influence media coverage of attacks that take place within the United States.

He goes on to argue that terrorist attacks are particularly attractive to the media:

> Media outlets have incentives to provide overly extensive coverage of terrorist attacks. This coverage can provide terrorists with a vehicle for conveying their political messages to mass audiences, and it can also distract from public understanding of the difficulty of preventing terrorist attacks and the steps that authorities take to achieve this objective.

Walsh finds significant evidence that the specific and focused attention the Western media have paid to "Islamic terrorism" has been a major cause of promoting and strengthening terrorist activities throughout the world and in generating both individual copycats in Western countries as well as organizational copycats in Muslim-majority countries.

We have seen from news coverage that the overwhelming majority of individuals who committed or intended to commit terrorist attacks in the United States, Canada, or Europe were from disturbed families, were involved in gangs, and were already in trouble with law enforcement or have otherwise demonstrated violent behavior—indicators of a tendency to become radicalized. This tendency is equally observed with Christian or other groups that attacked Muslim targets or were involved in white supremacist or neo-Nazi groups. Almost without exception, all of these individuals were influenced by news coverage from major media outlets and sought their attention to receive recognition for their "courageous" work for an "honorable" cause.

Walsh notes that media coverage has an impact not only on the terrorist but on the public audience as well and creates a bias for more muscular counterterrorism efforts:

> The tone with which the media covers terrorism influences the attitudes and behaviors of mass publics, including voters, as well as potential sympathizers with terrorist movements. There is considerable evidence that coverage of terrorism increases fear and anxiety and that these emotional changes influence the preference of some members of the public for counterterrorism measures that rely on force. This may make it more difficult for authorities to respond to terrorist attacks with other types of policies, even if these policies might produce superior results.

For example, immediately following the 9/11 attacks, news outlets used various slogans and captions to describe the attack and the US government's response. The captions or banners

> typically incorporated a patriotic red, white, and blue motif, along with an explicit graphic of the American flag. Examples include:

- "America Attacked," "A Nation United" (ABC)
- "Attack on America" (NBC)
- "A Nation Challenged," "Day of Terror," "Portraits of Grief" (*The New York Times*)
- "America's New War," "War Against Terror," "America under Attack" (CNN)
- "War on Terror" (Fox News)
- "America on Alert," "America under Attack" (MSNBC)
- "The Second Pearl Harbor" (*Honolulu Advertiser*)
- "War On America" *(The Daily Telegraph)*[280]

[280] https://en.wikipedia.org/wiki/Slogans_and_terms_derived_from_the_September_11_attacks.

The most dramatic and durable slogans were those of the two most watched news media outlets, namely Fox News and CNN. Under the Republican administration of George W. Bush, the Fox News "War on Terror"[281] slogan became the American slogan of choice. American news coverage also helped to make the war in Afghanistan a necessity and the Second Gulf War possible.

Due in part to justifications provided by "experts" on news talk shows, the American public's view was swayed toward harsh treatment of Muslims and "radical" Muslim groups throughout the world, with the eventual impact of transitioning radical Muslims toward violence and conservative and mentally unstable individuals to become radicalized, with some resorting to violence. The extensive media coverage of atrocities committed by Muslims make it almost impossible for American politicians to support ending the "War on Terror" and starting dialogue and positive reinforcement activities to end the root cause of such wars. Thus, the vicious cycle continues.

Muslims, however, have their own media outlets' coverage, as well as firsthand experience of terrorist attacks, such as the massacre of Muslim Rohingya populations in Myanmar,[282] the killing of women and children in Gaza by Israeli forces,[283] drone attacks killing dozens of innocent people, and the silence of Western governments—including the United States—in the face of atrocities committed by Israel and unscrupulous dictators in Egypt, Saudi Arabia, and elsewhere. The sense of injustice created leads easily to violence.

Terrorist organizations use media attention not only to propagate their messages to existing and potential supporters and those whom they wish to terrorize; they also use media coverage of their attacks

281 We note in passing the use of a similar term ("War on Drugs") to describe American efforts to counter illegal drug use, with a much longer history but a similar lack of positive results.

282 See, e.g. http://www.cbsnews.com/news/un-dozens-of-rohingya-muslims-massacred-by-buddhists-in-rakhine-burma; http://www.genocidewatch.org/myanmar.html; http://burmatimes.net/the-silent-massacre-of-rohingya/.

283 See, e.g., https://electronicintifada.net/content/un-complicit-israels-massacre-gaza/7904; http://www.presstv.com/detail/2014/08/03/373898/israeli-gaza-war-revives-nazi-genocide/; http://www.dailysabah.com/energy/2014/07/28/israels-gaza-massacre-operation-energy.

to compete against rival terrorist organizations. For example (as we write in April 2016) ISIS is actively competing with al-Qaida and the Taliban—and winning supporters from their bases. Numerous Taliban groups are reported to have switched sides and have pledged allegiance to ISIS because of the attention that ISIS has been able to garner from public media in comparison with the Taliban.[284] Al-Qaida groups are also reported to have transferred their loyalties to ISIS,[285] while radical United States–funded and equipped "non-jihadist" organizations such as the Hazzm Movement in Syria have joined ISIS as well. The special attention that ISIS has received from Western media outlets because of their incredibly cruel and barbaric methods has had an immediate effect of consolidating their power base and ensuring that ISIS became stronger and gained additional resources.

From these facts, we may conclude that the message, style, and coverage of terrorist attacks by Western media, but also by media in Islamic countries, play a significant role not only in informing the public but also in radicalizing both sides of the spectrum. The media contribute to radicalizing Muslims and moving them to violence (against civilian and military targets, against Muslims and non-Muslims), but they also radicalize voters and, by extension, politicians in Western countries, including the United States, leading them to take measures in reaction that further exacerbate terrorism by Muslim groups. Without a lowering of the level and tone of media coverage of terrorist events, the problems of Muslim radicalization and terrorism are unlikely to diminish. To hope that attention-driven, sensationalism-savvy, and profit-hungry Western media will change their approach is likely an unrealizable dream—with predictable results.

---

284 https://indbreaking.wordpress.com/2014/10/05/pakistan-taliban-switches-side-vows-to-send-jihadists-to-help-islamic-state-indian-express-topnews/; see also https://afghanhindsight.wordpress.com/2015/01/13/isis-and-afghanistan/.

285 http://warincontext.org/2014/08/11/fighters-abandoning-al-qaeda-affiliates-to-join-isis-u-s-officials-say/.

Chapter 18

The Imposition of Western Values

My Way or the Highway; I Decide What Is Wrong and What Is Right

Different strokes for different folks.[286]

The concept of globalization is frequently misunderstood—both in developed (Global North[287]) and developing (Global South) countries. Many observers in Global South countries—poorer and with weaker physical and information technology infrastructures—consider globalization to be a tool used by the Global North to extort Global South economic and natural resources. Many Global North citizens consider Global South countries as a threat to their material success and resistant to creating a better and more cohesive world. Both sides tend to take a partial and incomplete view of globalization, leading them to resist the trend itself and its effects.

---

286 This phrase apparently originated in the United States in the 1960s; perhaps the first pop-culture reference was in the song "Everyday People" by Sly and the Family Stone. See http://www.funtrivia.com/askft/Question137661.html.

287 Note that the terms Global North and Global South refer only generally to geography. Developed Southern Hemisphere countries such as Australia and New Zealand are considered to be in the Global North, while poorer Northern Hemisphere countries such as Morocco and Nepal are part of the Global South.

Two definitions of "globalization" that the authors find useful are:

> The process of international integration arising from the interchange of world views, products, ideas and other aspects of culture[288]

and

> The worldwide movement toward economic, financial, trade, and communications integration. Globalization implies the opening of local and nationalistic perspectives to a broader outlook of an interconnected and interdependent world with free transfer of capital, goods, and services across national frontiers. However, it does not include unhindered movement of labor and, as suggested by some economists, may hurt smaller or fragile economies if applied indiscriminately.[289]

The first definition is a possible cause of significant distress in many non-Western countries, because it implies more than just the interchange of worldviews and other aspects of culture, but also an integration of Western worldviews and culture into those countries. The second definition finds more resonance with all actors, as it is limited to "movement toward economic, financial, trade, and communications integration" rather than a wider-ranging cultural and social integration of countries. It is this second definition that the authors will refer to when evaluating the impacts of globalization on Muslims and the Islamic world.

Whereas the essence of the second definition of "globalization" is something that most people or countries cannot object to or resist effectively, it is the implementation and some of its excesses that have created significant objections and resistance in certain quarters. For example, the World Trade Organization (WTO) rules provide that its members should have equal access to the markets of all other members. One such rule prohibits members from enacting subsidies that can

288 https://en.wikipedia.org/?title = Globalization.

289 http://www.businessdictionary.com/definition/globalization.html.

inhibit exports by other members into their market. However, Global North countries in Europe, as well as the United States, have adopted extensive farm subsidies, so that such basic products as corn, beans, wheat, sugar, and cotton from the Global South have no effective chance of entering their markets, while the lower prices resulting to American producers from such subsidies mean that they can export to Global South countries at prices that make local production uneconomical, producing a dependency of these Global South countries on such exports. To take just one example, the cheapest beans on sale in Managua, Nicaragua, are those imported from the United States, where the average US bean farmer receives $21,000 in annual subsidies.[290] With these subsidies, US farmers are able to offer beans at below the production cost in Nicaragua, making local bean farming impossible and the country thus dependent on US-grown beans.

The Nicaraguan government has the right to complain to the WTO, which will then initiate a long and costly legal battle to decide if the subsidies are justified. The United States and European nations (particularly when they act through the EU, on behalf of all 28 member states) have greater resources to wage such legal battles than a poor country such as Nicaragua. Even should Nicaragua prevail in such a proceeding, its means for enforcing its rights may be limited in a practical sense and may result in other types of sanctions imposed by Western governments on their economies. It is in this context that the second part of the business dictionary definition—that such rules "may hurt smaller or fragile economies if applied indiscriminately"—becomes particularly pertinent.

Muslims as well as non-Muslims from Global South countries have no objections to access to technology, investment, and economic activity from any part of the world. However, many Global South residents object to the Global North using its cumulative financial strength to impose what they see as disproportionate restrictions on the Global South—and to the imposition of Global North values. Many of the disconnects between Muslim and Western cultures arise from what Muslims see as this imposition.

On a cultural level, Muslims often feel threatened by globalization. Chandra Muzaffar, president of the International Movement for a Just

290 http://www.globalexchange.org/resources/wto/agriculture.

World and professor at the Center for Civilizational Dialogue at the University of Malaysia (Kuala Lumpur), states that Muslims feel that the globalization and the ideas emanating from the West are harmful.

> There is the cultural dimension of globalization which Muslims are very conscious of. They feel that the sort of values and ideas, notions of living which are emanating from the West and beginning to penetrate their societies, influencing their young in particular—that these are harmful; at least some of the more obvious aspects linked to music and dance forms and films and so on. They see these things as injurious to their own culture and identity.
>
> . . .
>
> They're also conscious of the fact that the global political system is dominated by the United States, to a great extent, and some of the other big powers. And somehow there is perhaps wittingly, perhaps unwittingly, the exclusion of Islam from the global process. And they've also been reacting to that, I think.[291]

Prof. Muzaffar considers the difference between the Western worldview and the Islamic worldview as a main point of conflict in the interaction between these two communities. He sees the principal distinguishing element between them as being that the Islamic world is primarily faith-based, while the Western world is more reason-based. He says

> Islam is very much a faith-based civilization. Everything, at least in the theoretical sense, centers around faith, that you believe in God and as a result of that, you hold on to certain practices and rituals. And you believe that politics should be conducted in a certain way, the economy should be run along certain lines and so on. All that emanates from faith and the oneness of God and God's revelation over time and the place of the Prophet Muhammad—may peace be upon him. That's part of one's belief system, rooted in faith.

---

291 http://www.pbs.org/wgbh/pages/frontline/shows/muslims/themes/west.html.

> Western civilization, contemporary Western civilization as a product of the enlightenment, is a civilization that centers much more around reason. It's an enlightenment of the head, not of the heart. If you look at the way in which the Buddhists, for instance, talk of enlightenment, it is from the heart. But in the West, it's basically the head. It's a rational attitude, it's empirical, it's secular in the sense that it's not linked to the revealed truth or to a scripture. It's different in that sense.[292]

While there may be common ground among the two communities in, for example, concern about the environment, this different way of looking at the world makes being able to work together—an increasing need in a globalizing world—very difficult.

To cite just one example, the West considers the 1948 Universal Declaration of Human Rights to be a sacred, inviolable document—which is regularly violated by Muslims. Muslims, on the other hand, see most rights contained in this declaration as rights they will be able to accept and accommodate without any difficulty—e.g., freedom of expression, the right to a fair trial, the rights to food and shelter, the right to found a family. However, they have difficulty with the lack of a communitarian dimension, as the declaration focuses primarily on the individual's human rights—and not the rights of the community as a whole.

The case of the drawing of representations or caricatures of the prophet Muhammad is a good example of where the individual's right of free expression collides with the communitarian right of Muslims to revere and respect their Prophet. Muslims believe that, just as it is illegal in many quarters to shout "Fire!" in a crowded theater, it should not be legal for a cartoonist to insult the prophet Muhammad and, by doing so, insult the 1.6 billion Muslim community. As Pope Francis recently stated, freedom of speech should have limits;[293] he gave the example that his assistant could expect a punch if he cursed the Pope's mother. Many Muslims find puzzling the idea that the European Union

---

292 Ibid.

293 http://www.bbc.com/news/world-europe-30835625.

may impose jail sentences for merely denying the Holocaust,[294] but that a similar requirement is not applicable to criminalize insulting of significant religious persons of Islam and other religions, seeing this inconsistency as hypocritical and a violation of the essence of the Western value system.

For Muslims, communal rights are critically important; most believe that the universal declaration mentioned above should be supplemented to include such rights. Many Muslims will never accept human rights declarations if insulting the Prophet, or any person for that matter, dead or alive, is equated with an individual's right to express oneself. This understanding is rooted in the Quranic verse that prohibits the insulting of other people's God lest they insult Allah out of ignorance:

> *O believers*, do not insult those whom these *mushrikeen* [worshippers of gods other than Allah] call upon besides Allah, lest in retaliation they call bad names to Allah out of their ignorance. Thus We have made the deeds of every group of people seem fair to them. In the end they will all return to their Rabb and then, he will inform them of the reality of all they have done.[295]

Finding the appropriate limits to freedom of expression and thus addressing this difference in value systems is critical in an age of increasingly global Internet, television, and social media coverage.

Muslims are thus not against globalization or modernity; rather, they see it in a different light and propose that different values be highlighted. As Tariq Ramadan is reported to have said, "Anything good is Islamic, so allow me to quote to you a Chinese Islamic saying." So, by nature, a Muslim cannot be against something that is for the common good and that is in essence good. Globalization, as understood by Muslims, is a natural consequence of their creation. God has created mankind and divided them in tribes and races so that they may get to know each other for whom they are and to appreciate their diversity.

---

294 http://www.nytimes.com/2007/04/19/world/europe/19ihteu.4.5359640.html?_r = 0.

295 Sura Al-An'âm (6), verse 108.

> O Mankind, We created you from a single *pair of a* male and a female, and made you into nations and tribes that you might get to know one another. Surely, the noblest of you in the sight of Allah, is he who is the most righteous. Surely Allah is All-Knowledgeable, All–Aware.[296]

Getting to know each other implies the exchange of goods, services, relations, and friendships across cultures, societies, and nations. It is the definition of mutual coexistence and recognizing the essentiality of the family of citizenship of the world.

Such getting to know each other, however, does not mean imposing one value system on the other, whether it be in a direct and dictatorial way, as exercised during the colonial rule of Muslim-majority countries by the West, or in a subtle and indirect way, as exercised today. Unfortunately, for many Muslims in the world, the indirect effect of Western cultures is something that threatens the essence of the Islamic value system and the cultures of Muslim-majority countries. It is this essential threat that is often perceived and opposed by many Muslims, rather than globalization itself.

> Coming for those at the edge of Western modernity, like in Turkey . . . this was the formula. In order to be civilized, you have to be Westernized in your clothes, in your mind, in your education, in your habitation, the way you organize your interior space, nuclear family, even how you walk in the streets with a man.
>
> . . .
>
> I would say, Islam challenges this formula today. Islam wants to be modern, but civilized not in the Western way, but Islam. So they are trying to tell us, like with the "black is beautiful" formula, Islam is beautiful and trying to be a reference point in different sets of civilizations. You take it, you don't take it. You can be critical or not, as I am too, but they are trying to give a reference to a different source of being civilized in the modern world, with a lot of complexities.

296 Sura Al-Hujurât (49), verse 13.

> . . .
>
> Modernity is constructed, shaped, produced, invented by values which were not values of Muslim countries . . . [Earlier, there] was this either/or thing. If you are modern, you can't be a Muslim. Now we are going beyond this either/ or and you can be both Muslim and modern. [297]

Muslims thus want to share their understanding of the right, the good, and the beautiful—and then leave it for the observer to choose. Many Muslims see, however, globalization as based purely on Western values, particularly through Western media, and thus a threat to be resisted and fought. Muslims see this imposition as a sort of authoritarianism, coming from Western secularism or modernism.

> If these two [value systems] cannot work together, there will be always authoritarianism, either coming from secularism or modernity. Secularism or modernity will be imposed from above and by authoritarian means, or from any fundamentalist movement, religious or ethnic, seemingly opposing itself to that, but also imposing another kind of authority. So there must be a kind of give-and-take, a kind of borrowing between two different cultural values, between two different sets of values.[298]

Muslims see this imposition as a new sort of colonialism—indirect, as opposed to the direct form that prevailed before the mid-twentieth century.

> The average Muslim is anti Western-overbearing-influence. What do I mean by that? I mean by that that their governments are following the West, doing the bidding

---

[297] Nilufer Gole, Professor of Sociology at Bogazici (Bosphorous) University, Istanbul, Turkey, quoted in http://www.pbs.org/wgbh/pages/frontline/shows/muslims/themes/west.html.

[298] Nilufer Gole, Professor of Sociology at Bogazici (Bosphorous) University, Istanbul, Turkey, quoted in http://www.pbs.org/wgbh/pages/frontline/shows/muslims/themes/west.html.

> of the West. Their governments are trying to, or are seen as implementing programs, which are easily connected to what some have called the arrogant West. In other words, you don't rule us directly anymore; you rule us indirectly . . .
>
> I don't particularly think that the ordinary Muslim is necessarily anti-Westerner. By that, I mean I don't think the average Muslim is against the average Westerner. I think a lot of Muslims are against Western politics, Western governments, because of what they perceive that Western governments do, and the influence they have in their countries. . . .
>
> I think that any cultural export of the West which violates Muslim sensibilities [would] be considered threatening . . . [for example,] Western perceptions of what is correct, for example, for women to wear, how they appear in public. They are against, for example, certain kinds of music, certain kinds of movies, even certain kinds of discussions on radio. For example, VOA and BBC carry certain kinds of discussions, which Muslims find, not anathema, but against their moral values. Therefore they see this as a kind of imposition. You're imposing your values on ours. Our society should not become like Western societies . . . I mean, you're talking about differences in values.[299]

Muslims are offended by the threat of sanctions when they do not adhere to certain (Western) value systems and find such behavior difficult to accept:

> Here is another aspect of the West, and that is the attitude of the West toward the non-Western countries, in terms of trying to be presumptuous in telling them how

[299] http://www.pbs.org/wgbh/pages/frontline/shows/muslims/interviews/akbar.html.

> they should even live their lives in ways that they are not accustomed to.[300]

For example, when Uganda decided to pass anti-homosexuality laws, the United States and other donors cut off funding for Uganda.[301] Muslims interpret such sanctions as the imposition of Western value systems on an African nation with the threat of cutting international assistance for vital humanitarian and developmental projects.

This perception of having Western values imposed on Muslims is a critical factor in creating opposition to globalization and its consequences and, by extension, to encouraging groups that oppose US and Western influences. Such groups seek a convenient excuse to migrate from a radically thinking group to one willing to act violently, and eventually to move its violence beyond their local village or town to a national level and then beyond the borders of their country. Examples of such radical groups that migrated to violence and then extended themselves beyond their borders are al-Shabaab in Somalia and Boko Haram in Nigeria (both of which recently declared their allegiance to ISIS).

To eliminate Muslim terrorism, the West must avoid creating the impression that it is imposing its value system on Muslims and Muslim-majority countries by adhering to the true values of globalization—just, equitable free trade and the exchange of goods and services—while avoiding creating the sense of cultural and political imposition.

---

300 Imam Faisal Abdul Rauf of the Masjid al Farah, New York City, NY, quoted in http://www.pbs.org/wgbh/pages/frontline/shows/muslims/interviews/feisal.html.

301 http://www.bbc.com/news/world-africa-29994678.

Chapter 19

Western Support for Authoritarian Regimes

Value Systems Take Second Place to Short-Term Interests

When it is said to them, "Do not make mischief on earth,"
they say, "We make peace." Beware! They are the ones
who make mischief, but they do not realize it.[302]

These verses, from the second sura of the Quran, characterize the way many Muslims look at the Western world. While the West, including the United States, has no inhibitions about supporting authoritarian regimes in such countries as Saudi Arabia and Egypt, it regards Iran as an enemy because it oppresses its people. Whereas the United States and other Western countries (including Russia and China) have imposed sanctions against Iran for developing a nuclear energy capability at various sites inside Iran with the possible intent of someday building nuclear weapons, these countries raise no questions and remain silent about Israel's nuclear program. Many Muslims see these different approaches as hypocrisy, which goes to the root of the problems such Muslims have with the Western world. Such Muslims ask, "Where is honesty and decency in a relationship that is based upon double standards?" Now that the Group of 5 + 1 have reached an agreement on ending Iran's "nuclear bomb" ambitions, Muslims are watching

302 Sura Al-Baqarah (2), verses 11–12.

and waiting to see whether they will take a similar approach to Israel's atomic weapons program.

Many Muslims throughout the world feel offended, insulted, and aggravated by this double standard in Western approaches to Muslim-majority country governments. The Western approach appears to them to be "A good Muslim government is one that is friendly to the West, even if it imperils its own people, while a bad Muslim government is one that is unfriendly to the West, even if it governs for the good of its people." Some examples of Western support for oppressive regimes include the following:

Egypt

Egypt receives more than $1.5 billion in annual aid from the United States, even though the al-Sisi government toppled a duly (and by general agreement fairly) elected Muslim Brotherhood government. The al-Sisi government has killed hundreds of peaceful demonstrators on the Egyptian streets and has sentenced thousands of political activists to death (and many more than that to many years in prison, including national and international journalists). The United States and European governments, however, do not consider these detainees as political prisoners, while military and economic aid to Egypt continues uninterrupted. The sale of F-16 fighter jets and conduct of joint military exercises between the United States and Egypt have resumed after a short interruption—a policy many Muslims see as hypocritical.

Saudi Arabia

The Saudi government enjoys high esteem in international circles and receives billions of dollars in US weapons systems and other support, even though it violates human rights on many fronts, including the rights of women, children, foreigners, religious minorities, and political opponents. Saudi Arabia is known to be involved in every civil war of a Muslim-majority country; it produced 15 of the 19 members of the al-Qaida team that carried out the 9/11 attacks. Nevertheless, Saudi Arabia is categorized as one of the West's major allies in the region. Such policies violate publicly vaunted Western values; the West's hypocrisy in supporting such a regime does not go unnoticed among Muslims.

Bahrain

Bahrain receives significant aid from the United States and is home to the US Fifth Fleet at one of the largest bases in the Persian Gulf. With United States and Western support and silence, in 2014, Bahrain's king introduced new legislation to stifle dissent. Amnesty International called the decrees draconian measures to legitimize state violence:

> Authorities in Bahrain have, for years, abused existing legislation to suppress any form of dissent, but these new measures are taking their disregard for human rights to a completely new level. We fear that these draconian measures will be used in an attempt to legitimize state violence as new protests are being planned for 14 August.[303]

Despite a claimed 164 deaths since 2011 and thousands of injuries,[304] the Western response has been limited to reviews of existing aid programs and expressions of concern, with the United States using the same tone (that of a candid friend) it uses in admonishing Israel:

> For most observers, the lesson is clear: western and Arab governments alike badly need the Gulf region's energy and financial resources. That's why Bahrain's spring is already over.[305]

---

303 https://www.amnesty.org/en/latest/news/2013/08/bahrain-new-decrees-ban-dissent-further-protests-organized/.

304 http://www.tasnimnews.com/English/Home/Single/373903.

305 http://www.theguardian.com/world/2011/apr/16/bahrain-protests-us-supports-government.

Israel

Israel is the largest recipient of US funding for military and other purposes. As of April 2016, the United States had vetoed forty-two resolutions at the United Nations Security Council and has strongly opposed all Palestinian initiatives, including nationhood, membership in various UN agencies, and the stopping of illegal Israeli settlements in occupied territories. The United States has remained silent in the face of the killings at Sabra and Shatila (1982),[306] the deaths of thousands of women and children during the Gaza invasions of 2012 and 2014,[307] the economic suffering caused by the Gaza blockade since 2007, and to use Jimmy Carter's phrase,[308] the "apartheid-like" conditions experienced by Palestinians in Israel, the West Bank, and Gaza. American silence, coupled with its multibillion-dollar annual financial aid, active diplomatic support for Israel, and its condemnations of Palestinian leaders and militants, is noted and used by both radical and nonradical Muslims as a major reason to oppose US "colonialism" and its perceived double standard.

Other Countries

The United States and Europe have provided aid and military and political support to numerous other countries with regrettable track records of corruption, human rights violations, and support for terrorist organizations, including Algeria, Ethiopia, India, Jordan, Myanmar, Pakistan, and Tunisia—providing further fuel for the radical Muslim fire directed against the West.

From the perspective of a Muslim person or organization that is already radical or is in the process of undergoing radicalization, this Western double standard provides an incentive to transition to full radicalization and the use of violent action in the form of terrorism of anything directly owned by, of interest to or in support of the West.

---

306 https://en.wikipedia.org/wiki/Sabra_and_Shatila_massacre.

307 https://en.wikipedia.org/wiki/2014_Israel%E2%80%93Gaza_conflict.

308 Jimmy Carter, *Palestine: Peace Not Apartheid* (New York: Simon & Schuster, 2006), ISBN 978-0-7432-8502-5.

The authors recognize that US policy, whether under a Democratic or a Republican president, is unlikely to change in the near future. US alliances are long-established, and in many cases supporting a distasteful regime advances US interests better than abandoning or undercutting such allies (at least in the consensus opinion of an overwhelming majority of the US political and diplomatic establishment). Fighting terrorism is only one goal of American foreign policy; other goals, such as maintaining the balance of power and peace in volatile regions of the planet, may be a higher priority. Our point is rather that supporting allies with authoritarian and oppressive governments has costs—and these costs are likely to be ongoing, rendering the struggle against terrorism more difficult, if not ultimately futile. Any US policy to oppose terrorism must weigh these costs and seek to determine the appropriate mix of fighting terrorism and pursuing other goals; the chosen mix may often require policies that undercut the US ability to achieve its goal of defeating terrorism.

Which Organizations Should the United States Support?

In addition to supporting such regimes, the West has also become notorious (again, particularly in the Muslim world) for supporting organizations that have either directly engaged in terrorist acts or that have transitioned to terrorist activities. While virtually forgotten in the West, Western support for (and the intervention of the US Central Intelligence Agency in) the overthrow of Iranian prime minister Mohammed Mossadegh in 1953 remains a *cause célèbre* in the Muslim world and an ongoing source of tension with Iran.

> "Blowback" is a CIA term first used in March 1954 in a recently declassified report on the 1953 operation to overthrow the government of Mohammed Mossadegh in Iran. It is a metaphor for the unintended consequences of the US government's international activities that have been kept secret from the American people. The CIA's fears that there might ultimately be some blowback from its egregious interference in the affairs of Iran were well founded. Installing the Shah in power brought twenty-five years of tyranny and

> repression to the Iranian people and elicited the Ayatollah Khomeini's revolution. The staff of the American embassy in Teheran was held hostage for more than a year. This misguided "covert operation" of the US government helped convince many capable people throughout the Islamic world that the United States was an implacable enemy.[309]

The United States and European allies have funded and supported the equipping and operation of such terrorist organizations such as the al-Nusra Front (Syria—now affiliated with ISIS[310]), al-Qaida (global), Taliban (Afghanistan), al-Shabaab (Somalia), the Peoples' Mujaheddin (Iran), and the Syrian Revolutionary Front. In almost all of these cases, the organizations chose to engage in terrorist activities in their respective countries and some, such as al-Qaida, ISIS, al-Shabaab, and the Chechen Resistance Group,[311] initiated terrorist activities outside of their country's borders or they eventually violently opposed the United States and Western countries in a bid to undermine the United States' authority over them. Al-Qaida was responsible for attacks on the Twin Towers on September 11, 2001, and numerous other attacks in various parts of the world; al-Shabaab is actively recruiting young Somalis in the United States; ISIS is beheading American hostages; the Chechen Resistance Group was the motivation for the Tsarnaev brothers to launch terrorist attacks on the Boston Marathon, and the Taliban are active participants of a war against the United States in Afghanistan and Pakistan.

What Is a Terrorist Act?

In the domestic sphere, the United States is clearly limiting the term *terrorist* to Muslims committing and planning to commit terrorist acts, while classifying terrorist acts by non-Muslims against Muslims and non-Muslims alike as hate crimes and acts by mentally-ill individuals, even though the culprits have clearly indicated their political motives

---

309 Chalmers Johnson in http://www.thenation.com/article/blowback.

310 http://www.theguardian.com/commentisfree/2015/jun/03/us-isis-syria-iraq.

311 http://www.theguardian.com/world/2004/sep/08/usa.russia.

behind their attacks. This difference in treatment has been the case with Dylann Roof,[312] James Holmes,[313] Craig Hicks,[314] Robert Doggart,[315] and many more, who have committed or planned to commit politically motivated acts of terrorism but have not been categorized or tried as terrorists by law enforcement agencies. On the other hand, acts and intended acts by criminals, who happen to be Muslims, in every part of the world, are immediately categorized as terrorist acts, just because the culprit was a Muslim. For example, less than 2% of all terrorist attacks in Europe have been committed by Muslims, while 98% have been committed by ultranationalistic or right-wing or left-wing groups.[316] In the United States, the number of terrorist attacks committed by Muslims is less than 6%,[317] primarily because many terrorist attacks by non-Muslims are categorized as hate crimes or not at all categorized as politically or racially motivated crimes. If legitimate cases of crimes against Muslims, Blacks, gays and lesbians, Hindus, and other groups are properly categorized as acts of terrorism, the Muslim share would be significantly less than 2% in America.

The United States and Western world's double standard may not have been noticed by the mainstream media in America and Europe, but it has been clearly noted and criticized by media as well as organizations in Muslim-majority countries and has been consistently used as a tool to recruit violent extremists in various parts of the world, including in the United States and Europe. This challenge will continue to remain in place and prevent the peaceful coexistence of people everywhere for

312 http://fusion.net/story/152632/shooter-kills-9-at-historic-black-church-in-domestic-terrorist-attack/.

313 https://en.wikipedia.org/wiki/2012_Aurora_shooting.

314 http://www.nytimes.com/2015/02/12/us/muslim-student-shootings-north-carolina.html.

315 http://www.cair.com/press-center/press-releases/12991-cair-says-tenn-man-who-planned-religiously-motivated-attack-on-ny-muslims-should-face-terror-charges.html.

316 http://www.thedailybeast.com/articles/2015/01/14/are-all-terrorists-muslims-it-s-not-even-close.html.

317 http://www.globalresearch.ca/non-muslims-carried-out-more-than-90-of-all-terrorist-attacks-in-america/5333619.

as long as the United States and other Western governments do not put an end to their double standards.

As long as people and governments are selective in what they consider right, the problems of terrorism will not find an end. The concept of "One country's hero, another country's terrorist" needs to disappear. Hypocrisy must also end. A terrorist by definition should be the same in every corner of the world, even if the "terrorist" seems to be serving US purposes and causing disruptions to American enemies. The new motto should be "One country's terrorist, another country's terrorist" if we want to achieve a world free from terrorism.

Chapter 20

Toward an Islamic Reformation?

Does Islam Need Reformation? If Yes, How?

Do not raise your children the way [your] parents raised you, they were born for a different time.[318]

The current state of relations between the West and Islam, as we have described in previous chapters, is hardly encouraging. At least in the perception of most Muslims, the West proclaims lofty ideals that it adheres to only so long as it is easy, convenient, and to its advantage. Western support for such regimes as Israel, Saudi Arabia, and Egypt, tolerance for abuses such as Abu Ghraib and Guantanamo Bay, and restrictions such as French bans on wearing headscarves, show how quickly such ideals can be forgotten or ignored when it suits Western political interests. Many Muslims see libertarian initiatives such as legalizing marijuana, allowing gay marriage, and casual attitudes toward pornography as dangerous "decadence" and an assault on the values in Muslim-majority countries, in some cases tracing such values from the Quran and the ahadith, in others from local cultural customs that are independent of and may predate Islam.

The situation is scarcely better in the Muslim world, where materialism, the support for jihadist organizations, and abuses of

318 Ali Ibn Abi Talib, fourth caliph of Islam and cousin of the prophet Muhammad.

political power by ruling elites show similar levels of hypocrisy and where, as we have shown in chapter 3 and appendix 2, the societies are far from implementing Islamic values.

The failure of most democratic movements after the Arab Spring and the increase in terrorism by those claiming to act in the name of Islam have added fuel to a long-burning fire about reforming Islam. Many non-Muslims[319] and some Muslims[320] have claimed that Islam needs a Reformation. As we shall argue, however, the Protestant Reformation (Reformation) is an extremely complicated historical evolution, with a variety of both positive and negative ramifications.

The Reformation—an Inappropriate Model for Islam

While many claim that Islamic thought and practice need reform, the authors believe that the ultimate goal of the Reformation, namely to eliminate a monolithic understanding and application of religion dictated by a single authority, is not appropriate for the Islamic world. As we have shown in chapters 3 through 7, Islam is far from a monolithic religion, and the acceptance of different ways of practicing Islam has always been a cornerstone of Islamic religious understanding. The authors believe that changes should occur in the true understanding and practice of Islam, rather than in its structural framework.

The Catholic Church[321] that Luther was seeking to reform spoke (and continues to speak) with a single voice—the pope. While pre-

---

319 See, e.g., http://www.nytimes.com/2002/12/04/opinion/an-islamic-reformation.html, http://www.wsj.com/articles/a-reformation-for-islam-1426859626, and http://www.newsweek.com/we-need-muslim-reformation-316906.

320 See, e.g., http://www.huffingtonpost.com/raza-rumi/islam-needs-reformation-f_b_6484118.html, http://www.clarionproject.org/analysis/farzana-hassan-islamic-, http://www.libertiesalliance.org/2012/01/27/liberal-islamic-reform-and-the-prospect-for-an-islamic-reformation/reform-daunting-needed.

321 In Catholic countries such as France, Italy, and Poland, even though they are rapidly secularizing, it is still common practice to refer not to the Catholic Church but rather "the Church"—as if there were no other.

Luther Christianity had defined views binding on all believers (despite the efforts of prior reformers such as John Wycliffe and Jan Hus, who generally paid for their heterodox views with their lives), one of the results of the Reformation was the development of a multiplicity of views—even more pronounced within the reform movement itself (contrast the different views of the churches established by Luther, John Calvin, Ulrich Zwingli and Henry VIII).[322]

This diversity of views already exists within Islam. Islam is, and has been since its beginnings, radically Protestant in its structure and organization—as in Protestantism, all believers are theologically on the same level, and each believer is responsible for understanding God's revelation and implementing it in his or her life. Clergy in both Islam and Protestantism have no superior standing or claim to special status; their authority comes only from greater study and reflection and their ability to provide guidance to the members of their community. Restrictions in freedom of thought in Islam are thus not structural or organizational; they come rather from politics, culture, and tradition within Muslim communities.

Luther as a Model for Reform?

Martin Luther is considered a hero among Protestants for launching the Reformation. He was, however, a very human vehicle for advancing reform and, particularly in the light of 2016 values, held many views that most observers today find highly objectionable. For example, Luther

> demanded that German peasants revolting against their feudal overlords be "struck dead," comparing them to "mad dogs," and authored On the Jews and Their Lies in 1543, in which he referred to Jews as "the devil's people" and called for the destruction of Jewish homes and synagogues. As the US sociologist and Holocaust scholar Ronald Berger has observed, Luther helped establish antisemitism as "a key element of German culture and national identity."

---

322 See, e.g., http://history-world.org/reformation_and_counter_reformat.htm.

Luther is thus hardly a poster boy for reform and modernity for Muslims in 2016.[323]

The Use of Religion for Political Purposes

As we noted in chapter 12, political leaders in the areas where Protestantism spread after Luther found it a very useful tool to consolidate and reinforce their control. In 1555, the Peace of Augsburg and the adoption of the principle of "Cuius regio, eius religio,"[324] allowed the political ruler to impose his religion on his population—and neatly enabled Lutheranism to supplant all of the other Protestant variants such as Calvinism or Anabaptism in the German lands. This principle has been followed in a number of Muslim-majority countries, with the alliance in Saudi Arabia between the al-Saud family and the Wahhabi movement and the establishment of Pakistan as a religiously based state; Israel is following a similar path in seeking recognition as a Jewish state.

The Move toward Reason and Science

As noted in chapter 12, one immediate consequence of the Reformation was the religious violence that plagued Europe throughout most of the sixteenth and seventeenth centuries. The Reformation, however, did not have only negative consequences; one of its more positive effects was the opening it left for the pursuit of reason and scientific inquiry. While neither Luther nor the other Protestant religious leaders were particularly interested in science or reason, they created a climate that was propitious for their development.

> The Lutheran influence on the development of science was generally positive. Luther, and also Calvin, rejected the idea that religious vocations are superior to secular ones.

---

323 http://www.theguardian.com/commentisfree/2015/may/17/islam-reformation-extremism-muslim-martin-luther-europe.

324 "Whose realm, his religion," as cited in https://en.wikipedia.org/wiki/Cuius_regio,_eius_religio.

> Men and women should serve God by performing honest and useful work with diligence and integrity. Scientific work reveals God's handiwork in a universe which is both rational and orderly. It also gives results that can be used for the benefit of mankind. As Johannes Kepler wrote to Michael Maestlin, his former professor at Tübingen, "I wanted to become a theologian, and for a long time I was restless. Now, however, observe how through my effort God is being celebrated in astronomy." Kepler considered astronomers to be priests of God in the book of nature.
>
> . . .
>
> Luther was not primarily interested in science. But the Reformation created a climate of openness and acceptance of new ideas, which generally encouraged scientific development. With the development of printing, new scientific as well as religious ideas spread rapidly. After Galileo's trial in 1633, the Protestant areas of Europe dominated scientific discovery. [325]

Has Islam Already Had Its Reformation?

If the Reformation represents a purification of a long-established religion that has been corrupted by its political leaders and a return to the claimed values of its founders, Islam has arguably already had its Reformation, and the results are hardly what many Westerners are seeking—namely, the Wahhabist-Salafist synthesis, and with Ibn Abdul

---

[325] http://www.leaderu.com/science/kobe.html.

Wahhab as its Luther (if not Abu Bakr al-Baghdadi). Mehdi Hasan, a commentator on Al Jazeera English,[326] argues provocatively that

> The truth is that Islam has already had its own reformation of sorts, in the sense of a stripping of cultural accretions and a process of supposed "purification." And it didn't produce a tolerant, pluralistic, multifaith utopia, a Scandinavia-on-the-Euphrates. Instead, it produced . . . the kingdom of Saudi Arabia.
>
> Wasn't reform exactly what was offered to the masses of the Hijaz by Muhammad Ibn Abdul Wahhab, the mid-18th century itinerant preacher who allied with the House of Saud? He offered an austere Islam cleansed of what he believed to be innovations, which eschewed centuries of mainstream scholarship and commentary, and rejected the authority of the traditional ulema, or religious authorities.
>
> Some might argue that if anyone deserves the title of a Muslim Luther, it is Ibn Abdul Wahhab who, in the eyes of his critics, combined Luther's puritanism with the German monk's antipathy toward the Jews. Ibn Abdul Wahhab's controversial stance on Muslim theology, writes his biographer Michael Crawford, "made him condemn much of the Islam of his own time and led to him being dismissed as a heretic by his own family."[327]

---

326 Al Jazeera English, owned by the Al Jazeera Media Network (belonging to the Al-Thani family, the ruling family in Qatar), produces programming for the English-speaking world other than the United States. It is an entirely separate network from Al Jazeera America, a sister company, which produces news and programming targeted at an American market. Almost 53 percent of American households with television service have access to AJAM. The authors consider it to be an excellent and relatively unbiased source of news—a worthy competitor to the British Broadcasting Corporation's World Service. The authors much regret its leaving the air in April 2016. https://en.wikipedia.org/wiki/Al_Jazeera_America.

327 http: //www.theguardian.com/commentisfree/2015/may/17/islam-reformation-extremism-muslim-martin-luther-europe.

Does Islam Need a Counter-Reformation?

If Islam is to experience the beneficial effects of the Reformation such as the opening to various views and an embrace of scientific thought, the Counter-Reformation, the Catholic response to the Protestant Reformation, may be a better model. While Catholicism and Islam are fundamentally different religions (more so than Protestantism and Islam), there are elements in the Counter-Reformation that suggest that perhaps that it is a somewhat better framework for considering desirable changes in the Muslim world than the Protestant Reformation. While the specific events and main characters of the Counter-Reformation do not suggest Islamic equivalents, some of the elements of the Counter-Reformation that could benefit Islam include

- greater clarity with regard to doctrine,
- bringing accrued superstitions under control,
- an openness to constructive change and a recognition of past corruption, and
- a recognition of past failings and a willingness to reform, rather than ignoring faults.[328]

The situation in the Muslim world today shows many similarities to that of the Catholic Church at the beginning of the sixteenth century. Since the fall of the Ottoman Empire in 1920, Muslims have been facing a power vacuum in terms of religious as well as political authority. In the mid-1970s, with the merging of the Wahhabi and Salafi movements in Saudi Arabia and with the defeat of the Soviet empire in the hands of the Afghan resistance fighters (supported by the Saudi government as well as the United States and other Western countries), a new power base, religious as well as military, began to take shape. Wahhabi-Salafi Islam—antimodern, antiprogress, and violently opposed to any sort of opposition—is being imposed on Muslims by small groups of well-funded and well-armed people. Their goal is to take as much control of the Muslim world as possible and to achieve their form of political power and influence. Muslims in every part of the world are defending

---

328 http://www.historylearningsite.co.uk/the-counter-reformation/how-successful-was-the-counter-reformation/.

themselves against this brutal movement and are struggling with the negative consequences of this merciless violence.

If Islam is to emerge from its Dark Age and return to the flourishing, energetic, curious, and open spirit of the Islamic Golden Age, the change must come from within. But where is that change likely to come from?

Chapter 21

And the Sun will Rise from the West

Muslims of the West Are the Solution

The Internet changes everything.

A hadith quoting the Prophet says:

> The hour will not come until the sun rises from the west; and when the people see it, then whoever will be living on the surface of the Earth will have faith, and that is (the time) when no good will it do to a person to believe then, if he believed not before. [329]

For many Muslims (particularly of the *how* school), this passage should be read literally—that at the end of the world, the sun will physically rise from the western horizon. Many Muslim scholars and scientists of this persuasion have spent valuable hours trying to explain how this phenomenon can occur,[330] while others following this interpretation admit they do not know how it can happen (except that nothing is beyond God's power).

Some Muslims, however, interpret the same text metaphorically. The Quran is filled with figurative references, and the Arabic language

329 Authentic hadith narrated by Abu Huraira in Al-Bukhari.

330 http://www.harunyahya.com/en/Articles/8533/one-of-the-signs-of.

then (and now) is quite poetic; Arab writers may equate a beautiful face with a flower or a tall and slim figure with a poplar tree. For those who accept such interpretations, the sun may be equated with light and interpreted as knowledge, wisdom, or enlightenment—a metaphor for God's guidance to mankind (and for Muslims, Islam—God's chosen religion for mankind). Whereas previous enlightenments have come from the East (namely all major world religions), this hadith may indicate that the new or next enlightenment will come from the west—or the West, namely the United States and Europe. Thus, some Muslim scholars interpret this hadith as meaning that the new enlightenment for Islam, after centuries of deviation from the true message, will come not from Muslim-majority countries (every Muslim-majority country except Morocco and Mauritania, hardly Islamic thought-leaders, has an eastern longitude), but from the West.

Islamic thought in the West is evolving very differently than in Muslim-majority countries. Western Muslims are taking advantage of the free exchange of ideas, the Internet, and social media to demonstrate to young Muslims in both Muslim-minority and majority countries a different vision and understanding of traditional Muslim values. While previous debates over values and practices required centuries to change attitudes and behavior (e.g., the evolution of the different Sunni schools and the various branches of Shi'a Islam), the instant diffusion of and wide access to new interpretations will mean that the twenty-first century discussions will take place in greatly accelerated "Internet time."

When our author Rafaat was growing up, his sources of learning about Islam were quite limited—reading the Quran and the ahadith himself, his parents, his teacher and the imam at the local mosque, and his immediate surrounding community—all of whom were linked to a specific culture and tradition concerning Islam. This culture included often a very narrow interpretation of texts that suited the government or his community's narrow-minded mullahs' understanding of Islam. This limited exposure meant that a young and curious Muslim had only a limited ability to look beyond what the local society was able to provide in understanding and interpreting Islamic teachings. Because of limited abilities to travel and communicate with the outside world, a young Muslim was hostage to the limitations of mind and thought of local geography. Without exposure to other ways of thinking and other views of life, including other worldviews, how can a young person jump over their own shadows to develop an in-depth understanding of one's own faith? This environment was the jail that housed young Muslims for many centuries in every part of the Muslim world.

Today's young Muslims, however, have access to their smartphones, computers, the Internet, and social media. They are no longer limited to their local community and the government-sponsored and approved sources of knowledge about Islam. They have the whole world at the tip of their fingers, with access to scholars such as Hamza Yusuf, Tariq Ramadan, Khaled Abou El-Fadl, Jamal Badawi, Hakim Murad, Suhaib Web, and others to learn about Islam. They have access to YouTube videos of lectures and presentations about different topics. Some scholars such as Tariq Ramadan have iPhone Apps that give access to lectures, writing, and viewpoints on various topics, political as well as religious and social. Hence, young computer-literate Muslims in Afghanistan, Saudi Arabia, Pakistan, Bangladesh, Indonesia, and elsewhere have the ability to access independent of government or other controls, the entire range of Islamic thought, from Boko Haram and ISIS to Tariq Ramadan or Hamza Yusuf. Thus, young twenty-first-century Muslims have at their fingertips the whole corpus of 1,400 years Islamic thought and tradition. They are no longer a hostage of their minds, thoughts, and geography but are free to think and learn what they want to think and learn. They may still be limited by their upbringing and their intellectual abilities to comprehend complex issues and concepts, but if they manage to free themselves from those chains, they are enabled by the vastness of their access to knowledge to fly beyond their country's or even continent's borders. The prophet Muhammad instructed Muslims to "seek knowledge even if you would need to travel to China." The Internet and modern communication tools enable a young Muslim to go beyond borders to unimaginable distances with a click of a mouse or the tab of a keyboard.

Islamic thought in the West has evolved very differently than it has in the so-called Muslim world. In Muslim-majority countries, similar to other non-Muslim third-world countries, Muslims are often subject to tyrannical governments such as Saudi Arabia and Iran that restrict thought and innovation. Even in many less-repressive countries—such as Egypt, Afghanistan, Pakistan, and Libya—the local Muslim communities have a very limited toleration for new ways of looking at established Muslim thought and practices and little ability or incentive to question the application of fundamental Islamic teachings to a changing world. Thus, a Muslim scholar in a Muslim-majority country wanting to engage in topics of current importance such as the prohibition of *riba* (bank interest) in the world of twenty-first century finance, the evolving roles of men and women in families, the distribution of inheritances, and the role of scholars in interpreting the Quran and the ahadith can find it dangerous or even life-threatening to do so. Thus, more often than not, scholars in such countries choose to remain silent on critical issues where they deviate from the accepted thought and practice, preferring to adhere to local community norms. For example, even though discussions are beginning to occur about whether the prohibition of riba should apply to commercially accepted interest rates (such as 5–10 percent) or rather to more usurious rates of, say, 30–100 percent, most Islamic scholars, particularly in Muslim-majority countries, prefer to stay away from this discussion altogether for fear of being labeled a liberal or, even worse, for diverging from the long-accepted ways of thinking.

Most often scholars in Muslim-majority countries have not yet learned to engage in the *why*, rather than the *how*, questions. To quote anecdotally one head of the world-renowned al-Azhar University (founded AD 972) in Cairo,

> 99% of the graduates of the University spend half of their life to memorize Islamic text and the rest of their life to repeat what they have learned.[331]

Most scholars do not use the opportunity to expand on what they have learned but rather prefer to stay limited to their literal narration of the existing knowledge.

As discussed in chapter 7, the Ash'ari school of thought with the teaching that

> all that is to be known about the religion is already known, and there is no need to inquire more about the

[331] Anecdotal narration from the sheikh Al-Azhar (President of Al-Azhar University).

> religion; all are required to focus on learning what is already known[332]

has gripped the Muslim world since about 1200 CE and is still alive and well in most Muslim-majority countries, guiding and limiting the religious discourse even in the twenty-first century.

The educational system in most Muslim-majority countries further restricts the scope of Muslim thought. From kindergarten through the university, Muslim students in developing countries are taught to memorize rather than analyze, understand, and internalize concepts. Rote memorization is more highly prized than interpretation or problem solving—even at universities in disciplines such as medicine, science, and engineering. The result is that Muslim students often do not develop the ability to analyze complex ideas and to apply them to evolving situations. In short, Muslim education does not teach how to ask *why* but only *how*. For this reason, Muslim countries have produced very few Nobel Prize winners and great thinkers or sophisticated thought leaders for the past hundreds of years. The same phenomenon occurs in applying religious learning and practices to rapidly changing societies.

Muslims like to quote Ali, the fourth caliph and cousin of the Prophet, who said,

> Do not force your own customs upon your children for they are in other times than yours.[333]

However, many Muslims fail to adhere to this advice themselves and continue with the same approach and with the same mind-set with which they were raised. They often refuse to adjust to changing situations and fail to keep up with the times. Political leaders in Muslim-majority countries, often out of fear of upsetting the local population, fail to implement policies to promote change and development. As a result, Muslims in these countries continue to suffer from poverty, a lack of sustainable development, oppressive leaders, and failing institutions, just as their parents and grandparents did. Also, their comprehension

332 http://www.thenewatlantis.com/publications/why-the-arabic-world-turned-away-from-science.

333 http://www.imamreza.net/eng/imamreza.php?id = 9206.

of Islam is limited by their upbringing and their critical-analysis-free approach to understanding their religion, which has been a curse for most Muslims in developing countries.

The contrast between Muslims living in a Muslim-majority country and Muslims living in the United States is striking. Muslim children in US schools, along with their non-Muslim colleagues, learn already in kindergarten and in primary school to analyze simple concepts. Muslim children everywhere inquire about things such as why do we pray, why do we fast, why did God create the world, why did the prophets come, why are we Muslims, etc. Parents of American children have asked the same questions when they were children and are ready to answer them because they have engaged with the essence of each of those questions.

On the other hand, Muslim parents living in mostly developing countries have been systematically disciplined when they dared to ask these questions at home, in school or in public. Hence, they have no answers for their children. As a result, they often opt for the same response as they received growing up, namely, "Don't ask these questions," "These questions are for adults!" etc. Failure to obey has also led to their children being disciplined. All one has to do is to spend any significant time in a Muslim-majority country in contact with Muslim families to become aware of this contrast with the United States.

Since the beginnings of widespread access to the Internet roughly two decades ago, one can already see a significant change in Muslim world youth. Some of that change is negative, such as the evolution of radical terrorist groups such as ISIS and their command of the Internet and social media. However, much of this change stemming from the Internet is very positive. Many Muslim youth are now significantly better connected and better informed about events and ideas throughout the world. They are better informed about their religion and other interpretations of their religion that differ from what their parents taught them. They have become much more mobile in their ability and willingness to "seek knowledge from the cradle to the grave"[334] or to "seek knowledge even if it is in China, because acquiring knowledge is

334 Hadith from Prophet Muhammad narrated in ibid. Tradition 327 (http://messageofthaqalayn.com/39-pearls.pdf).

obligatory for every Muslim."[335] This change in the youth is expanding with the passage of each day; the numbers of youth becoming aware of ideas and events outside their borders, as well as their access to alternative sources of knowledge, continue to grow.

Even small children in developing countries are able to play games on iPads and similar devices that enhance better understanding of complex concepts and that seek to challenge their abilities to analyze situations and to think outside the box. These children, when they grow up, will not be the same as their parents and will not think as their parents thought. They will refuse to accept challenges to their desire to ask the *why* questions. They will pose these questions and will want to have answers. Where such answers are not provided by their parents or their teachers, they will rush to the wider world through the Internet to seek answers and thus will also have access to Western Muslim scholars' opinions on their questions and see how Western Muslims are dealing with these issues.

Such children—and adults raising such issues—will, however, face the same challenge that non-Muslims throughout the world face—namely, that the solutions proposed by the modernist Western Muslim scholars are difficult; they require thought and effort to reach a new level of understanding. The solutions proposed by radical Muslims are angrier and as such much simpler; they require less thought and effort. The growth of Western megachurches and the continuing popularity of televangelists show the ongoing appeal of such simplistic solutions to an American audience, and Muslims have access to similar arguments. Clearly hate and anger always require less sophistication of thought and insight and are a tempting path to mobilizing young and emotionally unstable people. Achieving an understanding of religion that reflects the complexity and diversity of the globalized twenty-first-century world is a challenge that extends far beyond the Muslim world.

Muslim scholars in the West benefit from the open society, the freedom of expression, the technological advancements, the fast access to information, and their upbringing as thinking, feeling, and questioning persons; they are not at all hesitant to pose the *why* questions. They are not afraid of a government that chastises them or even imprisons,

335 Hadith from Prophet Muhammad narrated in ibid. Tradition 324 (http://messageofthaqalayn.com/39-pearls.pdf).

tortures, and prosecutes them for blasphemy. Their only concern is what fellow Muslims may think of them, most often a burden that is not, unlike in Muslim-majority countries, too heavy to carry. As a result, they mimic the life of the early Muslims from the Mu'tazila school of thought who believed that because the Quran was created, it is man's responsibility to interpret Allah's teachings to fit the circumstances of the time in which they live—and thus their extensive willingness to raise questions about seemingly established doctrines and practices of Islam.

Some scholars question the essence of some of the Muslim practices and demonstrate that they need to be changed to match the changing circumstances in the world. Some examples are ruling on the leading in prayer of men by women,[336] the permissibility of bank interest in Islam,[337] inheritance and divorce rights for women,[338] the right for women to marry without a male relative's consent,[339] and others. Western Muslims can advance these arguments because they live in countries where freedom of expression and significant protection from prosecution are the norm. This freedom of exploration and expression is little different from the conditions in early Islam, when Muslim scholars could question all aspects of their religion, including some that are critical belief systems, and were able to expose themselves to criticism and to open challenge by other scholars. As a result, Islam and Muslims advanced not just geographically but also scientifically, literarily, politically, socially, and humanly.

In the Western world, we see scholars who are able to answer to the *why* questions competently, freely, and in detail. Many are able to question the essence of some practices and positions of scholars held for

---

336 http://en.wikipedia.org/wiki/Amina_Wadud and http://www.independent.co.uk/news/uk/home-news/first-woman-to-lead-friday-prayers-in-uk-1996228.html.

337 http://www.academia.edu/4822162/Reform_in_Finance_Riba_vs._Interest_in_the_Modern_Economy.

338 http://www.al-islam.org/rights-women-islam-ayatullah-murtadha-mutahhari/part-nine-question-inheritance

339 http://www.wluml.org/node/4009.

centuries and as such open a completely new window for Muslims to the twenty-first century and beyond.

The critical aspect of this new generation of Muslim scholars is their ability not only to build knowledge based on strong, sustainable foundations achieved with the best scholars in the Muslim world (living in Saudi Arabia, Egypt, Jordan, Iran, Pakistan, Indonesia, Malaysia, Turkey, and elsewhere) but also to excite and motivate young Muslims to follow in their footsteps. Hence, we see large numbers of Muslims joining similar institutions, Muslim business people offering scholarships for Western Muslims to gain Arabic and Islamic education in Muslim-majority countries, and opening new doors for them to gain traditional knowledge. Upon their return, these Western Muslims utilize the skills acquired as children and growing adults to interpret, question, and analyze concepts and not to be limited to repetition of the already acquired knowledge. This combination of the Western inquisitive spirit and knowledge of traditional Muslim practice and wisdom in turn helps them to question the essence of their knowledge and to progress to the next level of knowledge, namely a deep-rooted understanding for the *why* in everything that they believe in.

The sheer growing number of such young and dynamic scholars has achieved two critical additional effects.

- More Western universities in every part of the Western world are establishing Muslim chairs, Islamic studies departments, and other vehicles that serve as think tanks for Islamic thought. Such thought centers create a new environment that enables yet more young Muslims to have an opportunity to learn more about their religion in an open-minded environment free of political and social constraints. By 2001, 57.9%[340] of American universities that were members of the Council on Graduate Studies in religions, and 9% of all departments of religious studies, had an Islamic studies specialist on their faculty, an increase from 36% and 4.6% respectively since 1981. Since 2001 more universities and colleges have hired Islamic studies specialists in their ranks, which in turn has significantly enhanced the quality and quantity of Islamic studies programs

340 http://www.unc.edu/~cernst/pdf/romes.pdf.

in these universities, producing yet more Western Muslim scholars.

- Muslim scholars have teamed up to establish Islamic high schools, universities, and graduate schools to enable the training of Muslim imams, scholars, and leaders. The first accredited Muslim liberal arts college in the United States of America is Zaytuna College[341] in Berkeley, California, cofounded by Hamza Yusuf and Hisham Alalusi in 1996; many others have followed.[342] More universities are being established every year that mostly ensure the creation of homebred scholars of Islam with a Western mind-set and education base.

In the long run, not only will the existing Muslim scholars grow in wisdom and skills, but they will also produce new generations of scholars that will not at all be inhibited by the restrictions of developing Muslim countries. These new scholars will use their open mindedness as well as their analytical skills to ensure that Islamic thought resumes the course that it enjoyed from the times of the Prophet and the Salaf until around 1200 CE.

These young Western Muslim scholars will use modern technology such as smartphone apps, YouTube, Twitter, Facebook, websites, and other tools to communicate their views and messages to the Muslim population of the world. They will lecture, initiate discussions, raise questions, challenge people to thoughtful pondering, and guide them to

---

341 http://www.zaytuna.org.

342 Other colleges and universities founded and run by Muslims in Western countries include the Cordoba University (Virginia), the Institute of Islamic and Arabic Sciences in America (Virginia), the Islamic American University (Michigan), Mishkah University (Minnesota), Tooba University (Maryland), the American Islamic University (Mississauga, Ontario, Canada), the Islamic Institute of Toronto (Canada), the Islamic Online University (Qatar and US), the Islamic University of Rotterdam (Netherlands), Islamic University of Europe (Netherlands), the Institute of Islamic Studies (Austria), the Islamic College for Advanced Studies (UK), Hijaz College (UK), Ebrahim College (UK), the Muslim College (UK), the Islamic College (UK), Tayyibun Institute (UK), and Azad University (UK).

> the Way of those whom You have favored, not of those who have earned Your wrath, or of those who have lost The Way.[343]

With the young generation of Muslim-majority countries as a critical component of the audience of the new Western Muslim scholars, it is only a question of time until sufficient numbers of young people in Muslim-majority countries receive and are affected by these arguments. Slowly and gradually, the old concepts of "There is nothing more to be learned about Islam," "Don't ask *why*, ask *how*," and "Memorize the Quran and everything else as well" become history, to be replaced with an open-minded, enlightened young Muslim generation that seeks "knowledge from the cradle to the grave" and that "seeks knowledge even in China." Increasingly, it will be these Muslims who will take charge of their countries and will guide the Muslim world to prosperity.

The future is bright, because it can only be bright. The essence of Islam is reading, knowledge, and thinking. The first revelation of the Quran starts with "Read!" Numerous verses in the Quran end with a call to people who think, people who understand, and the like. The Quran reveres people with knowledge instructing to ask God for increasing their knowledge[344] and clearly differentiates between those that know and those that do not know.[345] Islam is a religion that is based on intellect and logic and has a strong alternative solution to today's challenges. When properly understood and then communicated, Islam can be a satisfying and fulfilling alternative to the Western way of life.[346] It is with the ability and the vision of the Western Muslims that the true nature of Islam will be revived and sent back to the East to emulate. When this revival happens, the prophecy of the prophet Muhammad will come true: *the enlightenment of the world will rise from the West*, or *"The sun will rise from the West."*

---

343 Derived from Sura Al-Fâtiha (1), verse 7 of the Quran.

344 "And say: 'Oh my Rabb! Increase my knowledge,'" Sura Tâ-Hâ (20), verse 114.

345 "Say, 'Are those who know equal to those who do not know?' In fact, none will take heed except the people of understanding," Sura Az-Zumar (39), verse 9.

346 *Islam: The Alternative* by Murad Hoffmann.

Appendix 1

Comments of Non-Muslims Concerning Muhammad

Napoleon Bonaparte—Quoted in Christian Cherfils's *Bonaparte et Islam* (Paris, 1914)

"I hope the time is not far off when I shall be able to unite all the wise and educated men of all the countries and establish a uniform regime based on the principles of Qur'an which alone are true and which alone can lead men to happiness."

M. K. Gandhi, *Young India* (1924)

"I became more than ever convinced that it was not the sword that won a place for Islam in those days in the scheme of life. It was the rigid simplicity, the utter self-effacement of the prophet, the scrupulous regard for his pledges, his intense devotion to his friends and followers, his intrepidity, his fearlessness, his absolute trust in God and his own mission. These, and not the sword carried everything before them and overcame every trouble."

Lamartine, *Histoire de la Turquie* (Paris, 1854), vol. 2, pp. 276–77:

"If greatness of purpose, smallness of means, and astounding results are the three criteria of human genius, who could dare to compare any great man in modern history with Muhammad? The most famous men created arms, laws and empires only. They founded, if anything at all, no more than material powers which often crumbled away before their eyes. This man moved not only armies, legislations, empires, peoples and dynasties, but millions of men in one-third of the then inhabited world; and more than that, he moved the altars, the gods, the religions, the ideas, the beliefs and souls . . . the forbearance in victory, his ambition, which was entirely devoted to one idea and in no manner striving for an empire; his endless prayers, his mystic conversations with God, his death and his triumph after death; all these attest not to an imposture but to a firm conviction which gave him the power to restore a dogma. This dogma was twofold, the unity of God and the immateriality of God; the former telling what God is, the latter telling what God is not; the one overthrowing false gods with the sword, the other stating an idea with words.

Philosopher, orator, apostle, legislator, warrior, conqueror of ideas, restorer of rational dogmas, of a cult without images; the founder of twenty terrestrial empires and of one spiritual empire, that is Muhammad. As regards all standards by which human greatness may be measured, we may well ask, is there any man greater than he?"

Edward Gibbon and Simon Ocklay, *History of the Saracen Empire* (London, 1870), p. 54:

"It is not the propagation but the permanency of his religion that deserves our wonder, the same pure and perfect impression which he engraved at Mecca and Medina is preserved, after the revolutions of twelve centuries by the Indian, the African and the Turkish proselytes of the Koran . . . The Mahometans have uniformly withstood the temptation of reducing the object of their faith and devotion to a level with the senses and imagination of man. 'I believe in One God and Mahomet the Apostle of God', is the simple and invariable profession of Islam. The intellectual image of the Deity has never been degraded by any visible idol; the honors of the prophet have never transgressed the measure of human virtue, and his living precepts have restrained the gratitude of his disciples within the bounds of reason and religion."

Rev. Bosworth Smith, *Mohammed and Mohammadanism* (London, 1874), p. 92:

"He was Caesar and Pope in one; but he was Pope without the Pope's pretensions, Caesar without the legions of Caesar: without a standing army, without a bodyguard, without a palace, without a fixed revenue; if ever any man had the right to say that he ruled by the right divine, it was

Mohammed, for he had all the power without its instruments and without its supports."

Annie Besant, *The Life and Teachings of Muhammad* (Madras, 1932), p. 4:

"It is impossible for anyone who studies the life and character of the great Prophet of Arabia, who knows how he taught and how he lived, to feel anything but reverence for that mighty Prophet, one of the great messengers of the Supreme. And although in what I put to you I shall say many things which may be familiar to many, yet I myself feel whenever I reread them, a new way of admiration, a new sense of reverence for that mighty Arabian teacher."

Montgomery Watt, *Mohammad at Mecca* (Oxford, 1953), p. 52:

"His readiness to undergo persecutions for his beliefs, the high moral character of the men who believed in him and looked up to him as leader, and the greatness of his ultimate achievement—all argue his fundamental integrity. To suppose Muhammad an impostor raises more problems than it solves. Moreover, none of the great figures of history is so poorly appreciated in the West as Muhammad."

James A. Michener, "Islam: The Misunderstood Religion" in *Reader's Digest* (May, 1955), American edition, pp. 68–70:

"Muhammad, the inspired man who founded Islam, was born about A.D. 570 into an Arabian tribe that worshipped idols. Orphaned at birth, he was always particularly solicitous of the poor and needy, the widow and the orphan, the slave and the downtrodden. At twenty he was already a successful businessman, and soon became director of camel caravans for a wealthy widow. When he reached twenty-five, his employer, recognizing his merit, proposed marriage. Even though she was fifteen years older, he married her, and as long as she lived, remained a devoted husband.

"Like almost every major prophet before him, Muhammad fought shy of serving as the transmitter of God's word, sensing his own inadequacy. But the angel commanded 'Read.' So far as we know, Muhammad was unable to read or write, but he began to dictate those inspired words which would soon revolutionize a large segment of the earth: 'There is one God.'

"In all things Muhammad was profoundly practical. When his beloved son Ibrahim died, an eclipse occurred, and rumors of God's personal condolence quickly arose. Whereupon Muhammad is said to have announced, 'An eclipse is a phenomenon of nature. It is foolish to attribute such things to the death or birth of a human-being.'

"At Muhammad's own death an attempt was made to deify him, but the man who was to become his administrative successor killed the hysteria with one of the noblest speeches in religious history: 'If there are any among you who worshipped Muhammad, he is dead. But if it is God you worshipped, He lives forever.'"

Michael H. Hart, *The 100: A Ranking of the Most Influential Persons in History* (New York: Hart Publishing Company, Inc., 1978), p. 33:

"My choice of Muhammad to lead the list of the world's most influential persons may surprise some readers and may be questioned by others, but he was the only man in history who was supremely successful on both the religious and secular level."

Sarojini Naidu (famous Indian poetess), "Ideals of Islam," *Speeches and Writings* (Madras, 1918):

"It was the first religion that preached and practiced democracy; for, in the mosque, when the call for prayer is sounded and worshippers are gathered together, the democracy of Islam is embodied five times a day when the peasant and king kneel side by side and proclaim: 'God Alone is Great'"

Thomas Carlyle—*Heroes and Hero Worship*
"How one man single-handedly, could weld warring tribes and Bedouins into a most powerful and civilized nation in less than two decades?

"The lies (Western slander) which well-meaning zeal has heaped round this man (Muhammad) are disgraceful to ourselves only . . . How one man single-handedly, could weld warring tribes and wandering Bedouins into a most powerful and civilized nation in less than two decades . . . A silent great soul, one of that who cannot but be earnest. He was to kindle the world; the world's Maker had ordered so."

Stanley Lane-Poole—*Table Talk of the Prophet*

"He was the most faithful protector of those he protected, the sweetest and most agreeable in conversation. Those who saw him were suddenly filled with reverence; those who came near him loved him; they who described him would say, 'I have never seen his like either before or after.' He was of great taciturnity, but when he spoke it was with emphasis and deliberation, and no one could forget what he said."

George Bernard Shaw—*The Genuine Islam*, vol. 1, no. 8, 1936.

"I believe if a man like him were to assume the dictatorship of the modern world he would succeed in solving its problems in a way that would bring much needed peace and happiness. I have studied him - the man and in my opinion is far from being an anti–Christ. He must be called the Savior of Humanity.

I have prophesied about the faith of Muhammad that it would be acceptable in the Europe of tomorrow as it is beginning to be acceptable to the Europe of today."

Appendix 2

How Islamic Are Islamic Countries?

To what extent do self-declared Islamic countries actually behave as Islamic countries i.e. following Islamic teachings from the Quran and the life and sayings of the Prophet? In other words, are these countries truly Islamic or are they Islamic in name only? We believe that only once this question is addressed can one begin to measure and/or claim empirically that Islam either deters or enhances human development, human solidarity and economic performance.

On the Economic Islamicity Index's, 12 Fundamental Islamic Economic Principles are taken into consideration that include:

- Equal economic opportunities for all members of society & economic freedom,
- Economic equity,
- Personal property rights and sanctity of contracts,
- Job creation for all that can and want to work & equal availability of employment,
- Equal availability of education,
- Poverty prevention and reduction; basic need fulfillment of food, shelter, clothing and rest; and alms giving to charity,
- Taxation to meet the unfulfilled needs of society & to address social issues generally,
- Appropriate management of natural and depletable resources to benefit all members of current and future generations,

- Abolition of corrupt practices,
- Establishment of a supportive financial system,
- Financial practices that includes the abolition of interest, and
- The effectiveness of the state in achieving the above (general economic prosperity).

AREA		**SUB-CATEGORY**[18]
A	**ECONOMIC OPPORTUNITY AND ECONOMIC FREEDOM**	*A) Gender Equality Indicators* *B) Other Non-discriminatory Indicators* *C) Labor Market Indicators* *D) Ease of Doing Business Indicators* *E) Economic Freedom Indicators* *F) Business and Market Freedom Indicator*
B	**PROPERTY RIGHTS AND THE SANCTITY OF CONTRACTS**	*A) Property and Contract Rights*
C	**JOB CREATION AND EQUAL ACCESS TO EMPLOYMENT**	*A) Equal employment and Job Creation*
D	**EQUAL ACCESS TO EDUCATION**	*A) Education Index Indicator* *B) Education Public Expenditures Indicator* *C) Education Equality Indicator* *D) Education Effectiveness Indicator*
E	**POVERTY, AID AND BASIC HUMAN NEED**	*A) Poverty Effectiveness Indicator* *B) Provision of Healthcare Indicators* *C) Alms/Charity Indicator*

F	**ECONOMIC EQUITY**	*N/A[1]*
G	**TAXATION AND SOCIAL WELFARE**	*A) Fiscal Freedom Indicator* *B) Tax Level Indicator* *C) Taxation Level Indicator* *D) Freedom From Government Indicator*
H	**MANAGEMENT OF NATURAL AND DEPLETABLE RESOURCES**	*A) Quality of Economic Spending* *B) Savings Indicator*
I	**CORRUPTION**	*A) Transparency International Indicator* *B) Freedom from Corruption Indicator*
J	**SUPPORTIVE FINANCIAL SYSTEM**	*A) Investment Freedom + Financial Freedom* *B) Banking Sector Indicator* *C) Financial Market Risk Indicator* *D) Investment, Portfolio, & Capital Flows Indicator*
K	**ISLAMIC FINANCIAL SYSTEM *(FINANCIAL PRACTICES THAT INCLUDES THE ABOLITION OF INTEREST)***	*A) Absence of Interest Indicator*
L	**OVERALL STATE EFFECTIVENESS IN ACHIEVING ECONOMIC PROSPERITY (GENERAL ECONOMIC PROSPERITY)**	*A) Macro Economic Indicator* *B) Economic Development Success Indicator C) Degree of Globalization & Trade Indicator* *D) General Prosperity Indicator*

(2) Legal and Governance Islamicity Index (LGI2)

This index is an attempt to capture the two key areas of the legal and governance environment of a country. In doing so it measures degree of effectiveness and competence of government governance and legal integrity (including degree of military interference). Table III describes the various measurements, variables, and proxies for the Legal and Governance Islamicity Index.

TABLE III

AREA		Subcategory:	Measurement proxy
A	GOVERNANCE		
		A. Government Governance	
			Voice and Accountability Indicator
			Political Stability and Absence of Violence Indicator
			Government Effectiveness Indicator
			Regulatory Quality Indicator
			Rule of Law Indicator
			Control of Corruption Indicator

B	LEGAL INTEGRITY INDICATORS		
		A. Legal & Judicial Integrity Indicator	Judicial independence—the judiciary is independent and not subject to interference by government or parties in dispute
			Impartial courts—a trusted legal framework exists for private businesses to challenge the legality of government actions or regulations
			Integrity of the legal system
		B. Military interference Indicator	Military Interference in Rule of Law and the Political Process Index

Legal And Governance Islamicity Index (LGI2)

(3) Human and Political Rights Islamicity Index (HPI2)

This index represents an attempt to measure the degree of human and political rights in the 208 countries. It uses specific measurements for civil and political rights, women's rights, other rights, political risk, and genocide prevention, which can be found in more detail in Table VI.

TABLE VI

AREA	Subcategory:	Measurement Proxy

Human and Political Rights Islamicity Index (HPI2)

A	CIVIL AND POLITICAL RIGHTS		
		A. Civil Rights Indicator	Freedom Index
		B. Political Rights Indicator	Freedom Index
B	WOMEN'S RIGHTS		
		A. Woman Rights	Proportion of seats held by women in national parliament (%)
			UN HDI Seats in lower house or single house held by women (as % of total)
			UN HDI Seats in parliament held by women (% of total)
			UN HDI Seats in upper house or senate held by women (as % of total)

			UN HDI Women in government at ministerial level (as % of total)
			UN HDI the Year Women Received Right To Vote
C	**OTHER RIIGHTS**		
		A. Military Service Policy Indicator	Use of conscripts to obtain military personnel
D	**POLITICAL RISK**		
		A. Political Risk	Political Risk-PRC Group-Country Risk
E	**GENOCIDE PREVENTION**		
		A. Genocide Prevention	UN HDI International Convention on the Prevention and Punishment of the Crime of Genocide

(4) International Relations Islamicity Index (IRI2)

This index is an attempt to capture a country's relationship to the global community with respect to several keys areas of environmental contribution, globalization, military engagement, and overall country risk. Table V describes the various measurements, variables, and proxies for a country's relationship to the global community as embodied in our International Relations Islamicity Index.

TABLE V

International Relations Islamicity Index (IRI2)

AREA		**Subcategory:**	**Measurement Proxy**
A	ENVIRONMENTAL PERFORMANCE INDEX		
		A. Environmental Index	Environmental Health
			Air Quality
			Water Resources
			Productive Natural Resources
			Biodiversity and Habitat
			Sustainable Energy
B	GLOBALIZATION INDEX		
		A. Economic Globalization Indicator	Globalization Index
			Restrictions

		B. Social Globalization Indicator	Personal Contact
			Information Flows
			Cultural Proximity
		C. Political Globalization Indicator	Political Globalization index
C	MILITARY/ WARS		
		A. Proportion of Military Spending Indicator	(Military Expenditures % of GDP/Total Armed Forces) and Armed Forces Index
		B. Military Spending Indicator	Military Expenditure % of GDP/Military Personnel % of total labor force
D	OVERALL COUNTRY RISK		
		A. Country Risk	Overall Country Risk Index

RESULTS OF THE ISLAMICITY INDEX

In Table VI below, we present the summary results of the Islamicity I2 Index, ranking 208 countries organized by the following subgroups: High, Upper- Middle, Lower-Middle, and Low Income Countries, OECD, and Non-OECD Countries, OIC Countries, and Non-OECD Non-OIC Countries, and Persian Gulf Countries. The results of the Islamicity Index I2 of 208 countries where additionally disaggregated to the four individual index rankings of Economic Islamicity Index (EI2), Legal and Governance Islamicity Index (LGI2), Human and Political Rights Islamicity Index (HPI2), and International Relations Islamicity Index (IRI2).

TABLE VI

Detailed Summary Results Of The Islamicity Index (I2)

SUB-GROUPS (# OF COUNTRIES)	**EI^2**	**LGI^2**	**HPI^2**	**IRI^2**	**OVERALL I^2 RANK**
ALL COUNTRIES (208)	104	96	104	75	**104**
OECD[19] (30)	24	28	29	37	**25**
HIGH INCOME[20] (60)	60	40	84	40	**60**
UPPER MIDDLE INCOME[21] (41)	83	84	88	87	**85**
NON-OECD NON-OIC (123)	111	101	110	89	**108**
PERSIAN GULF (7)	94	104	138	109	**112**
LOWER MIDDLE INCOME[22] (55)	116	124	115	112	**122**
NON-OECD (178)	118	112	116	99	**118**

OIC[23] (56)	133	136	130	115	**139**
LOW INCOME[24] (54)	170	154	126	107	**153**

These are very preliminary results, but they do tend to indicate that the so-called and self-declared Islamic countries have not by-and-large adhered to Islamic principles. As indicated in Table VI, the average ranking of the 56 Islamic countries is 139; well below the average ranking of the 208 countries measured.

If the Islamic countries (OIC) are compared with OECD countries, the disparities are even more pronounced. For example, the average I2 rank among the OECD countries is 25 while (as mentioned above) it is 139 for the Islamic countries. One could argue that a fairer comparison would be to the group of non-OECD or Middle Income countries. However, even then the Islamic countries do not perform well as a group. When compared with the 178 non-OECD countries (average rank 118), the 41 Upper-Middle Income countries (average rank 85), and the 123 Non-OECD Non-OIC countries (average rank 108), the Islamic countries group (OIC) performance is the worst, with an average rank of 139. The degree of failure of the OIC countries performance is most clearly demonstrated by the fact that the Islamic countries fared even worse on the ranking than the 55 Lower-Middle Income countries, which ranked at an average of 132.

We are not unduly surprised by the fact that the OECD countries (and High Income countries) have performed better in this ranking. The average overall **I2** ranking of OECD countries was 25 while the High Income countries average rank was 60 compared to the OIC average rank of 139. It is to be expected that the OECD countries would perform better in our index as Islamic principles are not only compatible with, but also promote, free markets and good economic governance, economic systems and policies that encourage economic- social justice, legal systems and governance that are fair to all members of society and which include global standards of human and political rights, and, lastly, but equally important, promote, and foster better international relations with the global community. Thus the industrialized countries high ranking in an Islamicity Index underscores that Islamic law indeed promotes the notion that governments are duty-bound to provide good economic, financial, political, legal, social governance, policy, and end results i.e. measurable performance.

Our very preliminary results show that Islamic countries are not as Islamic in their practice as one might expect; instead it appears that the most developed countries tend to place higher on our preliminary Islamicity Index.

Given our results, one can surmise that the lack of economic, financial, political, legal, and social development can be attributed to age-old problems of developing countries, such as inefficient institutions, bad economic policies, corruption, underdeveloped rule of law and equity, economic, and social systems failing woman and children, and other traditional developing country diseases. It is, in fact, the shortcomings of the governments and their respective policies, not religion, that account for the dismal economic, financial, political, legal, and social developments and progress in the Middle East (even those blessed with oil).

This is further reinforced by the Islamic economic, financial, political, legal, and social principles represented by 67 proxies used in the Islamicity Index. If examined closely, all 67 proxies of the Index are standard practices of good governance and good economic, financial, political, legal, and social policies, applicable to any country regardless of religious orientation.

Countries {208}	Overall Islamicity Index Rank (OIC countries are highlighted)
New Zealand	1
Luxembourg	2
Ireland	3
Iceland	4
Finland	5
Denmark	6
Canada	7
U.K.	8
Australia	9
Netherlands	9
Austria	11
Norway	12
Switzerland	13
Belgium	14
Sweden	15
Portugal	16
Germany	17
Bahamas	18
France	18
Czech Rep	20
Estonia	21
Costa Rica	22
Spain	23
Barbados	24
U. S.	25
Slovenia	26
Hong Kong, China	27
Latvia	28
Japan	29

Malta	30
Hungary	31
Slovak Republic	31
Italy	33
Chile	34
Lithuania	35
Cyprus	36
Singapore	37
Malaysia	38
Panama	39
Trinidad and Tobago	40
Poland	41
Mauritius	42
Croatia	43
St. Vincent and the Grenadines	44
Namibia	45
Greece	46
Jamaica	47
Kuwait	48
Uruguay	48
South Africa	50
Botswana	51
St. Lucia	52
Ghana	53
Argentina	54
Brazil	55
Mexico	55
Bulgaria	57
El Salvador	58
Philippines	59
Dominica	60
Israel	61
Monaco	62

Lesotho	63
Bahrain	**64**
Brunei	**65**
Romania	66
United Arab Emirates	**66**
Belize	68
Andorra	69
Cayman Islands	70
Seychelles	71
Fiji	72
Uganda	**73**
Tanzania	74
Antigua and Barbuda	75
Gabon	**75**
Jordan	**77**
Thailand	78
Grenada	79
San Marino	79
China	81
Nicaragua	81
Cape Verde	83
Macao, China	83
Tunisia	**83**
Colombia	86
Dominican Republic	87
Peru	88
India	89
Aruba	90
Russian Federation	91
Honduras	92
Greenland	93
Guyana	**94**
Netherlands Antilles	95
Mozambique	**96**

Mongolia	97
Macedonia, FYR	98
Oman	**99**
Suriname	**100**
Bosnia and Herzegovina	101
Ukraine	102
Turkey	**103**
Maldives	**104**
Liechtenstein	105
Korea, Rep.	106
Kazakhstan	**107**
Timor-Leste	107
Senegal	**109**
Albania	**110**
Moldova	110
Qatar	**112**
Puerto Rico	113
Armenia	114
Kiribati	115
Sri Lanka	116
Georgia	117
St. Kitts and Nevis	117
Morocco	**119**
Northern Mariana Islands	119
Papua New Guinea	119
Zambia	119
Bolivia	123
Gambia, The	**124**
Azerbaijan	**125**
Ecuador	125
Guatemala	127
Belarus	128
Malawi	129

Mali	130
Saudi Arabia	131
Burkina Faso	132
Vanuatu	133
Vietnam	134
Rwanda	135
Paraguay	136
Kyrgyz Republic	137
Korea, Dem. Rep.	138
Virgin Islands (U.S.)	139
Indonesia	140
Venezuela, RB	141
Madagascar	142
Palau	143
Kenya	144
Guinea	145
Samoa	146
Benin	147
Pakistan	147
Cuba	149
New Caledonia	150
Nepal	151
Bangladesh	152
Egypt, Arab Rep.	153
Cambodia	154
Tonga	155
Burundi	156
Swaziland	156
Lebanon	158
Zimbabwe	159
Algeria	160
Micronesia, Fed. Sts.	161
Cameroon	162
Iran, Islamic Rep.	163

Myanmar	164
Central African Republic	165
Bermuda	166
Bhutan	167
Sierra Leone	**168**
Afghanistan	**169**
Guam	170
Congo, Dem. Rep.	171
Togo	**172**
Turkmenistan	**173**
Nigeria	**174**
Uzbekistan	**174**
Haiti	176
Tajikistan	**176**
American Samoa	178
Cote d'Ivoire	**179**
Ethiopia	180
French Polynesia	181
Congo, Rep.	182
Equatorial Guinea	183
Lao PDR	183
Serbia and Montenegro	185
Syrian Arab Republic	**186**
Marshall Islands	187
Faeroe Islands	188
Niger	**189**
Guinea-Bissau	**190**
Solomon Islands	190
Sao Tome and Principe	192
Djibouti	**193**
Liberia	194
Mauritania	**195**
Libya	**196**

Chad	**197**
Yemen, Rep.	**198**
Angola	199
Comoros	200
Iraq	201
Channel Islands	202
Sudan	**202**
Eritrea	204
Isle of Man	205
Somalia	**206**
West Bank and Gaza	207
Mayotte	208

Appendix 3

Excerpt from Khaled Abou El Fadl's Book Titled "The Search for Beauty in Islam: A Conference of the Books"

Chapter 57 *"Corrupting God's Book"*

This Conference was founded on the beauty of the Book, and our Civilization was the civilization of books. Our way to God is guided by the Book, and we found our worth only in books. Our God manifested through the Book, and our identity was defined by books. So how can we become the corrupters of the Book and the betrayers of books?

What type of arrogance permits a people to name themselves God's soldiers and then usurp His authority? What type of arrogance empowers a people to inject their insecurities and hatred into the Book of God, and then fancy themselves the divine protectors? Of all the sins of this world, what can be more revolting than usurping God's Word, and then misrepresenting God's meticulous Speech?

God has promised those who alter God's Word unmitigated enmity and inevitable destruction (4:46, 5:13, 5:41, 10:64, 18:27). Those who say about God what they do not know or what they are not authorized to say are held by God in utter contempt (2:80, 7:28, 10:68). Yet, we live in an age and place where the word of God can be altered and corrupted, and all the fancy Islamic centers and bombastic leaders and preachers could not be bothered to care. We live in an age and place where the so-called protectors of the Holy Sites, Mecca, and Medina, have become the corrupters of God's Word.

Their arrogance has convinced them that they are authorized to cleanse Islamic texts of their contents, and become the guardians of the Muslim mind. Even the commentaries on the Qur'an have been cleansed, and Muslims remain largely oblivious to this grave sin. For instance, the commentary known as Hashiyat al-Sawi on Tafsir al-Jalalayn has been cleansed of passages that describe the Wahhabis as the agents of the devil. Even if one believes that the Maliki jurist Ahmad al-Sawi (d. 1241/1825) has exceeded the proper bounds, this does not give one a license to commit fraud and forgery by misrepresenting al-Sawi's text. Abu Hayyan al-Andalusi's (d. 754/1353) commentary on the Qur'an known as al-Nahr al-Madd has been cleansed of passages that refer to Ibn Taymiyya's views regarding God's throne. The cleansing of the printed text is made without any indication or reference alluding to the deletions—as if some barely literate bureaucrat sitting on the cushions supplied by some prince or king is remotely qualified to validate or authenticate the work of such esteemed jurists. But beyond editing the work of jurists, now the corruptions have been extended to the translation of the Qur'an in English and even the hadith of the Companions.

For five years or more now, a beautifully printed English translation of the Qur'an has been distributed for free in nearly every Islamic center in the United States. This Trojan-horse translation is found in every Muslim bookstore and in every English-speaking Islamic center. The authors of the translation are professors at the University of Medina, and the book is printed, no expenses spared, in Saudi Arabia. On the very first page of the printed text is a certificate of authentication and approval by the late 'Abd al-'Aziz Bin Bazz, the "Head of the Ministry for Islamic Research, Legal Opinions, Preaching and Guidance" (Idarat al-Buhuth al-'Ilmiyya wa al-Ifta' wa al-da'wa wa al-Irshad). Interestingly enough, Bin Bazz did not know a word of English, but he authenticated the text nonetheless. To be fair, however, the translation is a faithful reproduction of Bin Bazz's views with all their idiosyncrasies. On the cover of the book is printed the title: Interpretation of the Meanings of the Noble Qur'an in the English Language: A Summarized Version of at-Tabari [sic], al-Qurtubi and Ibn Kathir with comments from Sahih al-Bukhari Summarized in One Volume.

The impression created by this translation is that the reader is not only receiving the insights of the authors as to the meaning of the Qur'an, but is also receiving the insights and implicit endorsement of the text by the esteemed classical scholars al-Tabari, al-Qurtubi, Ibn Kathir, and Bukhari. In the text, the original Arabic is printed in one column, and on the opposite column is an attempt at a verse-to-verse English rendition of the Arabic text. At the bottom of the page, there are hadith-reports purporting to explain and elucidate upon the text. But the liberties taken with the so-called interpretation of the Arabic is nothing short of frightening.

The English text has all the appearances of a translation. This appearance is only confirmed by the fact that the regular English text is full of interjections placed within parenthesis, and these parenthetical interjections purport to be elaborations clarifying the meaning of the translated text. A reader who does not know Arabic is left with the unmistakable impression that what is within parenthesis is a natural elaboration upon the intended meaning of the Divine text.

To demonstrate the corruptions of the text, we will consider a few examples. The authors translated Surat al-Ahzab (33), verse 59, in the following way:

"O Prophet! Tell your wives and your daughters and the women of the believers to draw their cloaks (veils) all over their bodies (i.e. screen themselves completely except the eyes or one eye to see the way). That will be better, that they should be known (as free respectable women) so as not to be annoyed. And Allah is Ever Oft-Forgiving, Most Merciful."

In the above translation, the authors assert that God's command is that women should cloak themselves in a large veil, and cover everything except one or two eyes. The authors liberally equate a cloak to a veil and, according to the authors, God explicitly mandates that the cloaks or veils be drawn over a woman's entire body. The authors' assertions are indefensible in light of what the Arabic actually says. A conservative and literal translation of the first quoted verse (33:59) would read:

"O Prophet tell your wives, daughters, and the women of the believers to lower (or possibly, draw upon themselves) their garments. This is better so that they will not be known and molested. And, God is forgiving and merciful."

The operative words in the Arabic text are yudnina 'alayhinna min jalabibihinna. This could mean either "lower their garments" or "draw their garments closer to their bodies." Jalabibihinna literally means "their garments." A jilbab, singular form of jalabib, is a garment worn on the body, and not a veil. A jilbab is a garment, like a dress or Arab robe, which has stitches and threads. A single piece of cloth like a chador or ʻabaya, which some women wrap around their bodies in the modern age, would not normally be called a jilbab. Yudnina, literally, means to bring closer or to lower something, in this case a garb. Therefore, one can interpret this verse to require the covering of the legs, or a more vigilant covering of the torso or, simply, modesty, but the original text does not support the authors' rendition into English.

Muslim jurists have disagreed on the meaning of this verse. Some argued that it mandates the covering of the legs or bosom. The majority asserted that it requires the covering of the full body except the face, hands, and feet. A minority view held by 'Ubayda al-Salmani and Ibn 'Abbas maintained that the verse exhorts women to cover their faces. Importantly, however, the reports about Ibn 'Abbas's views are not consistent. Some reports claim that he did not believe the face or hands should be covered. A number of the jurists who held the minority view argued that women are asked to cover their faces and hands not because it is a religious obligation but because of the advisability of distinguishing between free and slave women. This point about the distinction between free and slave women raises a very important issue about the way this verse should be understood. Nearly all the commentators agreed that this verse was revealed to protect women from molestation. These commentators state that there was a group of young and corrupt men in Medina who harassed and sometimes molested women at night. Apparently, these men targeted only slaves and not free women. They distinguished a slave from a free woman by the cloth they wore; if the woman wore a jilbab, they assumed she was free and left her alone, and if she did not, they assumed she was a slave and harassed her. The commentators state that in response to this problem, these verses were revealed with the specific purpose of responding to this particular problem. Consequently, many jurists argued that the 'illa (operative cause) for the jilbab is to address this specific type of problem. Therefore, many of those who claim that the jilbab should cover the face also hinge the analysis on the operative cause of the law, and argue that this law is relevant only if there is an issue involving the distinction between slave and free women, and a problem involving harassment and molestation. If this particular type of problem does not exist, the exhortations of the verse are not pertinent.

It is quite possible to distill from this analysis a general moral call for modesty and a principle of safe conduct. It is possible to argue that these particular verses are establishing social norms of modesty and self-restraint. Relying partly on this verse, the majority of premodern jurists argued that the 'awra (private parts that must be covered) of a slave girl is different from the 'awra of a free woman. They maintained that the 'awra of a free woman is her whole body except her face and hands, and many jurists added the feet. his means that a free woman should cover everything except the face and hands and, perhaps, the feet. But the jurists asserted that a slave-girl does not have to cover her hair, neck, arms, and some even added the chest. This, of course, raises the question: What is the basis for this distinction? Is the hair, arms, or chest of a slave-girl less capable of inducing seduction than that of a free woman? The response cannot be in the affirmative; the body parts of a slave-girl are no less enticing than their counterparts in a free woman. The response largely depends on social norms. The social norms of the time did not consider it immodest for slave-girls to leave their hair uncovered, while it was considered shameful for a free woman not to have a jilbab that would cover her body and perhaps a part of the hair. This raises the larger questions: To what extent is this Qur'anic verse addressing a particular social institution, and to what extent can this verse be generalized beyond its specific social assumptions. One way to generalize the verse is to extract or distill the fundamental moral and normative values that are affirmed by this verse, and, in essence, these values seem to emphasize modesty and safety of conduct. This point is open to debate. For our purposes, however, the most significant point is that this verse raises some rather complex issues that merit reflection and study. But by forcing a single and quite specific narrow minority view upon the verse is, without a doubt, a corruption of God's word. The authors quite intentionally limit the text to a singular meaning that is designed to cater to whatever prejudices they have towards women.

In a similar example and on the same subject of veiling and women, the authors translate Surat al-Nur (24), verse 31, as follows:

"... And tell the believing women to lower their gaze (from looking at forbidden things), and protect their private parts (from illegal sexual acts, etc.) and not to show off their adornment except only that which is apparent (like palms of hands or one eye or both eyes for necessity to see the way, or outer dress like veil, gloves, head-cover, apron, etc.) and to draw their veils all over Juyubihinna (i.e. their bodies, faces, necks and bosoms etc.) and not to reveal their adornment except to their husbands, their fathers . . ."

But a literal and more honest translation of the above quoted text would read:

"And say to the believing women to lower their gaze, and guard their private parts, and that they should not display their adornments except what would ordinarily appear. And, that they should draw their veils over their bosoms and that they should not display their beauty except to their husbands . . ."

The Qur'anic Arabic instructs that women should take their khimars and cover their jayb (pl. juyub). The Arabic is wal yadribna bi khumurihinna 'ala juyubihinna, which means that women should take their khimars and strike with it or place it upon their bosoms. According to the authoritative lexicon of Lisan al-'Arab by Ibn Manzur (d. 711/1311), a khimar is a piece of cloth that is worn on the head. A man's turban may be called a khimar as well, and a man wearing a turban may be called a mukhtamir. A jayb is the bosom of a human being. It could also be where the neck and chest meet or the beginning of the cleavage area on a woman's chest. Furthermore, a shirt, garment, or pocket may be called jayb as well. The jurists add that the khimar was a cloth worn by women in pre-Islamic times on the neck and that it was normally thrown towards the back leaving the head and chest exposed. The verse apparently instructs that the piece of cloth normally worn on the head (the khimar) or neck be made to cover the bosom or to descend down to the point of touching the cloth. Commentators on the Qur'an repeatedly emphasize that women in Mecca and Medina were in the habit of exposing all or most their chests, even if their hair was covered. Consequently, it is quite possible that the point of the revelation was to call upon women to cover their chests. But whatever the case may be, nothing in the verse indicates that the khimar is to cover the face or hands. If the verse intended that the face be covered, it would have stated wal yadribna bi khumurihinna 'ala wujuhihinna (instruct them to place the khimar on their faces). But the verse does not allude or refer to the face in any way. In fact, what partially covers the face is usually referred to as niqab, and what covers the head is normally referred to as khimar. But the Qur'anic verse does not use the word niqab anywhere. Although the verse does not explicitly require the covering of the hair, it is possible to argue that the verse assumes it. But to extract more than that from this verse requires an incredulous degree of creative reconstructionism at best, or arrogant and malicious misogyny at worst.

One should also note that the verse states that women should not display their adornments except what would normally appear. The Arabic is illa ma dhahara minha, which is an ambiguous phrase. The closest rendering in English of this phrase is: "that which appears," or "that which would normally appear." This phrasing leaves open the question of whether customs or social standards may influence notions of propriety and modesty. The vast majority of Muslim jurists asserted that the phrase "what would normally appear" refers to two distinct elements, the first is 'urf or 'ada (custom and established practice) and the second is haraj (hardship). Meaning, this phrase refers to what are admittedly adornments, and perhaps objects of enticement, but they are adornments that do not have to be covered because they "normally appear" either as a matter of custom or because they need to appear to avoid and alleviate potential hardship. Therefore, jurists such as Abu Hayyan al-Andalusi (d. 754/1353) and al-Razi (d. 606/1210) explain that the operative legal inquiry is: What normally appears as a matter of practice, what needs to appear so that the law will not impose undue hardship, and how can these two elements be accommodated within the bounds of modesty? Modesty does not mean removing all forms of adornments or enticements. One, that is not possible without excluding women entirely from society, and two, the Qur'an acknowledges that certain adornments (zinah) are permitted to appear. Modesty, at a minimum, does mean lowering one's garment and covering the bosom area. Most Muslim jurists concluded, from this discussion, that the face and hands are adornments that do not have to be covered because it would create hardship to ask that they be covered, and because established social practices do not necessitate that they be covered. Some jurists evaluating these same types of considerations allowed the appearance of the ears, the forearms, the neck, the feet, or anything one-half of an arm's length below the knee. Other jurists argued that since the 'awra of a woman in prayer or ihram is the face, hands, and feet, in all circumstances, only these body parts may appear. A significant number of jurists thought that the comparison to 'ibadat is not relevant to the issue of determining which adornments may appear. The rules of modesty in 'ibadat involve a very different set of issues than those involved in determining established social practice and hardship. Some jurists such as Sa'id Ibn Jubayr (d. 95/714) disfavored exposing the hair although they did not consider the hair to be part of a woman's 'awra. The majority of jurists argued that the hair is part of the 'awra of a free woman but not a slave-girl.

As mentioned above, the distinction between the rules of modesty for slave-girls and free women is rather significant. Perhaps because slave-girls lived active social and economic lives, the vast majority of jurists concluded that slaves did not need to cover their hair, arms, or anything below the knees. Some went as far as saying the chest of a slave-girl did not need to be covered, but this seems to be in direct contradiction with the Qur'anic verse discussed above. Much of the distinction in the case of slave-girls seems to rely on the appraisal of the twin elements of established social practice and hardship. Relying on their evaluation of these two elements, the jurists concluded that the adornments of slave-girls that could appear were very different than those of free women. Interestingly, a rather small minority of jurists argued that the rules for poor women who need to lead economically active lives were the same as those for slave-girls.

Today, the distinction between free women and slave-girls, to say the least, is spurious, and the whole issue needs to be re-analyzed. Established social practices and hardship connote moral imperatives, but the factual identification of either of these elements is an empirical, not just a textual, matter. In other words, if the law incorporates two distinct normative values, the first of which is the established social practice and the second of which is the removal of hardship, these two normative values need to be balanced against the requirement of modesty. But determining what is, in fact, an established social practice or a source of hardship is an empirical factual question that is subject to re-evaluation and re-examination as the circumstances dictate in different times and places. The input and testimony of women as to what constitutes hardship in today's environment is crucial. Put differently, men cannot simply assume to know what should "normally appear" of a woman's adornment. This is a matter where those most concerned (i.e. women) must have a clear and decisive voice. There is no question that various textual sources establish the outer parameters of this negotiative process—for instance, the chest or anything above the knee may not appear. However, within the outer parameters there is room for negotiation, re-evaluation, and analysis. Most importantly, the Qur'an does not demand or expect that all sources of fitna (enticement) be eradicated in society. The Qur'an balances the various interests and rights, and unlike our dismissive friends, the Qur'an does not expect women to bear the full burden of modesty. The weakness of men cannot be the source of hardship and suffering for women, and any approach that does not acknowledge this fact, in my view, is not true to the spirit or letter of the Qur'an.

The authors of the translation, however, seem to be working under a very different set of assumptions. They seem to be under the misimpression that the Qur'an aims to eradicate all sources of enticement in society, and that women should bear the brunt of the burden in this process. Hence, women should be covered from head to toe except perhaps for one roaming eye, and men may happily prance around undisturbed by delectable female parts. Worst of all, this fundamentally male-indulgent view is presented as God's unquestionable truth. The only truth here is that the authors simply forced the idiosyncrasies of their own culture upon God's text. Consequently, none of the richness and equanimity of the text is reflected in their translation. Rather, the text is made to represent and embody their authoritarian and despotic constructions.

The text of the translation does not give any indication that the absurd renderings of the Divine Text are a result of the idiosyncrasies of the Wahhabi authors. In fact, the authors attempt to confirm the impression of the immutability of their renderings by twice quoting a tradition as a footnote to the above quoted verses. The footnote says:

"Narrated Safiya bint Shaiba [sic.]: 'Aisha used to say: "When (the verse): 'They should draw their veils over their bodies, faces, necks and bosoms,' was revealed, (the ladies) cut their waist sheets at the edges and covered their faces with the cut pieces." (Sahih Al-Bukhari, Vol. 6, Hadith No. 282)."

The truly shocking realization for anyone with a command of the Arabic language is the shameless dishonesty and the remarkable liberties taken with translating this hadith. The authors' translation of the statement attributed to 'Aisha (d. 58/678), the Prophet's wife, and reported by Bukhari is nothing short of an outright misrepresentation. The original in Bukhari states that when verse 24:31 was revealed, 'Aisha said: "[The women] took their garments and tore pieces of cloth from the edges and yaakhtamarna biha." Yaakhtamarna biha means that the women took the pieces torn from their garments and wore them as a khimar, and, as mentioned above, a khimar could be a piece of cloth worn on the head. So, presumably, the women wore the pieces torn from their garments on their heads. Another version of the same report, also in Bukhari, provides that only the women of the migrants from Mecca (al-muhajirin) were quick to comply. Other versions of the same tradition, reported elsewhere, state that the women of the Ansar were the ones who promptly complied. In either case, the original Arabic does not in any way indicate that the veils were worn on the face.

The most one can understand from 'Aisha's tradition is that women covered their heads. But one cannot help but wonder, if the women cut a big enough piece from the edges of their skirts to cover their heads and faces, did this mean that these women left their legs exposed? In any case, the authenticity of this tradition, with its many versions, has been questioned, and some versions indicate that the response of the women in Medina was to cover their bosoms. (https://www.certmanserv.com/training/cmsiwt/snhu.html). In yet another example, and there are many examples, of corrupting the text, verse 4:34 was translated in the following fashion:

"Men are the maintainers of women, because Allah has made the one of them to excel the other, and because they spend (to support them) from their means. Therefore the righteous women are devoutly obedient (to Allah and to their husbands), and guard in the husband's absence what Allah orders them to guard (e.g. their chastity, their husband's property, etc). As to those women on whose part you see ill-conduct, admonish them (first), (next), refuse to share their beds, (and last) beat them (lightly, if it is useful) . . ."

The original in Arabic does not refer to husbands as the recipient of women's obedience. The original talks about women who are pious, humble before God, and observant of God's commands. The corrupted text not only inserts a reference to husbands, but also equates obedience to husbands with obedience to God. Furthermore, the translation leaves the reader with the distinct impression that husbands may punish their wives for what, in the husband's judgment, constitutes "ill-conduct." This leads to a separate discussion all together. Why are husbands, as a category, given full authority to act as judge, jury, and executioner against women for what they alone deem as "ill-conduct"? What if a husband is less pious than the wife? Furthermore, the word used in the original is nushuz, which means a serious deviation or gross misconduct and, in either case, the verse does not authorize husbands to beat their wives. The word azwaj (husbands) is not mentioned in God's text and, as explained earlier in the Conference, the verse is talking about gross sexual misconduct, which is distinct from other types of "ill-conduct," particularly from the purview of Islamic law.

The Noble Qur'an translation/interpretation of the Qur'an is widely distributed in the United States. According to this translation, God commanded that women cover their faces, necks, bosoms, arms, legs, and hands. Furthermore, the reader is informed that God commanded devout obedience to God's self, and then mandated the same type of obedience for husbands. From the gross liberties taken in translating the text, apparently the translators believe that God wishes women to be like house-broken dogs—loyal, timid, sweet, and obedient. One can only ponder, what type of rotted and foul soul imagines that God wishes to imprison women in a sewer of squalid male egos, and suffer because men cannot control their libidos? What an ugly picture they have created of God's compassion and mercy. According to the translators, God ordered the veil, and the veil must cover the face, except one or two eyes, and only the palms of the hands may appear. The eyes are not supposed to be covered, apparently as a concession to women, so that they may be able to walk. What if a woman had a seeing-eye dog—would she need to cover her eyes as well? But, of course, dogs are devilish abominations in Wahhabi thought, and so perhaps a woman could hire a slave to guide her through the streets. So in this nightmarish and macabre world, a slave would guide another slave to the altar of male divinity.

Furthermore, I cannot help but wonder how does a woman cover the back of her hands, but still show her palms? The translation mentions the wearing of gloves, but again, I wonder, since gloves, as they exist today, were probably unknown to the Prophet, why aren't gloves considered a heretical innovation (bid'a)? There is a tradition attributed to the Prophet in which he reportedly forbids women from wearing a quffaz (hand cover) or niqab while in a state of ihram (a state of ritual consecration during pilgrimage). Scholars, however, have doubted the authenticity of this tradition. The scholars asserted that this was simply the opinion of Ibn 'Umar, and it was wrongfully attributed to the Prophet. In any case, quffaz, as used in that tradition, meant either a decoration made of cloth worn on the hand as a form of beautification or a loose piece of cloth stuffed with cotton and having buttons on the side worn as protection from the cold. These hand covers were loose, dark, and large. Isn't the tightness of today's gloves a fitna (enticement), and shouldn't women wear loose black bags on their hands so that no one may be enticed by the attractive contours of the hand? Truly, ugliness can only beget utter absurdity.

The reader is left with the impression that the idiosyncratic understandings of the authors of the translation are supported by the traditions of Bukhari and the Qur'anic commentaries of al-Tabari, al-Qurtubi, and Ibn Kathir. But Bukhari's reports are grossly corrupted, and the commentaries of al-Tabari, al-Qurtubi, and Ibn Kathir do not support the authors' understandings. In fact, these Qur'anic commentators report a variety of views and conclude that women may show their faces, hands, and feet. In other words, the authors of The Noble Qur'an translation usurped the authority of these distinguished scholars, but apparently did not bother to read or correctly represent what these scholars actually said. This translation is nothing more than a faithful reproduction of Bin Bazz's extremely conservative and intolerant views, and the views of the scholars serving in the Saudi dar al-Ifta'.

It is clear that the authors of the translation and their supporters do not like women, and that they projected their inadequacies and deformities upon God's text and the whole Islamic intellectual tradition. Truly, the agony of the Muslim plight in the modern world cannot be expressed either in words or tears. What can one say about those people who seem to have declared an unmitigated war against women and who brandish the weapons of grotesque misogyny? What can one say about those people who, in their utter ignorance and maniacal arrogance, subjugate even the word of God to their ugliness and deformities? "Who is more unjust than those who suppress the testimony they received from God, and God is not oblivious as to what they do" (2:140). Truly, "These folks, the cult they are in, is destined to ruin, and false is what they practice" (7:139).

Index

B

C

N

O

P

Q

R

S

Y

Z